FOR THE LO[VE]
OF PRA[GUE]

Author's note: From the first three editions of this book, I have been blessed with hundreds of loving letters. As this book is about love – and written for love – these letters and reviews are my payment!

"Hi - Just a quick note to say thanks For the Love of Prague. What a beautiful book! I must say it is helping me understand why it is the way it is here. No other book has given me the perspective about the Czech way of life, way of thinking, acting, doing, etc. a wonderful story and lives full of rich experiences and love. Thanks for the inspiration. Your stories mean a lot to me - on Saturday, when I finished reading your book, I had so many emotional reactions. I was sad that I finished the book...it had become my comforting friend over the past couple of weeks. I relished coming home and reading and getting more educated in the most interesting way. I was also feeling very safe -somehow I felt like I would muddle through the emotional challenges I'm dealing with about living in a new place and getting used to everything new. I have a calendar of quotes; today the quote was 'Our illusions of separation disappear when we hear stories of another's struggles or discoveries.' Your book helped me feel less separate here."

Regina Miller, (upon moving to work in Prague.)

"The guy is so young that it's hard to think of him as 'The Oldest American in Prague.' But Gene Deitch writes with a passion of a young man in love – with life in Prague, with the woman who risked everything for him, and like her husband, won the game of life despite communism, a Soviet invasion, and the everyday hassles and shortages of living behind the iron curtain. But this book is more than an eye-witness account. For The Love of Prague is a great love story!"

Alan Levy, editor-in-chief, The Prague Post

The New York Times

hundreds of cartoons shown in the United States were actually
Kat, and Popeye, as

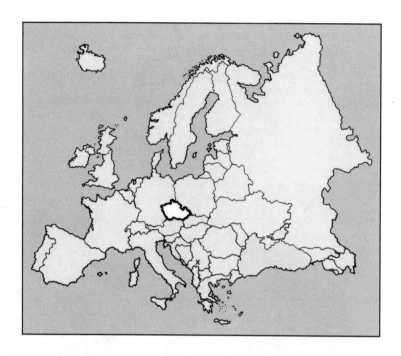

As a special service to our readers we present a true-scale map of

Europe!

That little blobby-shaped country in the exact center of Europe,
is the Czech Republic. Hugging it on the west is Germany.
On the northeast is Poland. Directly south is Austria.
(I'm sure you know all the other countries on the map.)

Even when there was a **Czechoslovakia,** its name shared *only three
letters-in-a-row* with Yugoslavia, o-s-l, yet many people lumped
the two countries together. And when Yugoslavia was being bombed,
many tourists stayed away from here! But Yugoslavia is *five countries
south* of The Czech Republic! (Note the little X)

FOR THE LOVE OF PRAGUE™

How it really was during
the communist times,
The love story
of the only free American
living in Prague
during 30 years of
the totalitarian regime.

*Love and cartoon films
were the secret!*

Told by Oscar-winning
animation filmmaker

Gene Deitch

New Fourth Edition! Revised,
expanded, updated. More stories,
and 16 pages of color photos.

For The Love of Prague™

FOURTH UPDATED EDITION

Cover design and most photos by Gene Deitch.
Typography by AG Design, spol. s r.o., Prague.

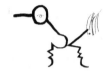

genedeitch@traveller.cz

www.fortheloveofprague.com
www.genedeitch.com
genedeitch.awn.com

Baset Books
Plovdivská 3400
143 00 Praha 4 - Modřany

Index:
1.Gene Deitch 2.Zdenka Deitchová 3.Prague 4.Czechoslovakia 5.Communism
6.Cold War 7.Cuban Missile Crisis 8. Every Day Life Under Communism 9.1968
Prague Spring & Soviet-Led Invasion 10.Velvet Revolution 11. Czech Republic
12.Motion Pictures 13. Animation 14. A Dangerous love affair 15.Bridging
Czech-American Cultural Differences 16. Outwitting the Communists

A successful American cartoon animator finds himself in hard-line communist Prague at
the height of the cold war. Under extremely difficult conditions he finds
love and creative fulfillment, wins a Hollywood Oscar, and outwits and outlives the
communists. A true memoir of a man in a unique situation in a magical but deprived place, during times of galvanic historic events.   How it really was to live under
communism, the bad, the ugly, the good, and the hilarious, through the eyes of an
American who lived through it for 30 years, yet was not under control of the regime.

ISBN 80-86223-09-4

Czechia is not only important, but also weird. We have called it Absurdistan. The president of the place was a writer of absurdist plays. The Czechs revel in the absurd, and the communist rulers were the most absurd of all. Strange things happened here. Kafka was only one of the strange things.

Here is the story of Gene in Wonderland; a young American dropped into Stalinist Prague in 1959, and all he wanted to do was make cartoon films and win the love of a remarkable woman.

```
I did see it as my main chance,
   and with Zdenka, I took it.
This book is for her.    G.D.
```

G&Z At home
Photo by Adam Trachtman - January 2000

Introduction

There has been a steady flow of interest in Prague since 1989's "Velvet Revolution," when communism was finally overthrown and democracy allowed to bloom. In the years since, thousands of Americans have flocked to this great city, many settling here for the long term, others, with only a few months or a year to kill, coming simply out of curiosity. The stories of Prague's older expatriates have already begun to be written - in memoirs, plays, poems, news reports, short fiction and even a novel or two. Inhabiting many of these tales is a growing nostalgia for the city before Big Macs and Hypermarkets were a common presence, when the joy of liberation still swelled the streets and an anarchy of goodwill ruled the land. But even those fearless explorers who came during democratic Czech Republic's earliest days are little more than newcomers beside Gene Deitch.

As an American who has lived and worked here continuously since 1959, Gene scooped us all, making all our stories appear woefully incomplete. In fact, he is the only American citizen to have been continuously resident in Prague during 30 years of Communist rule. Yet he was not a Communist himself, he was not of Czech origin, not a political refugee, and nobody's secret agent. He was simply and incredibly an American animation cartoonist assigned here by a New York film distributor to direct animated children's films, seemingly a „perfect cover" in the early days of James Bond.

In the course of doing his work - and concurrently falling in love with a Czech woman who single-handedly changed his life - Gene was in the remarkable position of being able to observe and actually live the life of everyday Czechoslovakia, without getting involved or becoming subject to it. In this unique situation he was his own wife's customer! (she being an employee of a State-controlled film studio), and he became a living symbol of the free world for every Czech who knew him. Even more amazing, he managed to pull this off *continuously for 30 years!*

What follows is Gene's story - part history, part memoir, part love story. This is his personal account of how it came to be, how the unpredictable events of his new life played themselves out, and how life in a hard-line

communist country truly was. It's the kind of story no reporter who rushed in, interviewed a few dissidents, and rushed out, could ever tell. Gene had a "fly's eye" view, as he puts it, of what was happening on the ground: sad, funny, serious, ironic, absurd. He was here during the dismal Stalinist period, during the Cuban Missile Crisis, during the euphoria of 1968's Prague Spring and its heartbreaking destruction at Soviet hands, during the 20 years of renewed darkness that followed, and finally he was a joyous witness to the "Velvet Revolution" of 1989. He came with a contract assuring he need not stay more than 10 days... and he has been here more than half his life so far!

Gene's story, like the story of the Czechs and Slovaks themselves, is one of courage, hope, and perseverance in the face of an adversity most of us from the West can never know. It is also a story of love, and how the human heart, no matter what our mind tells us, can take us places we've never dreamed of.

David Speranza, Prague

Prague: The Vltava River and Charles Bridge.

Contents

A guide to Czech pronunciation

To help you with pronouncing the Czech names used in this book, here is the Czech alphabet (abecede), with approximate English pronunciations. Czech is nearly phonetic, with only a few exceptions. But watch it! Those little "hook" marks over certain letters, (ěščřžňť), make for a whole new letter with a different pronunciation! They are called "háčky"(hahtch-ky), little hooks.

a=ah, **b**=beh, **c**=tseh, **č**=tcheh, **d**=deh, **e**=eh, **ě**=yeh, **f**=f, **g**=geh (never j !), **ch**=ch as in loch, (ch is considered as a single letter in the Czech alphabet) **h**=ha, **i**=ee, **j**=yuh, **k**=k, **l**=l, **m**=m, **n**=n, **o**=aw, **p**=p, **q**=kveh, **r**=r-r-r, **ř**=r-r-r-zh, voiced and unvoiced. (don't try this at home), **s**=s, **š**=sh, **t**=t, **u**=oo, **v**=v, **w**=v (v&w are pronounced the same!), **x**=ix, **y**=eu (like the German "ü"), **z**=z, **ž**=zh.

The marks áéíóúý are called "čárky" (tcharky), which simply means "marks," and are used only on vowels. They are a subtlety that escapes me. They indicate only a slight lengthening of sound, but not an emphasis, as in English or French. All Czech words and names have the accent on the first syllable, one of the few easy things about Czech. There is also a special little "ů" which isn't pronounced all that differently from a normal u, but such cuties are sacred to Czech speakers. But unlike English, Czech is at least mainly phonetic. Once you master the sounds of the letters, you can pretty much count on them being consistent. Certain exceptions apply, but don't worry about them!

Zdenka

Zdenka is the real subject of this book. She changed my life and I changed hers. She made it possible for me to live through 30 years of communism in a strange land with my wits generally intact. I came through it all with a head full of stories; all true, many absurd, and told here with real names and places. We happened to be thrown together into a unique relationship, in a place few outsiders cared about, cautiously feeling our way over slippery cobblestones, through narrow gas lit streets, and around hazardous corners concealing events that constantly threatened our footing. But we won a Hollywood Oscar, flummoxed and outlived a hard-line communist regime, baffled our families and friends, and found a full and happy life in a place where few would have even looked.

And it all was just by chance. Just the merest, most outside chance...

1 – Fright Flight

"...There's a little girl over there whom you are going to love!"

I was transported, confused and very nervous, into communist Czechoslovakia on October 10, 1959, smack dab in the dark days of the Stalinist regime. *But what in hell was I doing there?* That was the question I asked myself as the Soviet-built DC3-copycat began its descent toward the murky Prague airport.

There were other questions too: "Who is this guy Snyder? Why did he recruit me? Am I being set up?" (Remember, this was the time of early James Bond.) And most intriguingly, *"Who is this person I'm supposedly going to love?"*

I'd been nervous enough simply getting into that plane, which squatted gray and forlorn on the Zürich tarmac amid all the sleek western airliners, its paint drab and flaking. There were only four passengers on board, including an increasingly tremulous me, and even as we filed in, the stale dusty odor seemed oppressive - faintly beery, airless, frayed.

The captain asked us not to all sit on the same side of the plane – presumably his only hope of keeping it on an even keel. The tiny plane, innocent of soundproofing, rattled and howled down the runway, and as it lifted, groaning, into the air, my nervousness rose with it.

The flight from Zürich to Prague is a relatively short one; hardly enough time to contemplate one's fate, especially when faced with stout Pilsner beer poured into real glasses from large, half-liter bottles. This was accompanied by thin slices of fatty but savory Hungarian salami - the unvarying menu, I later learned, on the Czechoslovak Airlines of the day.

As I ate, I glanced out past the plane's dual propellers, determinedly chopping the foreign air. Restricted as we were to a low altitude, I could make out the exact moment we crossed from West German to Czechoslovak airspace. It was when the neat patchwork of carefully plowed German fields suddenly gave way to vast and amorphous smears of unkempt collective farms.

The barbed wire fences and the wide belt of the no-go border zone told me I had crossed the point of no return. Possibly even the pilot was thinking, *"Why am I willingly returning?"* In his case it was likely his wife and kids were there, virtual hostages until his return. My own family was back in

Tarrytown, New York, with little or no idea how fateful this adventure of mine would be. I was equally clueless, and only knew that I was dropping into a pit from which so many were trying to crawl out of.

On my lap I had my trusty 16mm Bolex movie camera. But the moment I lifted it to my eye and pointed it out the window, the stewardess, horrified, rushed up to put her hand over my lens. *"It is forbidden over the territory of Czechoslovakia to photograph!"*

I wasn't about to argue. As we touched down on the patched Prague airport runway with a fateful bounce, I looked down at my whitened knuckles and

Bill Snyder Welcome Gene Deitch to Prague 10/10/59

once again asked myself, *"Gene, what the hell are you doing here?"*

Before I could come up with an answer, the plane had taxied up to the cheerless wooden terminal building, no more than a shed, crowned, so help me, by *a neon hammer & sickle,* glowing grotesquely through the mounting fog.

The plane's door creaked open and a rickety metal stairway was wheeled up. A military looking officer with a red star on his cap appeared, and as I descended into the gloom he reached out his hand.

"Your pesspor-r-r-t, plizz!"

My passport? My God! My brand new United States of America virgin passport! The first and only one I ever had, bought just a week before in New York. Here I was, in the godless bowels of Iron-Curtainland, at the mercy of an inscrutable-language and a hostile ideology, and already I was having my passport confiscated! What do I do now?

As visions of doom loomed before me, I noticed the dim figure of a small woman emerging from the fog. Loping across the tarmac toward the plane, she arrived out of breath, but with a broad smile and one hand extended.

"Mr. Deitch?" she panted, "If you thought you were going to be taken from the airport directly to the jail, that is not true. Welcome to Prague!"

It was my first encounter with Czech humor, and right then the fog seemed to lift a little. *Was this middle-aged woman, I wondered, the one I was going to love?*

2 - Snyder

The circumstances behind my sudden dislocation to this strange land had begun over a year earlier, in New York, where I had reached the top of my craft as creative director of CBS-Terrytoons. This was a huge animation studio in New Rochelle, which produced cartoon shorts for 20th Century-Fox. While there, I'd created Tom Terrific and Mighty Manfred the Wonder Dog for the Captain Kangaroo children's TV show, and won Terrytoons its first Oscar nomination. But I'd inherited a disgruntled staff from founder Paul Terry, and a scheming business manager in whose way I most definitely was. He was clever enough to sabotage my efforts, and after three years there was nothing left for me but to strike out on my own.

In May 1958, I set up my own animation studio on West 61st Street. Gene Deitch Associates, Inc. was ensconced on the cheaper West Side of Manhattan in the Sophia Storage Building. I had some very talented people working with me; some from my earlier days as creative head of the UPA New York studio, and some from Terrytoons, including the budding Jules Feiffer.

Jules had created a hilarious satire on bureaucracy about a four-year-old boy mistakenly drafted into the army. It was called "Munro," and the storyboard was pinned to my wall, waiting for an angel to flutter in and feather it with financing.

On another wall was a story my dear friend, actor Allen Swift and I created, "Samson Scrap & Delilah," about a dedicated Brooklyn junkman and his lady horse.

While awaiting cash-heavy angels, my little group was relegated to the bread and butter business of TV commercials. I was not at all happy being the president of a company. I am no businessman, and the weight of responsibility was unnerving, even though we started with some lucrative contracts.

What I wanted to do were story films, which I had so much fun doing at Terrytoons. The bitterness of my expulsion made even my name, glistening over the door of my own studio seem a bringdown, and it brought tension to my 15-year-old marriage.

Columbia Pictures' Screen Gems division offered me a contract to produce Samson Scrap & Delilah as a series. They were the original backers of Hanna -Barbera, also just then starting. They appeared to want to use me as a buffer against H-B. Their contract was nearly an inch thick. My lawyer waded through it and advised me that maybe, if our series was a roaring hit, my grandchildren might see some money. What had seemed like my ticket to the Big Time, had to be reluctantly nixed.

Into this gloom materialized William L. Snyder. He did not at all look like your average angel. He was 40 years old; prematurely gray, wore a striped seersucker suit, and expelled paralyzing clouds of smoke from his contraband Cuban cigars. His most penetrating features were his Paul Newman-blue eyes. He was a man who could talk anybody into anything, as I was soon to find out. He exuded confidence, enthusiasm, and charm. He referred to himself as "beautiful," and considered himself irresistible, and a mover.

He had earlier phoned, claiming he had been looking for the best animator in New York. I didn't inform him that he possibly had the wrong number. What he had was an unappealing proposition.

"I have some animated films in production," he began, "but they're in trouble, and I'm told you're the only one who can straighten them out."

"If you mean you'll assign your films to my studio, I'll gladly look them over and decide if we can do what you want done with them."

"That's the only catch," he said, delicately drawing on his stogie. "The work has to be done in my facilities."

"Well, that's out. As you can see, I've got my own studio to keep busy. I can't undercut my own staff by directing films elsewhere. Anyway," I said, "I have no interest in kibitzing to another animator's films!"

He kept after me. Showing up nearly every day for a couple of weeks. "Look," he insisted, "These are very interesting children's films, beautifully done, but they just don't have the timing and pizzazz that I need." What I wanted to do were the two projects pinned to my wall.

My phone rang, and as I spoke I noticed Snyder was looking over the two storyboards. The moment I hung up he turned toward me with an offer he was sure I couldn't refuse.

"I'll tell you what I'm gonna do," said Snyder, exhaling another numbing cloud of smoke. He then proceeded to make me the Golden Proposal: *"If you will help me with my films, I will finance your "Munro" and "Samson Scrap" projects. You can direct them, and if they don't come out the way you want, you can throw the film in the trashcan, and keep the rights."*

"Why shouldn't they come out the way I want?" I asked.

"Well, it is barely possible that you may not like the way the animators in my facilities do them. If I back the films, they must be produced in my facilities."

"So just where are your facilities?" I asked, succumbing inevitably to Snyder's persistence, but hoping it would at least be within walking distance or a short taxi ride

"In Prague," he said, coolly examining the "Munro" storyboards at closer range.

Prague? I was incredulous. My mind flashed back to my Army days in World War II. I'd done my basic training at Camp Gruber - which looked just like it sounded - in Muskogee, Oklahoma. Look at a map: Just a few miles to the southwest of Muskogee is a poke town named Prague, where we used to go to a bar while on weekend leave.

"Come on!" I hooted, at last catching on that this was some sort of gag. *"You're not going to tell me that you have an animation studio in Prague, Oklahoma?"*

"No, no!" Now he thought I was the one who was joking. "My studio is in Prague, Czechoslovakia.

"What??!! Isn't that one of those communist countries?" I had, after all, heard of the country whose betrayal at Munich had precipitated World War II, and which had ultimately fallen into the red clutches of the Soviet Union. "I am certainly not willing to go there! *No way!*" But he wasn't about to give up now.

"It's not what you think! There are some great people over there, and this has nothing to do with politics. They need hard currency; I need films. It's strictly business. They've even set up a special 'Snyder Unit' to do my films. And then he delivered what he assumed would be the piece de résistance:

"And there's a little girl over there, the production manager, whom you are going to love!"

In the years leading up to that fateful day, Bill Snyder had been a marginal distributor of 16mm films, specializing in the educational and institutional markets. This was long before video. After World War II, he began scrounging around Europe, looking for bargain films he could acquire for U.S. distribution. He had a special love for puppet films, and had been looking for some in Munich. "The very best puppet films," he was told, "are by Jiří Trnka of Czechoslovakia. But unfortunately, no one can go there."

That was all Bill Snyder needed to hear: that there was somewhere he "couldn't" go. The challenge was irresistible. But he soon found he could hardly even *telephone* there. In fact, it took all day to finally arrange a call for the following day to Czechoslovak Filmexport, the official state-run film trade organization. His smooth talking and broad hints of Big Money actually elicited a business visa-the first, Snyder later claimed, issued to an American since the Communists seized power in 1948.

The great man first arrived in Prague in 1955. He screened films for days, buying many. He had excellent taste, and had good results with the magical puppet films of Jiří Trnka, along with several other cartoon gems. They sold well in the school and library market, and some did well in art house movie distribution, receiving rave reviews. Seeing that he had stumbled onto a good thing, and beginning to scrape the bottom of the barrel of existing films, he wondered if the Czechs might actually produce new films for him, on order. For as beautiful as those early Czech classics of animation were, they were not American in character or pace, and their U.S. distribution possibilities were limited. It was clear the Czechs could do beautiful work, so why not do it on stories supplied by Snyder?

One of the *why-nots* was that this was a "socialist" country with a "socialist" cultural agenda. Why should they lower themselves to produce bourgeois stories for "imperialist Amerika?" But when Snyder mentioned what he would pay for such work, ideology quickly took a back seat to pragmatism. Actually, it was peanuts for Snyder, and even a few dollars were hard to come by in Czechoslovakia during the 1950s.

So it was arranged for Snyder to visit the animation studio. It was called the "Brothers in Trick" studio, and still is today. This strange name is a play on the European tradition of calling animation films "trick" films. Playing with this, one of the leading animators of the studio, Zdeněk Miler (pronounced Mill-air) drew three little curly-haired boys wearing striped T-shirts as the studio trademark. In case you've ever wondered why T-shirts are called T-shirts, it's because they are made of cotton *tricot*. So the "tricot brothers" formed a visual pun for a group who made "trick" films!

BRATŘI V TRIKU

The studio stood on the exact spot where the Malostranská metro station sits today, on Klárov Square, which is why the animators referred to their studio as "Klárov."

On the big day William L. Snyder, with his self-assured American bearing, his bright blue eyes, and his incredible seersucker suit, was to visit the Klárov studio, waves of whispered excitement pulsed through the "temporary" wooden structure. (The building actually had a sign on it, "TEMPORARY STRUCTURE," though no one there could remember when it had been put up.) The most pressing question was: who could speak English and would be able to show Snyder around? The answer was a small bundle of energy named Zdenka.

Bill Snyder, Lulka Kopečná, Gene, Zdenka, at Bursa 1959

3 - The Little One

At the time of Snyder's arrival at Klárov, Zdenka Najmanová was thirty years old, married, and had a four-year-old son named David (the first "David", she claimed, in Czechoslovakia, and later the most popular boy's name - a point of pride with her). As the absurd P.C. term "vertically challenged" had not yet been floated, she could only be described as short, petite, little, tiny. Specifically: 1 inch short of 5 feet. But that was only in tape measure terms. In actual stature, the little chief of Klárov's animation group was tall, self-assured, in control, in *command,* unshakably optimistic, fearless, competent, talented, and in no need whatsoever of Western notions of Women's Lib. She was (and still is) a workaholic and intrepid organizer, ever at the ready to help straighten out anyone's badly managed life. In addition to being blonde, with bright blue eyes and her long golden hair done up in a bun, she was - in contrast to Snyder's theatrical facade - *genuinely* charming.

What could such a woman have known about the West? In this "socialist republic," any chance of experiencing the lands of "capitalist imperialism" was on a par with experiencing a trip to the Moon. Though her attempts to master textbook English remained undaunted, her approach to the language was unimpeded by mere grammatical rules. She rolled over all such obstacles like a verbal juggernaut.

After all, who could doubt there was a great bear of a constellation in the heavens known as the *"Big Diaper?"* Or that New York was crowded with *"skycrappers?"* Or that the Earth might be threatened by *"investors from outer space?"* (I imagined a row of little green men coming down the gangplanks of their flying saucers, each carrying a briefcase.)

"Impossible" was the operating word at the time, and even Zdenka used it when confronted with the startling requests of a brash visiting American. But to William L. Snyder, *nothing* was impossible, and he relished the opportunity to shock and bewilder his isolated and deprived hosts. What he proposed was to shake up the system, shaking up more than a few lives along the way.

On the day he arrived, Zdenka was there to greet him, tripping down the steps in her white, studio-issued smock, one hand smoothing her yellow hair. She showed Snyder around the studio, explaining "ze all," as she put it. Snyder knew nothing about animation production, but he was fascinated by Zdenka. After the grand tour, he took a long puff on his cigar in the office of Vojen

Masník, the studio manager. "OK" he announced, "if you'll set up a unit for me, I'll guarantee a minimum of eight films per year at $5,000 each - but only on one condition..." Masník and the representative from Czechoslovak Filmexport leaned forward with concern... *"That girl,"* proclaimed Snyder with his usual panache, "must be my production manager."

These people had never met anyone like Snyder. With no idea whether or not he was kidding, they promptly appointed Zdenka head of the "Snyder unit." She picked the best people for her crew, and three floors were commandeered in a building on Maxim Gorký Square that once housed the Prague stock exchange, long since abolished by the Communists.

Back in New York, Snyder now needed stories to produce. So from his East 59th Street office he ducked around the corner to the Doubleday Bookstore on 5th Avenue. He happened to have very good taste. He bought three *"Madeline"* books and *"Fifi,"* by Ludwig Bemelmans, *"Many Moons"* by James Thurber, *"The Smiling Prince"* by Crockett Johnson, *"Anatole"* by Eve Titus, and several other children's picture books of equally high quality.

In those days there existed only a minuscule 16mm school and library market for films based on children's books, so acquiring the film rights was a simple matter: Snyder just opened each book to its title page, noted the publisher, and gave them a ring. They were thrilled that some fool was willing to invest money in a film version of their books. Realizing that a film could increase book sales, they were naturally eager to give Bill the rights, often for as little as fifty bucks each!

He sent the books back to Zdenka in Prague, where she and her staff set diligently to work. When the filmed results started coming in, Snyder saw that it was indeed beautiful work: the animation was smooth, perfectly following the style and color of each book, and was accompanied by lovely original music. There was, however, one unexpected problem: The films lacked pace. They were ponderously slow. At that moment it dawned on Snyder that he had forgotten one thing: *to hire his own director.*

The trail led to me.

Can't help it. This is how I looked when I came to Prague.

4 – Ten Days That Shook My World

After signing me up and explaining how to obtain a passport, Snyder once again took off for Prague. I had to laugh at his promise that I would "love" the animation studio production manager. Obviously, this desperate ploy of his was on the assumption that a bit of philandering in a remote location would surely be the hook to grab me. He professed to be a great freelance lover, and figured I too would leap at the chance to taste some exotic fruits.

"Don't get me wrong," he said, drawing deeply on his genuine, illegal Cuban stogie, "I maintain a strictly moral standard when I'm abroad: I never fuck a girl less than half my age."

"Look, Bill, I don't go in for that sort of thing. I'm a happily married man." – (I really did say that!) The fact was I was not interested in fooling around, taking risks, or having to concoct lies. One could easily describe me as an overly cautious person. In any case, I dismissed this proffered bonus to the deal. I was interested only in getting my two pet projects produced, that was all. My plan was to do the absolute minimum of messing with these people's work, get my own projects into production and then get safely home, the sooner the better.

When Snyder arrived in Prague, he hastened to convey his "good news" to Zdenka.

"Darling," he said, placing a reassuring hand on her sturdy little shoulder, "I am bringing you the best animation director in America to show you how to improve these films."

Zdenka was so thrilled with this news she promptly resolved not to speak to me. I can only imagine the torrent of nasty Czech words that must have cascaded through her head. The thought of some smart-assed American hotshot hob-nailing over her finished films created in her a generous serving of advance hostility.

But not knowing my actual agenda, she certainly wasn't about to give up her weekend for me. She refused to even meet me at the airport, and sent her secretary instead. So it was the similar-sized, but 20-years-older, Ludvíka Kope_ná who met me at the airport that first day - and not the woman who, in less than two weeks, would completely change my life.

My plane touched down in Prague on Saturday, October 10, 1959. Along with my trusty Bolex, I was armed with a contract between William L. Snyder, "doing business as Rembrandt Films," and myself, which included, at my insistence, the clause: **"Deitch shall not be required to remain in Prague for a period of more than 10 days."** I wasn't taking any chances - though of course I had no idea what a joke that clause would turn out to be.

Ludvíka "Lulka" Kopečná, 15 years my senior, quickly steered me through customs, and retrieved my precious passport. All had been prepared for me, including a waiting car - in this case, a rattly Škoda 1950s Oktavia* wagon that belonged to the studio. We drove through the darkening streets of the town's outskirts and into its drab depths, Lulka enthusiastically pointing out how beautiful everything was. I was so happy to have an English-speaking host that I soaked up every word. Lulka, who was to be my guide and interpreter for those first awkward days, was an encyclopedia of Prague knowledge. "Hell," I thought, "I might as well get the most out of this adventure - after all, it's only for 10 days." I had that in black and white!

We pulled up to the Alcron hotel, located on a side street just around the corner from Prague's main drag, Wenceslas Square. A musty old relic of the bourgeois past, the Alcron and its lobby struck me as the perfect setting for a 1930s Marx Brothers movie.

I entered the building, and there he was - reclining in one of the well-worn overstuffed chairs, puffing on his powerful Cuban cigar. William L. Snyder.

---

* Not to be confused with the slick Škoda Oktavia, produced in the later Volkswagen-owned Škoda Auto company of the post-revolution Czech Republic.

5 – The Alcron

The faded and musty Hotel Alcron was reserved almost exclusively for westerners. You had little choice. There were a couple of other hotels in the center reserved for western businessmen - the Jalta, the Esplanade, and the Palace - while officials from other communist countries were always housed in the International, a long way off. Lenin forbid the twain should meet! There was even a mystery hotel, completely unmarked, near the Old Town Square, which was reserved for visiting Communist dignitaries.[1] But it was the Alcron that was the center of the town's wheeling and dealing, complete with genuine Old Prague atmosphere. It was staffed with reasonably courteous spies, and had quite a good restaurant, complete with potted palms and a Gypsy orchestra. My single room cost $1.75 per night at the black market rate - the rate, of course, that Snyder lived by.[2]

On arriving, I wanted to telephone home to assure my family I was okay. The woman at the Alcron switchboard told me, "No problem - I can probably put you through to New York at around 3PM tomorrow!" The switchboard was one of those walnut-veneered monsters shaped like an upright piano. Cloth-covered cables with brass jacks were plugged into various holes to make the connections. The whole place was a living museum of former

[1] If you get as far as the Epilog, you can read what happened to the Alcron Hotel.

[2] One of the great mysteries at that time was the Czechoslovak crown's actual worth. The "official" rate was seven crowns to a dollar; the "tourist" rate was 15 to a dollar. What Snyder actually got from his private suppliers was 35 to a dollar. I should explain: Snyder was a collector of antiques, of which Prague was overflowing. The antique shops, like everything else, were state-owned, but the managers of these collection points for family heirlooms - which were sold to raise money for necessities - were happy to spot and reserve choice items for a magician whose wand could make some US dollars appear in their pockets. For Snyder, and thus for me, everything was dirt-cheap. The Czechs were not so fortunate. One of the first jokes I heard was, "They pretend to pay us, and we pretend to work."

elegance, worn but evocative of more glamorous times. I half expected Fred & Ginger to waltz gaily in and sidle up to the bar.

There was only one elevator, with brass pantograph doors and a real live elevator operator. No Czech would enter that elevator to visit one of the foreign guests without first leaving his or her identity book with the porter. Only a very reckless person would risk being added to the national shitlist for such an act. Aside from Czechs officially doing business with foreigners, few dared to be seen even in the lobby of that place. Later, when I got to know a few people, they would always ask to meet at a less conspicuous venue, especially since they would be speaking English with me. The first time I was actually invited to a Czech person's home, I was instructed before entering the building to "Please not speak in the hallway!" Every apartment house had a "housekeeper," who recorded in a special book the names of all visitors. God forbid it should be a foreigner!

The Alcron was full of foreigners, all huddled in little groups in the lobby, often with representatives of the official import/export organizations. At any one time they could be seen conducting whispered under-the-counter deals for Bo-hemian glass, assignations, and who knows what else. There were plenty of winks, suggesting pay-offs, gifts, or that greatest inducement of all, invitations to business meetings abroad. Exit Fred & Ginger, enter Sidney Greenstreet.

32

When checking in at the Alcron, or any hotel for that matter, you were required to leave your passport and visa at the front desk. These were sent to the police for registering and stamping. If you stayed in a private home, or at a relative's or friend's apartment, you had to go to the police personally to register. If you didn't have the stamp in your visa showing you stayed at a "proper" place, you might have trouble leaving the country. The authorities wanted to know just where you were, and with whom you bunked. At the Alcron, your passport and visa were returned the next day.

Bill Snyder took me to dinner at the nearby Čínský restaurant, the only "Chinese" eatery in town. It was said to have been set up by cooks from the Chinese People's Republic back when Czechoslovakia and China still had good relations. Now, however, it was operated by locals, whose idea of Chinese food was that it should be spicy enough to make your ears smoke. It was the first time I'd seen waiters in a Chinese restaurant who weren't actually Chinese.

Soon after dinner I bade Snyder goodnight. Tomorrow was to be the Big Day, when I would see the animation studio for the first time, and start the job I'd been hired for. So off to bed I went, to let the hidden microphones in my hotel room record my every seditious snore.

The pohotos of the Alcron in this chapter are from the owners' archives, and date from the time I lived there. They are used here by permission.

6 - Bursa

The next morning Lulka met me in front of the hotel. Gorky Square was only a short walk away from the Alcron, near the Prague Central railway station, (once called Masaryk Train Station, but renamed Central Station by the Communists for reasons of "clarity"). The largest building on the square formerly housed the Prague stock exchange, called *bursa* in Czech, from the French word *bourse*. For this reason, "Bursa" was the staff's everyday name for the studio's "Snyder Unit," located on the fourth, fifth, and sixth floors.

Snyder taught me at least one thing of value, for which I duly credit him: it's actually easier to climb stairs two at a time than one at a time - especially if you have long legs like mine. Make a note of that. As Bursa had no functioning elevators, I did a lot of stair climbing in those days. And of course the animators did it regularly. That's probably why the first thing they did every morning while recovering enough breath to actually work, was to water their plants,s (there wasn't an office in Prague without plants lining every window sill), and make themselves a cup of "turecká káva".

Vaguely related to Turkish coffee, káva Turk was made by treating finely-ground coffee as if it were instant. Real instant coffee did not yet exist here. It took a great deal of expertise to drink káva Turk without getting a mouthful of grounds. After you poured boiling water over the ground coffee, you put in your sugar and gave it several seconds of diligent stirring. Then you *waited*. Patience was the key. It smelled marvelous, but too eager a gulp and you swallowed grounds. Only after they had settled to the bottom of the cup could you take a sip. And of course you had to know when to stop. Once I'd figured all this out I had to admit it was great coffee.

I was offered my first cup soon after entering the studio, and I realized then that working with the Czechs was going to be a lot like preparing káva turk: just enough stirring so as not to stir up the grounds. I did my best to explain what I was reluctantly there to do, and hoped they wouldn't hold it against me personally. Actually, they were very attentive. After all, I was an American, and America was considered "*vonderfool*" These people were by no means the hard-line communists I'd expected to meet.

Things started off well enough, but one early encounter pointed out the hazards of an unfamiliar language. I was carefully explaining a tricky suggested revision to Václav Bedřich, who I later learned was one of the country's best animation directors. To everything I said, as translated by Lulka, he responded "I know, I know, I know." At least I *thought* that's what he said. I wondered what I was doing there if he already knew everything I was proposing! It was only later that I understood: the Czech word for "yes" is "ano" which I heard as "I know." So Bedřich's "ano,ano,ano" actually meant, "yes,yes,yes!"

Later on we ran into a more serious stumbling block, and it was clear Bedřich was *not* saying "yes,yes,yes." It began to get a bit tense. During our exchange, I noticed a vague blur out of the corner of my eye. A small figure in a white smock would enter the room hefting a huge stack of boxes filled with animation drawings, set the drawings on top of a cabinet, glance in our direction, then zip out. On a closer look I saw it was a young woman. She repeated this action several times, sometimes bringing in more boxes, sometimes taking them out again.

Just when Bedřich and I seemed to reach an impasse, the small woman came in again. This time she put down her boxes, stepped quickly to our table, drew up a chair, and rattled off a barrage of vehement Czech. I watched in amusement, thinking, "There must be something to this socialism after all, if even an ordinary *gofer* has the right to put in her two-cents worth!"

It was my first encounter with Zdenka. Several more days would pass before she actually acknowledged my presence, but when she did, I finally realized my error: Lulka wasn't the production manager, Zdenka was! She had been watching me from a distance, sizing me up while letting her secretary take me in hand.

By the end of the first week, she was ready to speak to me. She strode up to me suddenly, as I was about to leave for the day.

"If you like, I go with you shopping on Satur-r-day."

Those were her first words to me, and it was the start, as they say, of a beautiful friendship.

* You will have a hard time finding Gorky Square today, the site of my first meeting with Zdenka and our first work together. Today it has erevrted to its original, pre-communist name, "Senovážné náměstí" (Haymarket Square), and the former "Bursa" building is now a part of the Czech National Bank. In fact, the once dingy dark corner where the entrance to the studio was, is now elegantly restored. I have yet to venture inside again myself!

Gene and Zdenka at the Bursa studio - October 1959

7 - Praha

Like so many Americans who have never before left their own country, I was a true babe in the European woods. I had never been to London, Paris, Rome, or any of the other obligatory first places to see in Europe. I was surely the only American in those days whose very first trip to Europe was directly to the planet Prague.

And it really was like another planet. "Praha" to its inhabitants, Prague at that time was as one might have imagined Old Europe to be. Western Europe had already become heavily Americanized and tourist laden, but Prague was behind the iron curtain, and that was no mere metaphor. The 28th of October, shortly after I arrived, was a national holiday, and Prague was festooned with thousands of flags. Czechoslovakia was founded on that date in 1918 by Tomáš Garrigue Masaryk, but the Communists co-opted the holiday by nationalizing industry on the same date. So October 28 no longer commemorated the founding of the "bourgeois state," but was "*Nationalization Day.*"

I didn't actually think that all those flags were out just to welcome me, but I was amazed at how many flags a poor little country could afford. I was also intrigued by their symmetry. Every window of every building sported two little flags, one Czechoslovak and one Soviet. The Communists were big on flags, but only in the prescribed twinned display of the red, white, and blue national flag closely guarded by the ruddy Soviet banner. The Czech flag was never permitted to fly alone. That would be considered a provocation. Every building was draped with giant twin banners. Every doorway, all the bridges over the Vltava River, even the old time streetcars rumbling and squealing down the undulating streets, bore the twin flags on their noses. I imagined that somewhere in a dark corner of Prague there must have been a giant warehouse crammed with flags. I later dreamed of the day when only Czechoslovak flags would fly - a day that would not come for another 30 years.

Meanwhile, there was still so much for me to learn. I wondered, "Who were these Czechs?" I learned that Czechs represent the farthest western tide of Slavic peoples. When one thinks of Slavs, one pictures Russians, Bulgarians, and the darker nationalities of former Yugoslavia. But Czechs rarely conform to these broad types. Look in the Vienna phone book and you'll see hundreds of Nováks, Dvořáks and Kubičeks. Most likely they were born in Austria and speak only German. Are they Czechs or Austrians? The Czech Republic's first Prime Minister, later parliament president is named Klaus.

He is a Czech, born in Prague, speaks Czech, but has a German name. There are thousands of Czechs with such straight German names, or names of German origin transformed into Czech orthography-such as Najman, pronounced "Nigh-mann," obviously derived from Neumann. Over the centuries, Swedes, Germans, and Austrians invaded this little former kingdom. Its historically brief union with the Slovaks, forming Czechoslovakia, and the 40-year domination by the Soviets left remarkably little influence or cross breeding on the bouncing Czechs.

The fact is, Czechs on the whole look far more like Germans, Austrians and Swedes than like the darker peoples of other Slavic nations. A derogatory joke in Poland once played up this fact, calling the Czechs "German whores who happen to speak a Slavic language."

So on that day long ago, Prague was flagbound as well as fogbound. The ancient town was gray with mist, its silhouetted towers receding in a variety of gray tones like cutouts on a stage set. The damp, narrow streets twisted this way and that as Lulka described for me the more significant places.

"Here is where Mozart conducted the premiere of Don Giovanni... Here is where Beethoven stayed when he visited Prague... Here is where 27 Czech noblemen were beheaded in 1621, after the defeat by the Hapsburgs at the Battle of White Mountain... Here is where Franz Kafka lived... Here is where Albert Einstein stayed... Here is the house where I was born... Here is where I went to grammar school... Here is where I played as a little girl... And here is where my father had his cosmetics shop."

Amazing. I had never lived in any one place in America for more than four years at a time, and yet here was a woman whose personal history took place amid the same settings as all those historic events before her.[1]

I recorded everything I saw on those first tours with my Bolex. (Apparently it was okay, once I was on the ground). Daytime revealed Prague's shabbiness. The buildings, all variations of dun color, were crumbling, a fact that was con-

---

[1] The cosmetics shop Lulka showed me, right at Můstek, the center of the commercial downtown district, was confiscated by the Communist government, along with her father's cosmetic factory. Lulka had become resigned to her low-income life, even though she had been raised as a rich girl. The building at Můstek was demolished a few years after I arrived, and the irony is that even now, in the new Czech Republic, the restitution laws cannot give her back her property, as it no longer exists.

firmed by the many "WATCH OUT FOR FALLING PLASTER!" signs that Lulka translated for me. Inside, tiles were cracked. Paint was distant history.

The shops were dismal. Goods looked like something from my earliest boyhood. Butter was carved off large blocks, weighed, and wrapped in scraps of paper. Loose items were poured into cones made from yesterday's pages of the Communist newspaper, Rudé právo - an excellent journal for this purpose. Medicines came in corked bottles with a bit of cloth over the top, tied with a string.

There were very few cars, and those were dulled with faded paintwork, resembling the failed tinny Kaiser compacts I recalled from 10 years earlier. The people seemed equally faded, shuffling along the streets in clothes like those from America's depression years.

*And there were no dogs...*or hardly any. As I found out later, this is a nation of dog lovers, but dogs eat meat, and there was little enough of that around even for humans. Today, dog shows abound, and every noble breed is proudly displayed - but the almost total lack of canines in those first days merely added to the gloom.

And the gloom was citywide after nightfall. During the '50s and early '60s, Prague was pitch dark at night. Due to a shortage of electrical power, there was no street lighting at all. It was definitely creepy, feeling your way across the cobbles on a moonless night. In today's Prague, with the castle and most towers and historic buildings floodlit every night of the year, I think back to the times when such lighting was only on special holidays, such as the annual celebration of "The Great October Socialist Revolution."

Yes, it was all very depressing. But even so, besides the fascinating historical aspects, there was something about the place that immediately spoke to me, made me feel cozy and comfortable, overcoming my initial unease. *What was it?* This city was as foreign to me as any place could be. I had no roots here that I could imagine. I was raised a California boy. Nothing and no one is old in California. But here, *everything* was ancient and musty. The buildings hadn't enjoyed any meaningful upkeep in over 50 years. The people were secretive and suspicious, not naive and open as I was raised to be. They spoke an incomprehensible language. All was drab and distant. It was all so *foreign.*

So what was it that grabbed me? The gas lamps? The historic center was still lit with them. A woman with a large dog and a long pole with a hook on one end would walk from lamp to lamp, hoist up the pole, then tug on a small ring which released the gas, causing the ornate cast iron lamps to plume with a soft orange glow. Charming, certainly, but that still wasn't it. *So what was it?* And then I knew. It was the *smell.* I was raised in California, but I was born in Chicago. In the 1920s, Chicago was heated with coal. My family moved to California when I was just a few years old. No coal heat in California. But from every chimney in old Prague there rose a flume of coal smoke that settled over the town, blackening the stones and the statues and filling the air with that pervasive odor of coal that went all the way back to my childhood. Smell is said to be the most evocative of the senses. Polluting or not, the smell of coal worked its magic on me! In this strange and foreign place, I began to feel at home.

There was one thing Lulka showed me that stuck in my mind for the next 30 years. She pointed me toward the city's and the nation's pride: Prague castle, at Hradčany. As we leaned on the balustrade at the river's edge, looking across to that magnificent castle high on the hill, Lulka told me that Bohemian kings had lived there from the year 900. Then, after 1620, the Hapsburgs occupied the castle for 300 long years, suppressing the Czech language and Germanizing the nation's culture. Finally, in 1918, Tomáš Garrigue Masaryk established the first democratic Czechoslovak state. He and his successor, Edvard Beneš, governed from the castle for barely 20 years, however, until Hitler's forces moved in during the brutal Nazi occupation of 1939 to 1945. And now the Communists were here - one hostile regime after another. "But," added Lulka significantly, *"The castle is still there"*-a symbol of Czech continuity. Musing over this, I thought, "History doesn't stop. Today a Communist leader sits in the castle, but this too shall pass!" But no one I subsequently met was prepared to believe the communists would pass away in our lifetimes...

When we walked to the center of the Charles Bridge, Lulka said, "If you stand here and turn 360 degrees, you won't see anything you could not have seen two and a half centuries ago." I looked all around at the spires, seemingly hundreds of them, silhouetted and receding in the mist. Incredible. But wait...

"What's *that???*" I asked. It was an immense granite statue of Josef Stalin, seeming as large as our Statue of Liberty and a likely match for the Colossus of Rhodes. It loomed on the highest bluff along the far shore of the eternal river Vltava (Moldau), dominating and mocking the heritage below. It seemed built to last as long as the Sphinx of Egypt.[2]

"We don't see it," said Lulka quietly.

To get an idea of the grotesque hugeness of this thing, note the two people in the photo below, standing beside it. At least the people of Prague did inherit a magnificent view, previously seen only by the stony eyes of Stalin. The view was always there if you were a bird, but previously there was no easy way to get up there, nor was there a place to stand. It's now easily accessible by an impressive stone staircase.

[2] The immense statue of Stalin was demolished in 1962, jack-hammered into shamed submission. It took two months to do the job, with crews working night and day. I experienced great pleasure watching it day by day, as it seemed to twist and grimace, then slowly surrender itself to granite dust. The statue was gone in a final dynamite blast, but the huge plinth remained to remind all below of the vast stupidity and waste that monstrous figure signified. I was told it cost as much as a complete hospital and housing development combined. It was constructed in 1952 of fourteen thousand tons of granite. It took 495 days and 623 workers and stonemasons to build it. It stood a full 30 meters high! Stalin's head was carved from a block of stone weighing 52 metric tons. The widespread joke was that Stalin, posed with his hand in his coat, Napoleon style, was reaching for his wallet, but when he heard how much his statue cost, the Man of Steel turned to stone!

8 – An American Sportsman

Zdenka had heard from Lulka that I wanted to find some gifts for my family, and after deducing that I was not so poisonous as she had imagined, decided to take charge of me. What convinced her, I later learned, was that I was wearing a heavy red sweater that somehow conveyed to her that I was a *"sportovec"* - a sportsman. Apparently the idea of a non-sportsman wearing sportswear had not yet penetrated these parts. It was a rare error of perception for Zdenka, one she rues to this day! Of course, I was just 35 years old, still had my hair, and my mother swore I was handsome. Zdenka had been watching me, and I had been watching her. There were actually *two* items of clothing I wore on that first visit which helped break the ice. The first was the heavy red sweater, and the second was my "plastic" suit. I wore one of the first polyester suits, and its olive green sheen attracted a lot of attention from the animators. They couldn't believe that cloth could be made from plastic. For them, it was yet one more Wonder of the West.

But while the animators stared awestruck at my plastic suit, I found it increasingly hard to keep my eyes off Zdenka. Granted, the studio was filled with gorgeous girls, and in my position as an exotic object, I suppose I could have done well with any number of them. Marrying a westerner was the one fairly sure way to get out of the country. But I really was not looking to get involved. And anyway, I was already married. Certainly Zdenka was no Barbie doll, but she had a magnetism and charm that was stunning. Just to watch her move, and to see her blue eyes flash, began to overtake all my previous convictions. I could see in this woman not only a unique person, but much more: the potential for a whole new way of life.

And what, you may ask, was wrong with my *old* life? To all outward appearances I had a loving relationship with my wife; I had three bright sons; I had reached a peak in my profession.

I didn't think of myself as trapped. But my world was small. Like most Americans, I couldn't imagine any better place. On top of that, I had recently endured my deepest creative frustration when my wife, against our agreement, had allowed herself to become pregnant in order to force me to give up my syndicated comic strip. Producing such a strip had been a boyhood dream, and if it had been given time to become successful I knew it could allow us to travel and live anywhere in the world. The smashing of that dream was a blow from which I never recovered. From that point on I lived in a funk, and just plodded along. My wife became prone to violent rages, and would cut me off for days, weeks sometimes, without speaking a word to me. Gloom set in as I bore my wife's outbursts of fury and rage as something I somehow deserved. I hardly even realized something was wrong until Zdenka and Prague made me see things in a completely new light. In my eyes, they represented that rare Second Chance I'd never imagined was possible.

Saturday, our day for shopping, finally came. Zdenka and I met downtown. As we strolled from shop to shop, I wanted to be a gentleman, so of course I pulled open the doors. But this only unnerved her.

"Don't open doors for me," she scowled. *"I am spor-r-ts woman!"* Armed with only my sporty sweater, I was in no position to argue.

We came to a coin-operated scale in one of the many arcades along Wenceslas Square, and Zdenka wanted to weigh me. She held my coat as I stepped onto the scales. It read 74 kilos (163 lbs.). This seemed to satisfy her. Clearly she was checking me out.

We continued on, and I found myself growing more and more fascinated. I wanted to know all about Zdenka Najmanová. She was for me an exotic person from a faraway land. I wanted to know where she was born, I wanted to hear about her childhood, her family; what life was like in this once-upon-a-time fairy tale kingdom… And before long, she told me.

My "plastic" suit, - early 1960s

9 - Dynamo

"I was born Zdenka Pavlína Hrachovcová, in Prague, on May 18, 1928," Zdenka told me matter-of-factly. I tried to figure out the meaning of her maiden name. The word "*hrach*," I learned, meant pea, so I was hoping I could call her "sweet pea." I was somewhat disappointed when she corrected me. *Hrachovec*, the masculine form of her family name, is nothing but a pea-shaped stone.

She was a hair or two under five feet tall, so I believed her when she told me how tiny she was as a little girl. "My mother put an enormous bow on my head that made me look even smaller," she said. "I was almost always late for school." (I believe that, too. I have 40 years experience of waiting, waiting, waiting for her to arrive at appointed meetings.)

"When I arrived late for school," she continued, "I had to wait for the teacher to come out and open the door for me, because I was too little to reach the doorknob!"

From her earliest years, charm was her weapon. "Even as a little girl I had a beautiful singing voice," she admits proudly, "and when my mother took me with her on the streetcar, I would sing loudly, and it would embarrass my mother when the other tram riders gave me coins!"

Tragedy struck when she was only seven years old. "My mother was shaking out a small carpet on the balcony of our apartment house when she suddenly lost her balance and fell. I was too scared to move. My older brother Fanina ran down the stairs to the courtyard, but Mother was quite dead."

So Zdenka, at the age of seven, became the "housewife" for her father and brother. "I had to stand on a box to do the dishes. I did the laundry, scrubbed floors, and carried buckets of coal from the basement."

She worked and studied, and to this day she is unable to sit still for long. Everywhere she looks she sees something that needs to be done. Dust and Disorder are her mortal enemies, and she fights them constantly. When I came to Prague, Snyder had already nicknamed her "Dynamo," and that certainly fit.

The tragic death of her mother at such an early age forced her to be self-sufficient. Her mother had been a seamstress before she was married, and her father was a stonecutter and a telegraph operator for the Czech railway. They lived in humble rooms above a railroad station. Zdenka was determined to make the most of her life. She had many basic talents and a perceptive intelligence. She was a marvelous singer and dancer, downhill skier, and graphic artist. She began to study languages, both French and English. "I became a member of a girls chorus," she told me. "We even did a concert in Krakow, Poland. I loved to be with people, and I thought I would like to be a tour guide, because I dreamed about traveling. But because I could draw, I also wanted to be a fashion designer."

The Nazi occupation and the war years were of course terrible for her. "There were so many bombs! It was frightening. They were always *American* bombing planes." I winced at this, even though the damage to this country caused by American bombers was in fact relatively light. During the Second World War, I trained as an Air Cadet. It was toward the end of the war, and the pilot training program soon ended. Still, I thought, *"What if I had actually become a member of a U.S. bomber crew, and had bombed Zdenka?"*

She lived through several bombings. "But my father moved me out of Prague to the South Bohemian countryside for two months during the worst of it." She managed, even during that time of great national tragedy, to attend language school and to learn both English and French. She also studied art at the Prague School of Practical Arts, but when the Prague Nazi *Reichsprotektor* Reinhardt Heydrich was assassinated by Czech patriots who parachuted in from Britain, all such schools and universities were closed in reprisal.

"When I was out of school and with no employment, I could have been sent to the 'Reich' to work, and that would be the worst!" Conditions for Czech workers in the sweatshops of wartime Germany were just a notch above the death camps. "I was lucky that I was put into the Philips light bulb factory. It was run by the Nazis, and was like slavery, but at least it was in my country." She spent four months in the repetitive job of winding light bulb filaments. "We had to be at work at six every morning, and when we entered the factory, a Nazi officer with his uniform and boots and a swastika on his arm watched each of us enter and punch the clock. A red light would flash on at random, and whoever was coming in at that moment was searched. It was a great terror. If you broke any rule you would be sent to the Reich." Zdenka told me she was only reprieved from light bulbs when American bombers put out the lights of the Philips plant.

When the war finally ended in 1945, Zdenka was just 17 years old and was looking for a job in fashion design. "I had a close girlfriend who was a good writer, and we had the idea to do a report on the Prague Barrandov movie studio. I would draw the illustrations, and we would try to sell our article to a magazine.

"When we were up there waiting to interview a Barrandov director, I saw a notice announcing that the Czech artist Jiří Trnka was restarting the animation studio. That sounded very interesting, so I hitchhiked back up there with my portfolio of drawings. The animation studio chief thought I was too young and was going to send me away, but the production manager, Jirka Veselý, came in and looked at my drawings. I think he liked my spirit, and he said 'she will be good!' And so I was hired."

Zdenka never looked back. Starting from the bottom, she did every job - cel colorist, inker, in-betweener, and animator. But her way with people, her incredible energy and élan, soon put her in organizational capacities. She became chief of the animation group. Her initiative, plus her personality and great ability to get things done, led Trnka to ask her to produce a film he was doing for the UN. By the time Snyder arrived, she already had experience in production management. In later years she became an executive producer, concentrating on custom production - which was work done for paying customers, as opposed to state-financed "artistic" productions made for Czech film distribution and film festivals. It tickles me when I think that for so many years during the communist times, I was not only her husband, but also her customer!

As I update this chapter, (spring 2002), she has worked in the studio 57 years and counting, is now the Studio Manager, and remains vague about retiring. Do you know anyone who has worked in one outfit for 57 years? Should I phone Guinness? She always had the same answer when asked why she couldn't just take a few days off. "It is my duty."

Zdenka is the "little Auntie" of the studio, always available to listen to her people and advise them on any troubles or problems they have. I've lost track of how many marriages she's arranged. But she is also a tough taskmaster. She constantly makes the rounds of the studio, a vast multi-story labyrinth, to make sure all are doing what they're supposed to. She had to give up wearing high heels. The "TIP-TIP, TIP-TIP" of her rapid short steps would instantly cause a dozing animator to snap to a working attitude!

The same goes for me, too. If I think that at 78 it is too much for me to climb up an 8-meter (25 foot) metal ladder to paint the topmost part of our cottage gable, she rolls out her favorite motto: "Only the strongest survive!" At 74, she shows no sign of slowing down, and I suppose that any sympathy for me will have to wait until her back is in the same shape as mine.

A while back her boss, the head of the parent film company, Krátký Film Prague, brought an American film delegation to tour the animation studio, and introduced them to Zdenka: "This is Mrs. Deitchová. She is our premier producer of animation, and has been in our studio for over 55 years. What's more, she lured an American here, and he has stayed for 40 years so far!"

Zdenka - 2001

10 – Magic City

One of Zdenka's first problems after breaking her silence was how to entertain me. The language barrier ruled out plays and movies, but I had noticed posters and records in shops that indicated there was jazz here. I've been a life-long jazz fan, and had assumed, from the anti-communist reporting in

America, that jazz here was forbidden. Well, at one time it had been, but recently it had occurred to the authorities - no doubt encouraged by the country's jazz music lovers - that jazz was a music of "black American freedom fighters in protest against bourgeois capitalist exploitation." So on that basis it was allowed to be played, and was even encouraged.

Thirty years later, American jazz and pop music would play a large role in bringing down the regime, but in 1959 there was only discreet Dixieland. One group of jazz veterans had formed a band called The Prague Dixieland, and were playing a concert at the famous Prague Lucerna hall, just a few nights after my arrival. I was amazed at how thoroughly the essence of American jazz had filtered through the iron curtain. After the concert, Zdenka took me backstage to meet the band members, and there I was zapped by my first experience of pure Prague magic, one of the weird manifestations that seem to weave through the strands of our lives.

Fifteen years earlier, as a fanatic young devotee of New Orleans jazz, I had drawn a series of cartoons and cover designs for a genuinely obscure jazz record collector's magazine called The Record Changer. I mailed in my cartoons and cover illustrations from Hollywood, where I lived. I never met the editor. It was just a hobby, but it led to my getting my first chance to work in an animation movie studio. Other than a few friends and colleagues, no one but dedicated old-timey jazz purists knew about that obscure magazine or of my cartoons in it.

But when I was introduced to the members of this faraway and isolated Prague Dixieland band, the guitar player, a doctor named Ludvík Šváb, stood up and asked in pretty good English, *"Are you by chance same Gene Deitch who drew cartoons in Record Changer magazine?"*

As my jaw dropped lower than the bottom string on his guitar, he groped under his seat for his valise. After pulling out a good length of sausage and half a bottle of beer, he retrieved, right there on the spot, six dog-eared copies of The Record Changer magazine!

Here I was, thousands of miles from my own country and behind an iron border, but I knew that I was "home." This was indeed a magic city!

11 – Love Spins

Zdenka took over as my Prague tour guide, making a point of showing me the "lovers lane" river bank on the little island of Kampa, where the washerwomen of Prague once lived and worked. In the evenings we wandered through all the romantic twisting gas lit lanes, and on Wednesday she took me to the little hide-away restaurant, "U Malířů" (At the Painter's). This candle-lit *vinárna*, or wine restaurant, has all its walls and ceiling painted with frescoes. In the 15th century, a poor artist earned his meals by decorating the interior, and his paintings are still there.

Zdenka chose a table for two, way in the back, and ordered vodka as an *aperitif.* "In our country," she instructed me, "we have this special habit." She demonstrated by interlocking our arms in such a way that after sipping from our vodka glasses, there was such a labial proximity that there was nothing to do but kiss. That was it. I was swept away.

This was entirely new for Zdenka, too. As with me, she had never considered having an affair. Under the glow of our circumstances, reason did not stand much of a chance. Zdenka's marriage was solid but dull. Her husband was not an artist, and had no interest in culture, which was Zdenka's passion. She told me that had I not materialized, her marriage would have ended anyway. It was above all her sense of duty, and especially her devotion to her son, that had kept the marriage going.

"Wouldn't it be fine if we could someday have a little nest right in this area?" I said, as this dream evening progressed. Amazingly, we actually now have our apartment no more than 100 yards from U Malířů! But then? Are you kidding? We were both married, with kids, and living on opposite sides of the iron curtain! Talk about *"Mission: Impossible!"*

But Zdenka had one more thrilling surprise for me. She laid on the table a gold chain with one of those little disks hanging from it that spin when you blow on it, making seemingly random marks on each side of the disc blend together to form the illusion of words - the most basic form of animation. I immediately blew on it, and the words said in Czech, "MILUJI TĚ" ("I LOVE YOU!")

I caught my breath. *"Where in the world did you find this?"* I couldn't think of anything else to say for a moment... but it soon came to me. Another kiss; this time for all time.

She found this rare spinner in a Prague antique shop. Even more amazingly, on my next trip I found an identical little gold spinner-disc that said on it... "I LOVE YOU" in English! To this day we both wear these little gold love discs on chains around our necks, and we never take them off.

My 10-day maximum contract with Snyder was already fading from my mind. Now the question was: How could I *prolong* my stay? How could I *return?*

We walked and talked. Each night Zdenka had to concoct excuses to her husband - "foreign customer" and all that. We became more and more distraught as the day of my departure neared. Everything was stacked against us. I had a one-time-visit visa, valid for just a couple of weeks. I was from the number-one Enemy State, the USA. This was Communist Czechoslovakia at its darkest time. Zdenka was a prisoner of the State, as were all Czechs and Slovaks. Leaving the country to the West was for her virtually impossible.

Yet there it was: an explosion for both of us. We both realized we were intensely in love. Theoretically it was a golden chance for a renewed crack at life, but in fact the future for a relationship was bleak. Only the brief and fleeting present existed for us.

We were in terrible danger: I, of being expelled and being denied re-entry, she, of being permanently locked in. We would have to wait, think, and hope...

This former "Tuzex" hard-currency shop, still to bee seen on Palackého ulice, could not be entered in the communist times, without first showing that you had at least some of the "Tuzex" hard-currency coupons actually in hand.

51

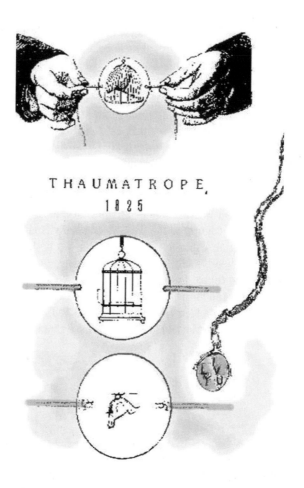

THAUMATROPE,
1825

Here is one of our original gold "love spinners,"
displayed on a reproduction of one of the earliest
animation devices. Both work in the same way.
If you blow on the spinner, letters on both sides
of the disc blend together, to form the words,
"I LOVE YOU." If you spin the disc of the
Thaumatrope between your thumb and forefinger,
the bird appears to be in the cage. So our
love spinners are appropriate to our profession!

12 - East Meets West

During those first days, I screened some of my UPA films for the staff. I needed to show them that I was really a professional, and that my advice was worth listening to. After that, I seemed to get increased respect, and was no longer viewed as a troublemaking interloper. That made things a lot easier.

The great moment came when I was finally able to get my own two film projects started. In animation, a scenario is in the form of many little drawings showing the action and scene continuity, all pinned to a large sheet of wall-board. We call this visual scenario, which resembles a long comic strip, a "storyboard." When explaining the storyboard to the staff, a pointer is used and the story acted out. What was hilarious in this case was that it all had to be translated.

I would enthusiastically act out the scenario, and each time I came to a gag point, there was a long pause while Lulka translated. Then, about 20 seconds later, everyone would laugh. It was like seeing a movie that was 20 seconds out of synchronization! It was talk-pause-*laugh*, talk-pause-*laugh*, talk-pause-*laugh*, throughout the entire demonstration! (Fortunately, there were no groans.)

I was delighted that they liked my projects, so culturally different from their own. I had brought with me the dialogue soundtracks for the two films, which I had recorded in New York, and I was ready to give the individual scenes to animators that Zdenka had recommended. So we were all into a working relationship.

I don't want to bore you with lectures on animation art and technology, but certain things have to be understood to fully appreciate the problems of my situation. Though the Czech artists who set up the animation studio just after World War II certainly had a passion for this art, they did not really know how to go about it.

All they had were bootleg black & white prints the Germans had duplicated from a couple of Disney features. They figured out basically how these films were made by running them on what they called a "Kinox" machine, a gadget made out of old projector parts that allowed a film to be run frame-by-frame and viewed on a plate of frosted glass. Working "backwards" in this way, they more or less figured out how the animation drawings and backgrounds should be organized.

The technology of animation had been formalized within the Disney studio during the '20s and '30s, and had subsequently been adapted in nearly all animation studios in the Western orbit and well beyond. So here I was, trying not only to instill some new animation philosophy, but having to cope with a technical system in nearly every way opposite to the day's standard! Of course, their system worked - they got their stuff onto the screen - but it was awkward and unnecessarily labor-intensive. The fault lay with a studio ruled by an old guard clique whose pride did not allow them to think there might be a better, easier, or more logical way to organize the work. It was a mindset I was to struggle against for the next three decades.

In spite of the language difficulties, I felt an immediate rapport with the animators and other artists and craftsmen in the studio. I don't know what I expected, but the popular American image of workers in communist countries at that time was of brain-numbed robots that marched to work in prison-like uniforms and attended constant lectures on Marx and Lenin.

This last item was almost true, but for the most part I found that, as with musicians, animators the world over are all instant colleagues. There were of course a few who were actual Party members, but no one showed any hostility towards me. Ironically, the only one who did at the beginning was Zdenka, and she had never been a member of the Communist Party nor any of its affiliated organizations. Not that they hadn't tried to recruit her. She was exactly the type they wanted: hard working, dedicated, and a natural organizer. She told me later that some of the more rabid Communists in the early fifties did try to have her thrown out of the studio, but they never succeeded. She was too valuable, and among her many friends were Party members who could protect her.

But now, with the two of us falling in love, she would be beyond saving if any official people suspected what was happening. Even though it seemed totally out of the question at the time, the smallest chance of her marrying a foreigner from the West would have meant the loss of a valued worker, not to mention an immense loss of political face.

They held all the cards - absolute power. Even a breath of suspicion would have meant my expulsion, with no chance for another visa. And of course Zdenka would be locked in!

But we were desperate to be together, and took enormous risks. As the work was being prepared, we managed to find ways to get together after hours. After all, she had to entertain her foreign "customer." Once she took me to a little bistro called Monika, in an arcade just off Narodní (National) Street.

There, as we ate dinner, the little orchestra played a sweet American song of that period, "When I Fall in Love." It had such a romantic melody that it immediately became *our* song. But we only heard the melody that night, as played by the little café ensemble. Only later, in New York, did I discover the words from a Nat King Cole recording. As a jazz and blues fan, I always held such sweet ballads in disdain. But when I heard the words, I felt my heart turn to mush. They seemed written just for us! It may be romantic pap, but all I can say is that 40 years later, they still ring true:

> *When I fall in love, it will be forever,*
> *Or I'll never fall in love.*
> *When I give my heart, it will be forever,*
> *Or I'll never give my heart.*
>
> *In the restless world that this is,*
> *Love is ended before it's begun,*
> *And too many moonlight kisses,*
> *Seem to melt in the heat of the sun.*
>
> *When I fall in love, it will be forever,*
> *Or I'll never fall in love.*

More about this song later.   © Victor Young & Ed Heyman

13 - "Na shledanou"

Zdenka tried to teach me a few Czech words. As the days drew nearer to my inevitable departure date, the one term I didn't want to learn was *"na shledanou"* - farewell. My only distraction from this painful reality was my work. I had prepared in New York all of the layout drawings, voice recordings and timing sheets for "Munro" and "Samson Scrap," and I had to explain everything to Václav Bedřich and the animators before they tackled the individual scenes. I was going to have to direct these films partly from New York, so I arranged for Zdenka to send me the 35mm film tests of the pencil animation scenes. I would then edit the scenes together on the Moviola viewing machine in my studio, and send back my comments and orders for revisions. It was cumbersome and took time, though we were able to make use of Czechoslovak Filmexport's access to airfreight. There were no international couriers, such as Federal Express, DHL, or UPS, to ship to Prague in those days, and no lightweight videocassettes.

On our last evening together on that tumultuous first visit, we went to an obscure little coffee house on Ječná Street called Kavárna Mocca. We sat on a little balcony all by ourselves. All I could think of was a film cliché: "Why can't we just do a slow fade-out, then a quick fade-in, and we'll be together again right here!"

In fact, it was to be *four months* - an excruciating time of trial. Would the cold bath of the "real world" wash away our exotic infatuation? After all, I had been in a desert island situation. Would it all just dissolve like some marvelous mirage? Would our sudden discovery of each other be strong enough to overcome the monumental obstacles our union would face? Political, cultural, language and geographic realities, personal responsibilities, loyalties, nationality, morality, family concerns, all flashed, "Stop!" "Danger!" "Falling Plaster Ahead!"

We walked slowly back to the Alcron Hotel, our heads full of all these doubts and concerns. Zdenka waited cautiously outside while I dashed upstairs to fetch my already packed bags and then check out.

"Is there anything I can bring you from New York?" I asked as the taxi pulled up.

"Yes," she said, "Some American *chevving goom.*"

Only after I was airborne, on my forlorn journey back, did I figure out what she meant.

My favorite Prague silhouette, the Týn church

14 – Hiatus

I remember it as the longest four months of my life, only comparable to my time in the army, when I was hoping World War II would end before I did.

An infatuation abroad was not a foreign concept to Bill Snyder. He enjoyed recounting uncountable affairs. I suppose I might be considered a weirdo, as I have been involved with only two women in my entire life, both of whom became my wives. I just don't find the complications of extramarital sex worth it. Yet here I was, allowing myself to enter the most complex time of decision in my life. As it happened, many lives were changed forever when William L. Snyder walked into my New York studio...

I was married to Marie Deitch, a brilliant woman one year older than I. We met during the war, when I was doing technical illustration at the North American Aviation plant, where the P-51 Mustang fighter and the B-24 Billy Mitchell bomber were built. Marie worked in the blueprint library. I needed to check out blueprints upon which to base my technical drawings; and thus we met. I had a model A Ford, and would get an "A" gas ration ticket from the plant if I carried a passenger to work. Marie became my passenger, and love bloomed. But the pressure of the war, the feeling that it was now or never, led us ahead too fast. I was just 19 when we were married, and was soon off to the Army. Kim, our first son, was born before I reached my 20th birthday. There were always underlying problems between us, often stormy, but perhaps, had I not gone to Prague, Marie and I might still be together. I don't know. She was a dedicated mother, a marvelous cook, a voracious reader, and someone I knew really loved me. That in itself seemed remarkable to me. I am a difficult person in many ways, with my own private inner world and plenty of obnoxious habits. I was good-looking when young, hard working, and I was honest. I was loyal. You could count on me to be true. I suppose that was what first drew her to me. But then, 16 years later, I was suddenly faced with being untrue.

If I had immediately opened up to Marie about my new feelings for another person, I would have instantly blown my neat and successful world into little bits. Of course, if this new strong love indeed proved inescapable, I would have to tell her. But the time was not yet right. I would hold the bomb inside my heart a little longer, bearing its terrible weight alone.

My studio, my work in New York, doing idiotic TV commercials - all began to seem pointless. What consumed me was what was happening in Prague.

Zdenka and I were exchanging daily letters, business-like, but coded with secret "I love you-s." The test reels of the films arrived. I edited and corrected them, produced the sound effects, and shipped back everything the Czech staff needed to continue the work.

Of the two films, Samson Scrap was intended as a pilot for a TV series. The other was Munro, adapted from a powerful satire by Jules Feiffer. Bill Snyder got it into his head that the latter could well be an Oscar contender. Yes, even cartoon films win Oscars each year, though few people ever notice.

Every year three or four animation films are nominated by the members of the Academy of Motion Picture Arts and Sciences Short Film branch. The final selection is by only those members who attend screenings of the nominated films. In order to qualify, the rules are that the film must be shown to a paying audience at a commercial movie theater in the Los Angeles area for at least one week prior to December 31 each year.

It was obvious these two films could not make themselves, which meant a second trip to Prague would be necessary. This one was planned for a month in March 1960. I began to count the days, and my daily correspondence with Zdenka kept the flame alive. Zdenka went to the studio's sound department and recorded a discreet but clearly loving message for me. I had found the Nat King Cole recording of "When I Fall in Love," and dubbed it onto a tape as a message to all the animators, but it was obvious to everyone that it was meant for Zdenka. By this time her closest confidantes in the studio knew about us.

I spoke a short introduction on the tape and then smoothly segued into Nat Cole's sensuous rendition. I heard later that they all assumed I was singing the song myself! They must have believed that in America anything was possible, and that I had rounded up a full orchestra with soaring strings to accompany my love song. That added more unearned points to my status than even my red sweater!

Later, when Zdenka found out I was 1) not really a sportsman, 2) did not ski, 3) could not sing, and 4) could not dance - *all things she loved to do* - it really had to be true love to overcome so many deficiencies!

Snyder had also caught onto my feelings for Zdenka. His off-hand prediction had actually come true, and he immediately sensed he had me in his clutches. He certainly had no problem getting me back to Prague.

My Gene Deitch Associates, Inc. staff surely noticed my distracted air at work, and it was more than likely Marie sensed my increasing emotional distance. All I could do was numb myself to the local scene and point my gaze toward March.

When the time finally came, I climbed aboard the plane with an entirely different set of feelings than on that first flight. My heart soared with the take-off. All I could think of was seeing Zdenka again, and I put all the negatives, all the obstacles, out of my mind. But would it really be the same?

15 - The Sportsman Returns

This time Zdenka met my plane. When she saw me, she joyously spun 'round on her heel! She had even colored her hair to an orangey shade, and was painted up like a kewpie doll. She wanted to look as she imagined an American would like. I told her I liked her just as she was.

Her message to me was, "Nothing change." That was her recurring love message, "Nothing change..." And it hadn't for me either. The time of March and April 1960, my first Prague spring, was an idyll.

Not only did our love mature, but also did friendships and working relationships with the staff of animators. They all wanted to talk to me about America, how perfect our country must be, and about how terrible it was in Czechoslovakia. I had to listen to a lot of grousing. I knew it was mostly justified, but there was nothing I could do about their situation. I tried my best to make them feel a little better about it. Insofar as I had observed up to that time, there were actually some very good laws in communist Czechoslovakia.

One good one was that you could not drink and drive. *At all!* Even one beer was not tolerated for an automobile driver, and the people really obeyed that law. If caught on the road with any alcohol whatsoever in your blood, you would lose your license. Tough policing did have some benefits. A woman could walk down any dark street or through any park in Prague without fear of assault. (Unless, of course, she was distributing anti-communist leaflets.)

I could not do anything about the *bad* laws. All I could do was try to comfort the complainers by trying to bring up all of the *good* ones I was hearing about. So whenever a complaining group surrounded me, I tried to play devil's advocate.

"Look," I would say, "It's really not all bad here. You've got guaranteed employment, cheap rent, free medical care, free university education, free recreational facilities, pensions..." But then I would be interrupted:

"It's easy for you to talk, Gene. You've got an American passport!"

End of discussion! That was their answer to anything good I tried to say about their country. I began to realize what my role here might be. If I wanted to play a hero, stand on a box in the town square and yell, "Down with communism! - Long live the USA!" I would accomplish only one of two things: either be thrown in jail or, more likely, be thrown out of the country. There was no way I could change anything. Communism in this country was not supported by the Czech majority; it was imposed and controlled by the Soviet Union. Was I going to fight the Soviet Union? Václav Havel had not yet surfaced. Other homegrown dissidents had been eliminated or jailed, with the keys thrown away.

But I began to see that I was really in a unique position, if I could just find a way to stay here. I realized that I was a guest in this country, without even the rights of the suppressed citizenry. I could not, and did not need to put out American propaganda. All I needed to do was be here. My presence alone was enough.

Everyone could see that I was earning money that could buy the kinds of goods their money could not. They saw I could travel anywhere I wanted on my U.S. passport. They saw I was free. *I didn't need to say a word!* Even if I'd gone so far as to point out that America was not a perfect place, they wouldn't believe it. If I did that, they would think I was a Communist! So I resolved to stay out of trouble, and just let myself be visible.

I suppose I was visible enough to the secret police. But I was thankful that they kept themselves secret from me. If they followed me, if they opened my mail, if they listened to my telephone conversations, I did not, and still do not, know for sure. I only assume that they did.

What I do know is that they never hassled me. They never knocked on my door. They never called me in for a little "chat." They never restricted my travel within the country or abroad. My only explanation for this is that I was not doing anything that would justify it. And I did have a value to them: My work was bringing in dollars. I didn't know any dissidents. I didn't attempt to smuggle in forbidden literature. I didn't make seditious speeches. All I did was work on my kiddy films and work on my love affair. That was my only dangerous activity.

Still, it's amazing this reckless affair didn't bring the roof down on both of us. By then, of course, events had taken on a life of their own.

16 - A Nest

The year 1960 was full of love and anxiety. One bit of stability was the eventual acquisition by Czechoslovak Filmexport of a tiny flat for me. For five months I had lived in the Alcron hotel, and it was impossible for Zdenka to come there. But getting an apartment was the number one difficulty - more like impossibility - for most Czechs. It was common for young married people, even with children, to have to squeeze into one of the parents' apartments, often for years. This was probably the main cause for the country's high divorce rate.

Zdenka had gotten her own apartment from the Ministry of Culture as a reward for her good work. Most people applied for apartments for their children soon after they were born, hoping the flat would be finally awarded when the kid reached adulthood! This required putting down a large amount of money as a down payment on a cooperative apartment. The money would sit all those years without interest, until the glorious day actually arrived. Zdenka did the same. She put several thousand crowns into a cooperative project for little David. (He never got it, but that's another story – many pages later!)

It was only due to my pull with Filmexport, and the fact that I was an employee of their customer, Snyder, that I got a tiny basement flat in an outlying development. It was made clear to me that this was the greatest gift imaginable.

The proliferation of outlying apartment houses with cheap rent was trumpeted as one of the "gains of socialism." The regime took special pride in adapting the "advanced building technology" of the Soviet Union, i.e., the assembly of prefabricated concrete panels. The Czechs called these buildings *panelaky*. They were stacked up like houses of cards. "Apartments for everyone" was the regime's principal promise to the people. These gray masses of identical buildings were eventually erected on all the peripheries of the city, looking for all the world like vast prison complexes. Certainly they are rabbit warrens. Every flat looked the same as every other; the same carpets, the same wallpaper, the same kitchen links, the same bathrooms. And they all smelled of plastic. The miracle is that none of these *panelaky* has yet actually collapsed. The communist rulers of this country were lucky that during their reign they did not have an "El Niño" year! Catastrophies such as the recent floods in Moravia would have likely brought the collapse of communism much sooner! Normally, there are none of the disastrous floods, tornadoes, forest fires, earthquakes, or mudslides here that regularly clobber America. The region's unremarkable weather definitely helped the Communists survive as long as they did.

I got a so-called *garsoniéra* in the outlying housing project of Petřiny. It was a damp basement one-roomer, with fungus growing on the walls, but at last I had a private place.

In those days you couldn't go far without seeing the ubiquitous Communist Party display cases, containing news of the latest "successes of socialism." Just outside my new apartment house door was one proclaiming, "BY THE YEAR 1970 THE HOUSING SHORTAGE WILL BE A THING OF THE PAST!" That was in 1960, so the 1970 prediction might have seemed safe enough. But by 1990 it was worse than ever. The Communists had to leave the housing problem to their capitalist successors.

I managed to find a few pieces of basic furniture, and Zdenka of course helped wherever she could. But I didn't yet have a refrigerator, so on my first night "at home" I left a package of butter and a bottle of Russian vodka on my outside window sill. In the morning, the vodka was gone. This was an item of great hilarity for Zdenka, which she told to one and all as an example of American naivité.

Another bit of American naivité was the idea of taking a bath or shower every day. Ours was a typical housing project building, and like all dwellers of these we were blessed with hot water on only Wednesday and Saturday, *if we were lucky.* So it didn't pay to work up a sweat on those off-days. The worst-case situations were when the hot water was on, but the electricity was off - taking a shower in pitch-blackness was just another of the routine hazards of life under socialism.

It was clear that I needed a refrigerator, another "narrow profile" item - meaning from a factory whose production chart barely remained horizontal, and thus a product difficult to obtain. Zdenka managed to get one. Everything one wanted was acquired through a network of friends who knew which counter to look under. The refrigerator was a tiny, thick walled crudity that made a rackety noise and cooled minimally. I held out little hope that it would make it through the warranty period, but amazingly this very same refrigerator still served at our mountain cottage 35 years later! It had never been repaired and it refused to die, even under the soggy and extreme summer and winter conditions. It outlasted a succession of much more modern refrigerators we've had in our Prague apartment. It was an unusual, shoddy-looking item, but it worked! In those early days at Petřiny it was my very first hard goods purchase, and it gave me a feeling of being at home.

My next household item was a vacuum cleaner. I have always had a whoosh for vacuum cleaners, considering them one of the most all-around useful domestic tools. Curiously, plain vanilla vacuum cleaners were always available on the Prague market.

One of the many things I used my vacuum cleaner for was to catch flies - another item of amusement for Zdenka. I would stand on a chair and pick off the little buggers as they circled the light fixture. I was even able to use it for daily dandruff extraction! Zdenka, however, remembers another vacuum cleaner incident.

She was trying to please me by attempting to make a real American-style apple pie. But as she was nursing it along in my oven, the oven door suddenly snapped shut, knocking soot from the inside down onto the baking pie. Zdenka was crestfallen. "Not to worry!" I shouted. "I have my trusty vacuum cleaner!"

Getting down on my hands and knees, I deftly approached the soot-sprinkled pie with my hissing vacuum hose, and ever so carefully brought it near to the blackened surface. According to well-known laws of physics, I reasoned, the light flakes of soot would be sucked up, leaving the pristine pie intact. But it didn't quite work out that way. *SH-LOOP!* The entire appled interior of the pie instantly found its way into the belly of my vacuum bag. We had no dessert that evening.

Otherwise, the year 1960 was pure joy for us, although we knew a time of decision was approaching. I had to make a couple of trips to New York for client meetings and dialogue recordings. At those times I stayed with my friend Allen Swift, who had done various voices for my films since we first met in 1951. But I was always eager to hurry back, not only to be with Zdenka, but for the enjoyment of being in Prague with my new colleagues and growing number of friends. These people had all been through so much, some of them overcoming the endless difficulties of the communist system to accomplish amazing things. I've learned much from these people, many of whom enriched my life and left me with a hatful of memories, for which I'll always be grateful.

17 – The Crunch

The Moment of Truth had arrived. During a trip back to Tarrytown, seeing me in an absolute state of the blues, my wife Marie took a sudden stab in the dark: "You're in love with somebody else!"

I confessed: Yes, I was. And from that moment on, a coat of ice formed over my old and comfortable life. There went my three boys, Kim, Simon and Seth. There went every bit of property I owned, all for the most elusive hope of another life. "Are you crazy?" Marie asked. It surely seemed so. Why else would I invite the scorn of family, friends and colleagues? God knows what they thought I was doing.

I knew I was doing devastating damage to my wife and to our boys, and I still know it. But I had two unpleasant choices: 1, damage them then, with at least some hope of their recovery; or 2, live with regret the rest of my life and make all our lives miserable forever. What I knew was that I had to go for my One Big Chance. I was ready to pay the price.

Zdenka's number-one problem, meanwhile, was her husband. He was the son of a furniture maker whose shop had been confiscated by the Communists after the 1948 putsch. He went to work as a minor foreman in a state-owned furniture company. He was just an ordinary guy who, through sheer persistence, managed to win Zdenka. She was pursued by many, but she never trusted the flamboyant artist types who fluttered around her. The one she accepted was not exciting, but he was solid, and Zdenka felt she could mold him into something. She supported him while he went to engineering school. She told me she never really loved him, but had been generally satisfied with her marriage. She was, as usual, able to be in charge.

Zdenka had to make up one excuse after another about why she was coming home late nearly every evening. One night I drove Zdenka home to her apartment to discover her husband waiting for us behind a bush. We found out right then, the hard way, that he knew the truth about us.

He rushed up to my car and I, hoping to brazen it out, rolled down the window. After all, I was just taking my production manager home after an important evening meeting. A flurry of fists to my face sent my spectacles flying, making it clear he wasn't buying. The time for charades was clearly over.

With his body pushed up against the car door, it was impossible for me to get out to defend myself. But Zdenka dashed out from her side of the car and scurried around, trying to drag him away from me. "What are you doing?" she shouted in Czech. I knew quite well what he was doing.

After Zdenka finally managed to drag him into the house - she was worried about what the neighbors might see - I was fired up and foolish enough to nsist to her that we go to the police and charge him with assault. It was dimwitted, but we actually went through with it. The whole time the police sergeant dutifully pecked out our complaint on his 1927 American Underwood typewriter, it was obvious whose side he was on. It's a miracle I wasn't thrown out of the country there and then.

It was an extremely dangerous time for us, and panic drove me to make some irrational moves. I even agreed to invite Marie to Prague, so she might better understand my feelings! Crazy, right? To this day, I do not understand what I was thinking. When Marie saw Zdenka, she said, "I knew she would have blue eyes!" I didn't get the point of that either. Marie also had beautiful blue eyes.

For Zdenka, it was an awkward situation. The last thing she wanted was a confrontation with Marie. Though she wasn't the one abandoning Marie, Zdenka felt as sorry for her as she did for her husband. It was just something that was happening, and she hoped it could somehow be done in a reasonable way. Marie, meanwhile, was refusing to give me a divorce, even though it was clear to her that our marriage could not survive.

Even if she had agreed, New York law made divorce nearly impossible, except for the rich. The only legal grounds for divorce at that time was adultery, but they had to catch you at it *en flagrante,* which meant you had to stage a bedroom scene and hire a photographer to record the "evidence." But that would have to be Marie's option, not mine, and Marie did not want a divorce.

The only alternative available to me was a Mexican divorce, and that required, a) Marie's agreement, and b) money. Nevertheless, it was my one and only option. To get Marie to finally agree to it would mean a settlement in which I gave up everything: custody of my three sons - one of them, Seth, still a lovable baby - our big house in Tarrytown - all of my life insurance, which I bought when I was 21, and which I could never afford to replace - most of my income in alimony and child support - plus a luxurious trip to Mexico for her - and even a trip to Prague and Paris. It left me with a thin lifeline of exactly $50 dollars per week for myself to live on. I understood that I had to pay the price and accept the blame, and I did both.

We signed a separation agreement, the financial terms of which meant I was now as effectively trapped in Prague as if I were a Czech citizen. I couldn't afford to live anywhere else!

Though few around us knew anything of these problems, I certainly felt the concern of Zdenka's family, who were afraid I might leave the country at any time and throw Zdenka's life into disarray. It required from her a lot of trust in me, but she invested in this high-risk endeavor without flinching.

After all, I was sentencing her to nearly the same losses and gains. We were going into a situation with no assurances and high risks. With my remaining $50 a week, I could now afford to do nothing else. Had I been fired by Snyder or expelled from Czechoslovakia, I could very well have ended up in a cardboard box on Times Square - something Snyder quickly caught onto. He signed me to seven years of low-pay contracts, which took me to 1968, that fateful year in Czechoslovakia's history, and yet another time of great upheaval. But that was still in the hardly imagined future.

I spent much of 1960 in New York preparing for my new life, the latter part of which offered seemingly endless confrontation with Marie. Additionally, the news from Prague was depressing. It was slow-going trying to direct animated films in a distant land by the tedious process of shipping heavy 35mm test reels back and forth, and with only a few opportunities to work together personally. With the year nearly over, we were still having problems with MUNRO, and the December 31st deadline was looming.

Zdenka knew how much this could mean for us, however unlikely an Oscar might be. *If* we could get it, it would increase our chances by several hundred percent of continuing our work in Prague-and thus being together.

But catastrophe struck. After Zdenka miraculously got the film shot in color within a comfortable margin of time, the studio's film laboratory accidentally *destroyed the entire negative.*

Zdenka was desolate. That evening she wandered out by herself onto the Charles Bridge, Prague's 14th century stone jewel that spreads its gothic arches and baroque statues across the river Vltava, and she cried her heart out. The entire film had to be reshot. With animation, that's technically possible, as all the artwork and timing sheets are still intact. But would there be enough time? We assumed not, and dropped our hopes. But not Zdenka.

She personally worked as assistant to her camera operator, also named Zdenka, night and day, reshooting the entire film. She organized all the needed elements, prodded the chagrined film lab and the generally lax

Filmexport shipping department, and got the film to us literally at "5 minutes to midnight!" The still damp print was rushed to a suburban L.A. movie house, and screened just in time to qualify us for the Oscar. It was Zdenka's supreme effort that did it!

The closing days of the year in New York were, of course, hellish. I wasn't sure Marie wouldn't murder me in my sleep. Perhaps some readers may think she should have. At our final parting, I nervously scrambled out from under the lowering garage door of our Tarrytown home.

I said, "So long."

She answered, "Goodbye."

18 - Czeching In

On New Year's Eve, 1960, I took off for Prague with the intention of establishing residence. There were no airport security checks in those days. Otherwise, what would they have made of the fact that I had a heavy microphone in each pocket of my overcoat? My main luggage was an Ampex 601-2 stereo tape recorder, the first stereo device of any kind in Czechoslovakia. It was to play a big role for me later, both socially and in regard to my work.

I was driven directly from the Prague airport to the New Year's Eve party going on at Klárov. It was also my welcoming party as a Prague resident. I had discovered that one key to my economic survival would be to have bona fide residence abroad for each entire calendar year. That would give me an IRS tax exclusion on my entire American-earned income. That's why I'd scrambled to be here by December 31. The gaiety of the party masked for the moment my worries and misgivings, and I felt right then that my new life was beginning. I was with Zdenka and all my new colleagues. I was locked into my new path.

A big difficulty during my first weeks was a lack of clothes, even socks and underwear. Zdenka helped me, but laundry was difficult to get done commercially, and there were no clothes for sale that I wanted to wear. I had left New York very hurriedly of course, but I did have time to throw some things into extra suitcases, which Snyder then shipped to Prague via slow boat. Finally, about 10 weeks later, I received a notice from Czech customs that my stuff had arrived. Zdenka took me to the customs office to help me with the clearing formalities. Naturally they were very suspicious of shipments from America, and a customs officer sharply quizzed me about the contents of the cases. With Zdenka's interpretation, I tried to sound as innocent as possible. "No books or magazines, no bibles, no printed material, no wrist watches, no pocket calculators or any other technical items, which might be sold on the black market," I assured him. "Just my clothes, extra shirts, and underwear."

Finally, with another officer present as a witness, the suspicious suitcases were opened. Zdenka was as shocked as were the officials when she saw the actual contents. I realized that I had been considerably more brain-numbed than ever when I threw my most precious personal possessions into these cases for shipment. Staring up at us from the open luggage was an assortment of my favorite jazz LP records, an African hand drum, a large Chinese drum, and a set of Cuban bongos - - but nary a pair of socks.

Famous Czech graphic artist Michaela Lesářová-Roubíčková made this symbolic portrait of us in our early years together.

Famous Czech graphic artist Michaela Lesárová-Roubíčková made this symbolic portrait of us in our early years together.

19 - Dining Out

MEAT! As the main emphasis of Czech dining, meat's availability or paucity was the leading indicator of better or worse times. Yet there were times when the only meat you could get was at a restaurant. When I was taken to a restaurant during my first visits, and still could not read the menus, I was always asked my choice in the following way:

"Would you prefer beef, pork, or veal?"

That was the primary choice to be made. Then it was a question of dumplings, boiled potatoes, or French fries (called "*pomfrity*" then). I soon learned to pass on the latter, as the fries were inevitably limp and soggy with grease.

Soup was usually offered, and came in two main types: chicken soup with a raw egg dropped into it, and goulash soup. The chicken soup was a sort of hot salted water with a few stray noodles and perhaps a few tiny lumps of chicken meat. The goulash soup was a thinner version of the goulash entree.

The main dish came ladled with gravy, and a tiny portion of grayish canned vegetables on the side, a few peas, diced beets, and slivers of carrot, all roughly the same deathly color. Presumably, these were intended as mere decoration, for no "real man" ate vegetables anyway. These were just pushed aside. It was the meat they were after, and that always came by weight. After each meat item listed on the menu, the weight, usually 100 or 200 grams of meat, was always noted. This was presumed to be the uncooked weight, but as there were no scales on the tables, you had to take their word for it. The glasses had little lines engraved on the sides to indicate the exact deciliters you should get of beer, wine, or what was called juice. The *volume or weight* of all goods in fact, was what was offered, with no reference available for quality.

The item universally accompanying the forlorn 100 grams of meat was the Czech knedlik, or dumpling, usually four or five slices. This amorphous material came in half-inch slices and was used to sop up the gravy. A Czech dumpling is a sort of boiled white bread in an elongated round mass, and then sliced for serving. For me, they have no particular flavor of their own, and thus take on any sort of gravy. They are mainly filling, and no doubt have their origin in poor times -a condition that continued nicely throughout the communist era. Czechs still love their dumplings, however, and continue to devour them even in better times.

Your cutlery was knives, forks and soupspoons, wrapped together in a quarter of a thin, generally non-absorbent paper napkin. That's right, one-*quarter.* The paper napkins at each restaurant were opened and carefully torn into quarters. That was all you got.

The hardest thing for me to adapt to was the method of eating. I was taught to eat and cut mainly with my fork, and to use my knife only for items needing to be sliced into bite-sized bits. A Czech holds onto the fork and knife continuously, using the knife to deftly combine and push the bits of meat, dumpling, and gravy onto the fork - certainly practical, and perfectly polite.

If you did get a vegetable, it was usually spinach. I wondered if Czechs had any idea what spinach actually looked like. All spinach in restaurants, or even when they later had it frozen in grocery stores, was a purée, with nary a hint that spinach actually existed as a leafy vegetable. It must have been a surprise to many, now that fresh spinach salad became a reality here!

Even when I learned to read Czech, I still could hardly make out the men-us. They were usually fifth carbon copies, hammered out on a 1925-model typewriter, or else run off on an ink-starved mimeograph or ditto machne, only faintly legible. It hardly mattered. What was common was a series of easy to see X's down the edge of the column, indicating those items not actually available.

If there was no more "beef, pork, or veal," there was often hen (greasy), duck (very fatty), trout (not bad), or venison with a few cranberries and a thin lemon slice a top your dumplings. That could be very good. That was about it, plus your beer, the primary Czech delight. Best beer in the world, without a doubt.

If you didn't want beer, wine, or vodka to drink, you could have mineral or soda water as a choice. What went by the name of "juice" was main-ly colored sugar water, and hardly justified its name. There was one drink that was unheard of in any restaurant: milk. I quickly became a laughing stock when I ordered a glass of milk. "Men do not drink milk," the waiter infor-med me, a look of derision on his face.

Food was described as "baked," "roasted," "stewed," "prepared on butter," etc., but most things seemed to be coated with breadcrumbs and deep-fried. There was a category called "dietetic," which meant it was fried in butter.

Now that modern kitchen gadgets are available, the biggest sellers are electric deep fryers. Czech men rejoice in the heavy diet of fried food and all manifestations of pig, by accepting early heart attacks as a normal and expected part of life.

The most devilish Czech food item is the so-called *sendvič* or *chlebíček*, which is just one angle-cut slice of a soft-crust baguette piled with perhaps bits of cheese, ham, salami, egg, tomato, onion, anchovy, and/or various cream cheese concoctions, all of which fall on your lap before you can get them to your mouth. Platters of these are routinely offered to test your skills.

You had to have more patience than hunger to enter a Czech restaurant. Interestingly, however long it took to get your order taken, and however long it took for your food to arrive, it was all nothing compared to how long it took to pay! Whenever a waiter did whiz by your table and you tried to flag him down, he would mutter, "Colleague," without slackening his pace. It always seemed to be a "colleague" who was the one to attend to you - and the "colleague" seemed to be invisible. When he or she did finally materialize, a fat wallet would be whipped out with file-like compartments for each denomination of banknote, and you would announce how much change you wished, in this way including the tip, usually 10%. Yes, though "not required" in socialism, tips were expected, and certainly never refused.

There were a few good restaurants in Prague, mainly at the hotels for foreigners, but the average eateries were grungy, with stained tablecloths, dirty ashtrays, and indifferent waiters. On each table was usually a glass container with two little open mounds of salt and pepper, with the finger dimples from previous diners. One simply took up a pinch of salt or pepper between thumb and forefinger. This, along with many of the other above -mentioned traditions of the lowly Czech pub, continue to this day.

Interior decor was achieved by running a patterned rubber roller, coated with a darker or lighter paint, over a base wall color. In fact nearly all walls everywhere - restaurants, apartments, or offices - were painted with these nondescript patterned rollers. The paint was mixed with water from a powder. If you leaned on or touched the wall, the color would rub off on you. The basic wall color was always sprayed on. If you called for your apartment to be painted, you would end up with everything in sight painted, including the light bulbs, wall switches, windows - everything in the line of fire of the spray guns, which were similar to the hand pump sprayers we used to use for the old time "Flit" bug killer. After the painters left, you would spend days scraping the paint off peripheral areas and objects. The main talent of these painters was their unnerving ability to "walk" on their ladders. To do the ceilings, the painters would straddle the apex of their stepladders, and by rocking back and forth, cause the ladders to step along in all directions. This was fascinating, and scary, to watch.

All restaurants had little signs on the wall giving their class and price category - I, II, III, or IV. Category IV meant you stood. No tables. In all of the categories, the restaurants were pretty much the same, only the meat got tougher and more gristled in each descending class.

A ubiquitous feature was the "Book of Complaints and Suggestions," which hung on the walls of all restaurants and shops, to which it was often coupled by cobwebs. Few customers were interested in wasting their time writing in those books, as it could get you in trouble if your complaint actually touched on the nub of the problem, the system itself.

Nonetheless, it was often a pleasant social event to go to a restaurant, and if you could afford class II, or I, there were some quite good ones. During the mid-'60s, when the animation studio was still downtown, Zdenka and I used to go for lunch in a really crummy local restaurant. The food was forgettable, but it was worth suffering through it just to get the bills. We loved those bills! The waiter there was a wizened old guy whose style indicated that he really took seriously the fact that our numerals are descended from the Arabic.

As we choked down the last of the meal and called, "Waiter! Check, please!" this true artist would sidle up to our table, whip out a thick pencil, and with sweeping strokes knock out the most elegant scraps of calligraphy to be found in any eatery. Each check was a work of art, and was worth more to me than the dinner it presumably recorded. Along with the gastritis, I have saved these nearly inscrutable checks over all these years.

A fond food memory of the early '60s is from the time when streetcars still ran up the length of the main business street in Prague, Wenceslas Square. As my tram lurched over the undulating track rails, it suddenly screeched to a halt, and the woman driver leapt out and disappeared into a food store. All of us passengers just sat and waited. No one but me seemed to think anything was amiss.

In due time the driver emerged, carrying a small parcel wrapped in pages from Rudé právo. She jumped aboard, gave a couple of clangs on her bell, and we were off again. Immediately two woman passengers rushed forward out of curiosity. With one hand on the controls, the driver opened the parcel with her other hand to show the women her prize. "What a lovely chicken!" they exclaimed, as the tram squealed around the corner at the national Museum and headed toward its next stop.

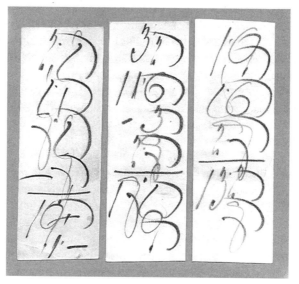

20 - The Great White Saab

One of the first Czechs brave enough to invite me into his home was Zdeněk Treybal, a tall, gray-haired, but still taut and tough photographer and former racing car driver. Like many Czech men, he was fascinated by auto technology, and was starved by the lack of it. He had the misfortune of coming from a wealthy family and living in an architect-designed modern house - not so great in socialist Czechoslovakia, where the only background worth having was one of humble "worker origin." As a former playboy and dashing competition driver, I supposed he was now paying the price. He had no chance of getting a job worthy of his skills and experience, so he taught himself to be a photographer. Photographers, authorized writers, and other qualified artists were among the very few allowed to be without formal employment, though they still had to belong to official "unions," which kept a close tab on their activities.

Despite his background (or perhaps because of it), Zdeněk had good contacts in the motor import/export ministry. He had been eager to make my acquaintance, and for more than personal reasons alone. Zdeněk was a man with a mission: He felt that if he could just get a Swedish Saab car into the country, and have it exhibited at the annual Brno city trade fair, it would result in some ministers ordering Saabs for themselves. This, he reasoned, would prove his ability to engineer the import of this sample, and as thanks he would be allowed to buy one of the cars for himself.

To swing this, he latched onto the one person around who could privately import the sample Saab: ME. All Americans were assumed to be rich, loaded with hard currency, and of course with the right to import a car duty-free, for personal use.

I realized that I would need a car if I were to live here. Getting a taxi in those days was near futility. On a dark night you could only recognize one by a single tiny light mounted inside the windshield. Taxis were mainly old Soviet-made Volgas, patterned roughly after a 1948 model Ford, but tinnier, and smelling inside like a couch stored in a moldy attic for 20 years. In any case, they would never stop for you. They could only occasionally be found at the very few and far between taxi stands.

So a personal car was a must, and I had already ordered a tiny Fiat 600. In fact, I had just sent a check for $600, which was about all I could afford. The Saab 96, the latest miracle car of its time, cost $1,600.

When Zdeněk Treybal first invited me to his home, his wife greeted me with the highest form of Czech hospitality. She brought out for me a portion of her dearest kitchen treasure, a thick layer of goose fat on a slab of solid Czech bread. It was obviously a sacrifice for them, and an honor for me, but the worst thing was I simply could not eat it! As much as I tried to feign delight, or even minimum politeness, I couldn't mask my revulsion at this gunk. I am not sure that Mrs. Treybal ever forgave me, but Zdeněk had more important matters on his mind, and got down to his Saab sales pitch.

"You don't want a rusty piece of tin like a Fiat!" he said. "The new Saab 96 has a revolutionary two-stroke engine! Freewheeling! The new sensation of Europe! Robust Swedish construction! A stainless steel bottom!"

He spun a tale of wonder about the Saab, and how he would personally do all the service and maintenance work for me for free - if only I would scratch the Fiat and order the Saab. I finally gave in. I did it, and let myself in for ten years of auto misery.

The $1,600 needed for a new Saab was money I did not have. But Snyder had it, and he advanced me half the amount. Later, whenever he saw the shiny white car parked at the studio, he never lost the opportunity to remind me just whose slave I was, deftly inserting his verbal dagger between my third and fourth ribs: "Which half is mine, Deitch?" he would taunt.

It was, I admit, an exciting idea to own the country's very first Saab. Czechoslovakia was a country with a proud tradition of automobile development and manufacturing, one that had long been rusted over by the Communist-mandated production of flimsy, degraded Škoda rattletraps. Škoda cars had once been great, and I'm happy to say they are now great again - but in that year of 1960, the nameplate had long been tarnished.

So it was a thrilling day when Treybal and I went to the dreary railway freight yard and saw that single white Saab lashed down in the center of an ancient railroad flatcar. It was raining and the water was running down the wax-covered car. That old model Saab looked very much like a large marshmallow with wheels. Treybal thought it was darling. The thick coating of wax protected it from rust on its long rail journey from Sweden, part of which was by sea in the belly of a ferryboat.

The very first thing that Zdeněk wanted to gaze at was the car's sweet little motor. We climbed up onto the flatcar. The Saab factory had sent me the set of keys in advance, so I was able to open the car and sniff that first rush of new-car-smell. I found the hood latch and we lifted it open. There was a motor in there all right, but even more charming was the bird's nest snuggled right on top of it, complete with mother bird and eggs! They had made the voyage from Sweden to Prague without benefit of passport or visa. We lifted out the nest very carefully, and found a place for it on the flat car. The mother was frightened off, but we felt sure she hadn't flown far, and would soon return to continue her family trip to God knows where...

After the customs formalities, the precious little car was rolled down a ramp, and its motor was sprung into sputtering action.

Treybal had already arranged for a garage to have the necessary detergents to remove the wax, which would enable us to see the car in its shiny newness. The service men there treated it as if it were a holy object. That Saab not only inspired awe, but *love!* Everywhere we drove in Prague, people gawked. When we stopped for a light, crowds would gather. It was just a little car, but it was The One! Snyder dubbed it "The Great White Saab."

In those days I could park anywhere, even on Wenceslas Square. Private cars of any sort were rare. People waited many years just to buy a Škoda, a Soviet Moskvich, an East German Trabant, or Wartburg, to name nearly the entire list of choices in those days. So my Saab was the unique dream car of Prague.

But as you may be aware, not all dreams are happy, and this car tended toward the nightmare. It took me a while to find this out, as, true to our deal, Treybal had the car for the first weeks, showing it to the foreign trade ministries and arranging to have it exhibited at the Brno trade fair. His ploy actually worked! The ministry agreed to import three more, and after some considerable weaseling (several other ministers wanted to grab one for themselves), they grudgingly allowed Treybal to buy his promised Saab.

But that took quite a while. In the meantime I had the one and only Saab in Czechoslovakia, and I was known in the country as the man with the Saab. More meaningfully, I was actually the one man who knew the *truth* about the Saab 96.

There were two things the car excelled at: 1) it devoured spark plugs; and 2) it ceased to proceed when wet. A 2-stroke engine runs on a mixture of gas and oil; it is basically a motorcycle, and it spewed out black smoke not unlike the infamous East German Trabant, only of course it was *Western* smoke. It was sturdy, neat, and comfortable. But I had to carry a cigar box full of spark plugs in the trunk at all times, and be prepared at any moment to change a plug. Its 3-cylinder motor instantly declined to the lameness of a 96-year-old granny whenever one of the plugs fouled, which occurred with depressing regularity.

Then there was dampness. The intake fan behind the radiator was cleverly designed to fling whatever moisture came its way directly onto the oh-so-vulnerable sparkplugs. Even the tiniest drizzle would stop the car, often in the most awkward places, such as the middle of a bridge or tunnel. But this didn't stop the car's sidewalk admirers. Once, a street worker was hosing down the roadway on Wenceslas Square just as I was entering from a side street. My Saab abruptly stalled right in the intersection. I had to get out and raise the hood in order to wipe off the sparkplugs. Immediately a large crowd gathered. If I ever wanted to make a public speech, all I'd have to do was raise the hood of that little car, and instantly a crowd would assemble! The police on traffic duty that day were apparently worried I was about to call for insurrection, prompting one alarmed officer to stride up to me and demand, "Sir, you must lower the hood of your car at once. You are creating a public disturbance!"

A much more alarming incident took place at another time in the Saab's career. In those days, when there were so few cars, parking was no problem. I often left the car behind our building in a little Malá Strana square I call "Beethoven Platz," because of a plaque on one building claiming that Ludwig van had briefly lived there. I had returned late one night from a recording session, and had rushed immediately home. The next morning I came out early, ready to embark on a long drive to Vienna. In each hand I held a suitcase, both of which I dropped in shock as I stared in horror at the space beneath my car.

"My God!" I gasped, blood pumping to my eyes, *"What have I done?!"*

There was a body lying there! It lay under my car, on its back, its two legs sticking out one side! In my haste to get home last night, could I have run over someone? I rushed forward in a panic, dropping to my knees and scrambling on all fours to see what I didn't want to see.

Immediately the body came to life, and a very embarrassed, not to say soiled, man scrambled out. "Please excuse me, sir," he babbled, "I just wanted to see your undercarriage." And then he pattered off, disappearing around a Baroque corner.

The Great White Saab, despite its front-wheel drive and free-wheel features, was no better on ice than baby Bambi. In the winter of 1961 Zdenka and I were returning from a country visit, coming up over an icy hill, when suddenly railroad-crossing gates loomed on the downgrade ahead. Fortunately for me, but not for its owner, a car stood between the oncoming train and me. There was no way to slow down, or even steer, so I did what I had to, and slammed into the rear of the hapless little Renault, one of the ancient variety with its motor in the rear.

My solid Saab lost one headlight and suffered only a dented front fender (it was sturdy), but the poor guy in front of me watched his car hemorrhage water, which immediately wedded with the ice on the road. That car wasn't going to take him anywhere on that dark, freezing night. I felt terrible about it, but there was nothing I could do for him aside from offering him my insurance.

In those days the railroad-crossing gates were cranked up and down by hand, usually by a sturdy woman, who crouched in a little booth waiting for her warning bell to ring. This booth even had a telephone. When the police car arrived, another crisis loomed. I realized that *I hadn't yet got my Czech driver's license!* The only document I had with me was my American passport.

Zdenka, quick thinking as ever, flipped through my passport to the page where it said *"Not valid for travel in North Viet Nam, North Korea, Albania, or Cuba."*

"See," she said, holding up the page to the English-deprived policeman, "This page of the USA passport is an international driver's license." The cold war cop bought it. A tow truck arrived for the maimed Renault, and we were miraculously on our way - carefully.

The Saab also gave Snyder a chance to defy Communist oppression, in his own, patented manner. On his first trip to Prague after the car arrived, I picked him up at the airport and drove him into town, toward the Alcron hotel. I was still not sure how to maneuver the maze of little streets, and I was zigzagging in the general area while Snyder shouted directions. "Turn left! Turn left!" he instructed.

"I can't turn left!" I protested, "It's a one way street. No entrance from this end."

"TURN LEFT!" he brayed. "This street leads to the hotel!"

A minor hindrance like a traffic law was no serious obstacle for a man of Snyder's stature. "OK," I said, "You pay the fine." I dutifully turned left, directly into the embrace of an officer of the Public Security. (The bourgeois term "Police" was not used by the Communists.) He flagged us down and politely saluted, which was the way a cop always approached a lawbreaker here. I wound down my window, hoping with my few words of Czech to explain my eccentric boss. But before I could open my mouth, or even before the cop could inform us of our obvious misdeed, Snyder leaned over me and put his policy of the best defense being a strong offense into loud operation.

"I demand to see President Novotný!" he shouted, waving his finger at the perplexed minion of road justice. Whatever the polite policeman tried to say, neither of us understood, but Snyder kept repeating, "I demand to see President Novotný!"

The officer was obviously as devoid of English as we were of Czech, but he surely caught the name "Novotný," the then Stalinist president of the Czechoslovak Socialist Republic. He also certainly observed that my car had the special colored license plates issued to foreigners. At that time, cars registered to foreigners bore plates of a distinctive yellow color with red numbers, whereas Czech citizens had white plates with black numbers.

With Snyder continuously repeating, "I demand to see President Novotný!" the hapless cop quite possibly had visions of a reprimand for interfering with high diplomatic personages. In any case he withdrew, with a few polite gestures indicating that we were after all going the wrong way on a one-way street. He saluted and waved us on. Snyder, in quiet triumph, tapped a few cigar ashes into my virginal Saab ashtray. Another blow struck against the Evil Empire!

At least Snyder had used the easily understood term, "Turn left." When Zdenka was navigating me at a crossroad, her instructions were invariably, "Go up," or "Go down."

"I'm driving a car, not an airplane," I would say, "I can only go to the left or to the right." But Czechs seem to be able to detect subtle inclines and declines at every fork in the road, which to them define direction. I have never perfected this perception however, and to this day I only know how to drive either forward, backward, left or right.

Of course, when trying to get around Prague, sometimes all the directions in the world don't help. One of the basic, everyday mysteries of this city is simply trying to find out what street you are on. It's not so bad in the historic center, but if you're driving in the outer neighborhoods, even a map won't help, because you'll rarely see a street sign! In America we have street signs on posts, usually on every corner. In San Francisco and other towns we even have prominent signs in the middle of blocks, so if you're driving, you'll know which street you're approaching. No such luck in Prague. The street names are on red enamel plaques, affixed to buildings on corners, or on fences along the way - sometimes.

I have often driven for blocks; scanning the sides of the street I'm on, searching vainly for a street sign while simultaneously trying to avoid being killed. If only Václav Havel had promised, "Comes the Revolution, you will have proper street signs" - the revolution might have come ten years sooner!

Inexplicably, I ordered two more Saabs before I finally gave up. In each case Treybal assured me that the "new model had all the bugs corrected!" Nothing however stopped the popularity of this car. After Treybal got his, he was able to finagle another batch for import, and got one piece for his friend and former co-driver Teodor Pištěk, who later won the Oscar for costume design on the Miloš Forman film, Amadeus. Then Karel Gott, the most popular singer in Czechoslovakia, who had plenty of money, bought one, and the Saab 96 became the status car of the country. It was a long way from the myriad Mercedes-Benz models, which glide through the traffic of today's Prague.

In those days, that was beyond even dreaming. No, it was Saab, which defined the upper crust for years to come. In 1969, after the Soviet-led invasion of the country, when the hardliners once again restored their rule, one such satrap was quoted as saying, "Now our asses will sit in the Saabs!"

Zdeněk Treybal was a fantastic manipulator, with great technical knowledge, an understanding of business, and an intense enthusiasm for what he believed in. I used to kid him that he should be the Czechoslovak Minister of Trade. But he came from a formerly wealthy family, was bitterly anti-communist, and the communist government was anti-him.

The tragedy is that he did not live to see the 1989 democratic revolution. Though an expert professional driver, one day on a Prague corner near us he got hit by another car, a simple intersection accident. Zdeněk was a diabetic, something he had never mentioned, and in typical Czech disregard for safety measures, he did not carry any diabetic information on him. This was before any personal injection device was available here. Ironically, he had been on his way to a clinic to get his daily insulin shot. By the time his condition was discerned, he went into shock and died.

For all of us who knew this colorful and daring character, it was a heavy loss, and though the government didn't realize it, it was a loss for them, too. Zdeněk was someone who could have single-handedly straightened out the hopeless ČSSR economy - if only they would have given him the chance.

My "Great White Saab" beneath the Charles Bridge, Prague, 1961

21 - Smashed Windows and Sliced Pig

The dampness and distance of my Petřiny digs were difficult to live with. Not only was there the constant threat of sinus revolt, but also the journey was daunting for Zdenka, who still lived with her husband and son on the opposite outskirts of Prague. I was of course grateful to have any flat at all, but I hoped that Filmexport could find me something more reasonable. My "contact" at Filmexport was a friendly woman, Jitka Markvartová, and she really did her best to make things easier for me. One day near the end of 1961, she phoned me with some good news: "Gene, I've found you a great flat in a great location!"

What she showed me was a building site, a half-finished structure in the ancient Malá Strana quarter - historic as hell, but a crumbling pit laden with soot from the hundreds of soft-coal-smoke-spewing chimney pots.

A lattice of rusted scaffolding webbed the naked bricks of the structure. The courtyard was mushy mud, decorated with random heaps of sand, cement, rotting wooden boards, and unidentifiable junk. In the middle of all this an old coot was continuously shoveling sand - and the occasional scoop of cement - into a battered and spattered cement mixer that groaned as if on its last go-round.

To get to the doorway, Jitka and I had to negotiate a wobbly series of boards laid over the mud. Inside was even colder than outside. "The heat will be connected soon," Jitka assured me, without giving her source of this information. Arriving at the top floor - no elevator and no hope for one – (I was being bureaucratically elevated from basement to attic), she produced a key, and we entered a tiny one-roomer built under the slope of the roof. A couch placed at the back wall of this room, with its steeply sloping ceiling, meant you would have to sit doubled over. Suddenly sitting erect could lead to brain concussion.

"And look at this charming little kitchenette!" said Jitka, leading me away from the wedge-shaped living room, into a tiny space containing a sink.

"And look," I said, turning the squeaky dry cast iron faucet, "No water!"

"The water will be turned on," Jitka said, again with unfounded assurance, "as soon as you move in. There are no tenants here yet. You will be number one!" So I was going to be first with something else. What an honor: the first tenant in this superb structure! "It has the most modern heating system in the city," she proclaimed proudly. "Not coal, but oil heat. No radiators taking up wall space, but radiant heat from pipes inside the ceilings and floors!" That part sounded good, assuming it would actually be turned on.

The warming plus to these frigid minuses was the flat's location - directly on the street leading to the 14th century Charles Bridge, the centerpiece of Prague. Who could imagine that 33 years later the front section of this very building would contain a McDonald's? Or that 101 *million* tourists per year would all be passing down our street and crowd into this now stone paved courtyard, all munching hamburgers?

But in that freezing December of 1961 all I could think of was water for washing, and water for flushing. I had to plod up and down those stairs, filling two buckets at a time from the one tap in the courtyard that issued water. I shared it with the cement mixer. For warmth I borrowed a small electric heater from a composer working on my films. Wonder of wonders, the electricity was working. But if my composer, Václav Lídl, hadn't had an ancient electric heater at home, I would not have been able to buy one. It was illegal to manufacture or sell electric heaters! Among all the other shortages, electric power was the most critical. Factories often closed on some workdays, because the cost of running and heating the plants was greater than the value of any goods they produced. One of the odd benefits of this situation was that the animation studio started to get Saturdays off. The five-day week finally arrived only because the cost of heating the studio on Saturdays was greater than the value of any work produced on the half day of work previously prescribed for Saturdays.

With only that one little electric heater, I was freezing, and with no water I was wondering just where the improvement was in my living conditions. Each day I went to the building manager's office, which occupied one of the apartments in the building's side wing, and immediately noticed one thing: It was nice and warm in there. They had an array of illegal electric heaters. When I mentioned Jitka's promise that the water and heat would be turned on "soon," I was told that everything was installed and ready, and all that needed to be done was to open the main valve. "Wonderful," I said, "So when can you do that?"

"Oh, we can't turn the valve. That must be done by the Chief Water Engineer on the project."

"Just to turn on a tap, you need an engineer?" I said. "Look, show me where it is, and I will do it and take full responsibility for the act."

Obviously, that would not wash. It had to be the water engineer, and only the water engineer. But where was he?

"He's taking a Christmas vacation."

By this time, several other freezing tenants had joined me, but as I was Number One, I was pushed as the water wangler. Even with my sparse Czech, they assumed an American could do anything.

I went over there the next day, this time armed with a heavy milk bottle. "Look," I said, "this is bureaucratic horsefall. You are the building chief; certainly you can open that valve! We are all freezing and unwashed. If you don't care about our comfort, I don't care about yours!" I flung my milk bottle through one of the windows by his desk. Icy wind immediately filled the room.

In a state of shock, (no one did such things in this country!), he leapt to his feet. "You can't do that!"

"I just did it," I said, "and I will be back tomorrow. And every day the water is not turned on, you will lose another window!" I was bravely counting on the fact that, since I was an American, he would resist the desire to beat my brains out.

I know it sounds wacky, foolhardy, and non-productive, not to mention entirely untypical of non-violent me. At the time I didn't even consider the possibility of the milk bottle landing on somebody's head. My only explanation, all these years later, is that those were early days for me here, filled with a whole slew of uncertainties, and I was edgy and not exactly rational. That building engineer was actually a nice guy, and the situation really was out of his control, according to the rules laid down in those days. But at that desperate, lonesome, freezing and insecure time, rationality was not my strong suit. I actually knocked out three windows in that building office. Each day I returned, they had taped a plastic sheet over the previous day's shattered glass. They had no extra glass available, and those windows remained broken for the next year, until a tenant actually moved in!

On the final day of my anti-window rage, the building chief yelled again his standard line: "You can't *do* that!"

I yelled back: "There's a policeman out on the street. *Call him!*" That was a long shot, but I already knew enough about the local scene to guess that he would not want to get involved with a cop.

"Look," he said, trying to inject some reason into my rampage, "The water engineer is out at his country cottage. They're having a Christmas pig killing.

If you think you can convince him to come back here and turn on the water, I'll drive out there with you."

So, on that freezing morning we set out in my pudgy white Saab to a pig-killing event. A pig-killing in this country involves an extended family, lots of large boiling pots, frying pans, a smoking oven, a brigade of meat grinders, sausage stuffers, not a few healthy appetites, and one fattened and unsuspecting pig. I had never attended such a ceremony, and I admit to a lack of stomach for murdering animals.

The road out there was as slick as the lard we were approaching. My car went into a dangerous spin on a remote country road. Fortunately, traffic was thin in those days, and we avoided getting smashed. Nonetheless, the incident did little to calm my nerves. Here I was, wasting an important working day on a fool's errand. That guy was not going to give up greasing his lips with fresh pork chops just so I could flush my toilet!

When we arrived at the scene, the pots were billowing with clouds of steam; the place was in high bustle. I was relieved to see we missed the actual slaughter, and that what I saw no longer resembled a pig. This was no day to be a vegetarian or cholesterol-phobe. With no hesitation, we were invited into the fray, and I have to admit it was terrific! Relatives, friends, wives and kids were all efficiently dismantling that pig, submitting its various parts to grinding, boiling, hand mixing, spicing, stuffing, smoking, chopping, breading, and frying in fresh, gooey lard. It was my first and final full-steam, no holds barred, pig out. After some good stomach-settling Czech Pilsner beer, we finally got down to my mission. To my pleasant surprise, the good man promised he would come the following day to turn the vital tap.

After that, the little top floor *garsoniéra* began to look better to me, and I began to appreciate Malá Strana, which was and is the most romantic and atmospheric part of Prague. Zdenka, of course, supervised the furnishing, and soon we had a charming little "Nest II." In the meantime, I became quite friendly with the building chief I had so rudely abused.

We still had to traverse the muddy courtyard for two more years, until the interminably building building was finally a building. It was in that courtyard that we had an encounter with the old sand and cement shoveler, who delightfully encouraged my progress in the Czech language. I was struggling to learn Czech, and was extravagantly proud when I could say one complete sentence.

Each day when I returned home from the studio, that old sand-shoveling coot would hail me in Czech, and I would try to exchange a few words with him. "Hello, how are you? How's the work going?" - trying out my linguistic proficiency. One day, realizing I was a foreigner, he got a little bolder. *"Pane, máte tabák?"* he asked. "Mister, do you have any tobacco?"

I've never smoked, but I went to the "Tuzex" hard currency shop and bought the guy a pack of good Dutch pipe tobacco. After I presented him with it he became my buddy, and every day he would greet me, and I would respond in my hesitant Czech. Seeing me come home one day with Zdenka, the old fellow hailed her. My moment of triumph was at hand...

"Young lady!" he called. "Your man there... He's not a Czech, is he?"

"No," said Zdenka, "He is not a Czech."

"Aha!" cackled the man in glee. "I *knew* it! I knew he must be a Slovak!" *

Our courtyard, December, 1961, when I moved in.

* At that time I took it as a great achievement - that I was at least in the Slavic-language ballpark. In January, 1999 I was on Czech TV doing an interview, and one of our friends was watching, with her 7-year-old grandson. The little boy piped up, almost in the same words of that old man 38 years earliere: "Grandma! That man on TV! He's not a Czech, is he?"

"No," our friend answered. "He's not a Czech."

"Aha!" said the lad, "He must be a Moravian!"

Look at a map of the Czech and Slovak Republics. In 38 years, I am proud to say that my Czech accent inched a bit closer to Prague!

22 – Stereo Daze

In the meantime, the year 1960 was like a dream. Not only was I able to spend the spring with Zdenka, but I was meeting more and more fascinating friends, and gaining a new perspective on life. People in Prague had lived through such a succession of difficulties, one would expect them to be complete zombies, but those very restrictions made many try that much harder to achieve their dreams.

One such person was Jiří Janda. "Jiří" is a difficult name for Americans to pronounce *(Yeer-rzhee)*, but it is simply the Czech version of George. Anyway, we call him Jirka *(Yeer-ka)*, which is much easier.

Jirka Janda was the husband of one of the studio animators, Irena Jandová. When she heard I was not only a music fan, but also a high- fidelity sound devotee she introduced me to Jirka. He had actually invented what I believe was the world's first all-transistor stereo hi-fi amplifier. What was most remarkable was that he was an electronic genius in a country where there were virtually no electronics. He basically had to make everything by hand, including actually making his own printed circuits.

Today, we are used to reading about microchips as big as a bed bug containing mega-million transistors. In those days there were only single transistors, each as big as a beetle. In Czechoslovakia there was no stereo of any kind. Jirka could make most everything he needed to demonstrate stereo except for three items:

1. The power transistors
2. A stereo phono cartridge
3. Some stereo LP records

None of these things existed in Czechoslovakia at that time. He hand-made his own printed circuit boards, incorporating his revolutionary design, and mounted on them the simple transistors, resistors, etc. he was able to wangle. He made his own amplifier case, even the control knobs. He made his own phono turntable and pickup arm. But the actual power transistors, the stereo cartridge, and of course the stereo records, could not be made by hand. He begged me to get them for him on my next trip to New York. He promised in return to build a second amplifier for me. It already had a name and logo: TRANSIWATT, and it would be the world's first all transistor stereo amplifier! There were none in America then, and none even in Japan. All amplifiers then on the market still used glass tubes.

Of course I agreed. Who would not want to participate in this significant advance in technology? Jirka wrote down the exact specifications of what he needed.

I assumed that as there were no stereo phono cartridges in Czechoslovakia at all, he would be delighted with any kind I could get. But no. Jirka may not have had a stereo cartridge, but he did have copies of recent technical catalogs he had managed to get free by mail order. So he knew the exact brand and model number of the best stereo cartridge, the Shure M3D, and that was the one he wanted.

In trying to find the power transistors he asked for, I had to hunt through the most advanced New York City electronic specialty houses. As Jirka had specified the very latest type, I discovered they were difficult to get even in America! That in itself made a terrific impression on me, and I found out this was typical of the Czech people. They may have had little or nothing, but they always knew which was the best of everything - and that was what they wanted.

I made a prediction right then, that if by some incredible miracle the Soviets would vanish, and this country became free, it would virtually overnight become the most bourgeois country in the world. Thirty years later the miracle happened, and that has actually come to pass!

After the 1989 Velvet Revolution here, Jiří Janda became the Grand Guru of Czech audio. Working with Austrian backers, he set up his own company to market his many inventions. He was the founding chairman of the editorial board on the Czech magazine, STEREO & VIDEO, as slick, beautifully printed, and technically up to date as any audio-video magazine anywhere. But in 1960, when he produced at home the world's first all-transistor stereo amplifier, he got exactly nowhere. A Czech citizen could not then form a private company, and could not deal with firms abroad. That could only be done via the official foreign trade organizations. There was also only one producer of electronic equipment, i.e., radios, primitive TV sets, professional sound systems for movie theaters, etc., and that was the Tesla organization, a typical národní podnik, or nationalized enterprise. Such establishments were only interested in staying out of trouble, avoiding risky innovation, and fulfilling their State-mandated plans.*

* Jiří Janda was one of my very first Czech friends in Prague, and over the years we had many ultra-sonic adventures together. His unfailing optimism allowed him to con-

More about the fairyland of socialist economics later, but in short, Tesla, within the ganglia of the Czechoslovak Socialist Republic, would not have been in a position to mass produce and market an advanced consumer product even if it wanted to. As a result, they missed a golden opportunity to get ahead of the Americans and the Japanese in audio and video technology!

But Jirka was an uncrushable optimist, and found all kinds of ways to get his inventions marketed, at least to the small but determined group of audio zealots in the country. If he couldn't form a company, he could form a "club," as long as it functioned under the umbrella of a socialist organization. Such was SVAZARM, an organization attached to the Czechoslovak army, which embraced clubs for model airplane builders, ham radio enthusiasts, balloonists, and many other potentially "dangerous" types. In this way, the government was pretending to allow these people to pursue their hobbies while at the same time keeping them under tight control. No such club could exist outside of SVAZARM.

So Jirka organized his audio "club" under SVAZARM, and managed in this way to produce a wide array of amplifiers, turntables, and loudspeaker units for the local market.

With the pilot amplifier he made from the parts I brought him, including the completed turntable with its one and only stereo cartridge, as well as the first stereo LPs every heard in this country, Jirka staged stereo demonstrations at various local "culture halls" and school auditoriums. Thus, under SVAZARM he was able, step-by-step, to acquire small quantities of the parts he needed to supply his tiny local market with the first all-transistor amplifiers and stereo loudspeaker units in the world!

From the very beginning of my work here I realized we had to have stereo soundtracks on our films if we wanted to have marketable products for the future. For this work I was able to bring into the country another technical miracle: the first stereo tape deck in Czechoslovakia. Stereo became even more important after we won the Oscar. The new projects that resulted called for stereo film soundtracks, and there was absolutely no stereo recording equipment in the country.

The film recording studio used massive Soviet built sound mixing consoles, with control knobs the size of hub caps. They couldn't even record on the world

tinuously accomplish the officially and technically impossible. He was a powerful example for me, and when he died, I had to face the fact that optimism does have its limits.

standard quarter-inch audio tape, but only on bulky 35mm sprocketed magnetic film of miserable quality, made in East Germany under the stolen trade name Agfa. On their own productions, the Czechs still did original recording and mixing on optical film soundtracks, long obsolete in the West.

Still, the studio sound engineers could hardly restrain a snicker when I walked into a session to record a 65-piece orchestra with only my little Ampex 601-2 stereo tape recorder, not much bigger than a briefcase (but still quite heavy, as it did use glass tubes and large power transformers), and my two small Electro-Voice dynamic microphones. The sound engineers generally used a battery of huge Soviet microphones, one for nearly each player. They assured me that there was no way I

The first stereo recorder in Czechoslovakia (1961)

could record this large orchestra with only my tiny gadget and two mikes. I urged them to just let me try.

All I had to control the sound was a little volume knob, and all I had to listen to my recording was a pair of the original bulky Koss stereo earphones. The engineers lined up to listen to my tape, and one by one they all nearly fainted. None of them had ever heard stereo, and it was a revelation! It would be years before they acquired studio standard stereo equipment, so in the meantime I recorded all of my early films with this little Ampex. I also used it at home to record my own narration and sound effects.

During our production of the MGM Tom & Jerry cartoons in 1962 I was editing all of my sound effects at home. For the T&J film CARMEN GET IT, I needed some really robust screams. In the movie, the human diva singing the role of Carmen is confronted by Jerry, the mouse, and she lets out a series of bloodcurdling shrieks.

I asked one of the more extroverted women from the animation studio, Kutula Zbyňková, to do the screaming, and we recorded her during a pause in our music session.

Editing the tapes at home in our apartment required playing the screams over and over again, to select and edit them precisely onto the soundtrack.

As I was running these window-rattling screams over and over, there was suddenly a furious pounding on our door. There stood two of my male neighbors in attack position, with clenched fists at the ready, prepared to rescue the rape or murder victim!

Showing them my tape recorders, and even playing them a bit of the recorded screams, did nothing to calm their fury. They were vibrating with anger.

"This apartment house is not a workshop!" they fumed, and stomped off. was careful after that to always edit drastic sound effects only through my earphones.

But the most fun, and the biggest sensation, came from my private use of this little wonder recorder. For all of us who take stereo for granted, it is hard to understand the effect this sound had on people here. It was a reaction you might expect from cocaine. When people would put on my earphones and listen to my tapes, they would fall into a trance, close their eyes and shout, "It's like I am right inside the orchestra!" Everyone shouted when they had on the earphones, assuming I could not hear them because they were surrounded by this intense sound spectrum.

When the great Czech puppet film maker Jiří Trnka heard about my stereo machine he invited us to his home, a beautiful renaissance villa on the island of Kampa, just a few steps from our Malá Strana apartment. "Be sure to bring your magic music box," he added. He wanted his other guests to hear it.

The first time he himself had tried the earphones, he immediately rolled back his great leonine head and went into a virtual trance. He was a music lover, as most Czechs are. He always engaged the finest musicians for his films. When he heard the stereo through my earphones, he exclaimed, "It's better than a real concert!"

The leading jazz groups were eager to have me record them, and I had no objections from club managers to setting up my microphones on their bandstands. I was recording organists in huge Baroque cathedrals, and classical guitarists in homes. That year was a veritable recording orgy! When my old friend Pete Seeger came to Prague in 1964 for a series of concerts, I also recorded him. The state gramophone company, Supraphon, issued several of my tapes on stereo LP discs. They were just beginning to issue stereo by that time, but had no stereo recordings of the various artists I had recorded on my little Ampex. Today I still record my favorites, only now with a pocket-size MiniDisc digital recorder.

Those 1964 Pete Seeger recordings have now been issued in full on a double-CD album by Interstae Music Ltd of Britain.

Perhaps our most ambitious effort was a plan to record the great maestro Leopold Stokowski, who was due in Prague that year. He was then 80 years old, and was about to conduct at Smetana Hall. Czechoslovak Radio technicians were rushing in and out, carrying huge loops of transmission cables and setting up their microphones. Jirka Janda and I, and a couple other stalwarts, including Jirka's sidekick Milan Vosáhlo, just as busily loped in, trying to look as much as possible like members of the technical crew. As it was unthinkable that anyone would try to do this without authorization, no one thought to stop us! I carried my tan recorder case, and the others carried our own cables and the two sensational-for-the-time ElektroVoice 666 microphones. These were sturdy enough to drive nails with, but had amazing sound fidelity. Certainly, there was nothing like them here.

We officiously climbed up to the highest loge on one side of the hall, lowered a string, with which we hauled up one end of my mike cable. Then we scurried down and across, and up to the loge on the other side, lowering the string and hauling up the other end of my cable, to which we had already attached the microphones. So there it was! My cable was stretched across the entire width of Smetana Hall, with my two mikes spaced a couple of meters apart, pointed right to where Leopold Stokowski would soon be majestically gesticulating.

As concert time approached I climbed up to the right-hand loge where I had set up my recorder, put on my earphones and listened to the stereo murmuring in the gradually filling hall. However, occupying this same loge, just in front of me, were the sound technicians from Czech radio. One of them, possibly hearing my heavy breathing, suddenly turned and asked in Czech, "Who are you?"

My Czech at that time consisted of somewhere between three and seven words, but I understood what the man said: "The Maestro has given explicit orders: no recording of the concert allowed!"

What could I do? I didn't want to let down my hi-fi brothers who had worked so hard on our installation, and who were depending on me to get this recording. There was nothing else to do but brazen it out.

"Where is the Maestro?" I asked.

Down behind the stage were the oak-paneled dressing rooms of the soloists and conductor. Around one impenetrable door, guarded by an equally impenetrable massively-formed woman, were throngs of people wanting a glimpse of Stokie. "The Maestro is preparing for his concert, and cannot be disturbed!" I made my case in English, earnestly enough to at least cause doubt to ripple across the large lady's face; only one tiny minute was all I wanted, etc. etc. She backed through the door while I waited. This was my one chance to escape and avoid making an unbearable fool of myself, but before I could do what needed to be done: (depart!) - the door opened just enough for a fleshy finger to emerge and give a beckoning twitch. Suddenly, the fat lady was out and I was in - alone with *Leopold Stokowski!*

He was lying on his back like a corpse, on a low chaise, with the heavy symphony score on his chest. It appeared he was absorbing the music by osmosis. He did not move, nor in any way recognize my presence. But there he was, lying no more than a foot above the floor.

To say my piece, I had no choice but to get down on one knee, as the supplicant I was, and begin to babble my plea:

"Maestro,-I-am-an-American-working-in-Prague-and-a-great-admirer-of-your-conducting-and-I-would-treasure-the-opportunity-to-make-a-recording-of-your-concert-tonight-just-for-my-personal-private-collection..bla-bla-bla-babble-bla.."

There may have been more, but I was blacking-out fast. The aged blue eyes finally fastened on my sweaty countenance and pronounced one word:

"No."

Sic transit gloria mundi. Later that evening Zdenka and I sat in the audience, waiting for the concert to begin. My microphones hung above our heads, deaf to the glorious sounds we were about to hear. Eventually Stokowski shuffled out. He was leaning on a cane, moving one painful step at a time. When he finally made it to the podium, he slowly hung the cane on its edge, then suddenly sprang erect, thrusting his arms and long slender fingers skyward It was a splendid, vigorous performance.

Ten years later, when Stokowski was 90 years old, he returned to Prague for his last concert here. But he failed to ask for his old friend Gene...

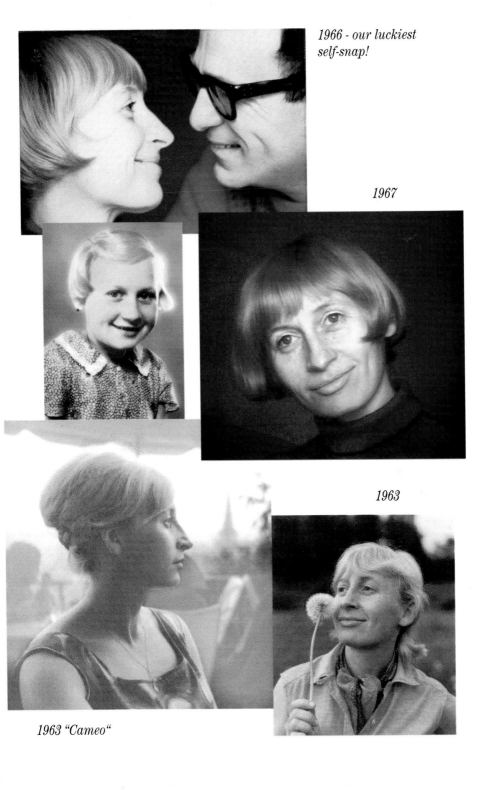

1966 - our luckiest self-snap!

1967

1963

1963 "Cameo"

In 1968 and again in 1970 the Czech
magazine Domov (Home) did articles on our new apartment. The mag was crudely
printed on cheap paper. I scanned these shots directly from the old pages, and did
the best I could with them. The mag's interest was in our taste, but also because we
had some things from the West. That's what really grabbed them!   Photos: Zdenek Podlesny

Zdenka enjoying Bill Snyder's Rolls-Royce, before his home in Larchmont – 1966.

A shot just inside our door. The photo poster was made on Oxford Street in London in late 1968, when we were on a film project. It became our classic personal image. The flag was a gift from Morton Schindel in response to a request from Zdenka. She felt it was a nice design.

*The Alcron
in the 1960s*

May Day, about 1963. The blurry high-ups, under giant photos of Marx, Engels, and Lenin, mechanically wave to the sullen throng plodding by below, carrying their required banners and signs. The banner above reads, "Wolkers of The World, Unite".

Parking was no problem in the early 1960s. I left my original Saab parked in front of the Rudolfinum concert hall, and went across the square to photograph this huge hammer & sickle in flowers. Today an underground parking garage has it's ventilator on this spot!

Our wedding day, November 24, 1964.

Later.

Reminiscing with Lulka, December 1999.

With Toshi and Pete Seeger at their mountain home. See: Chapter 33.

Bill Snyder, in his prime.
See Capter 58.

23 - Oscar!

By spring of 1961 we had almost forgotten about the Oscar ceremony in Hollywood. Snyder informed us earlier that "Munro" had been nominated; we were thrilled and satisfied with just that, realizing how close we'd come to missing the qualification date. As director of the film, I should have been at the ceremony, but I was happy to be in Prague with Zdenka. Anyway, we were busy with several new films.

Out of the blue came a telegram, not from Snyder but from some American colleagues. Then another came from my mother, and from many friends and other relatives: **We had *won!* We had *actually won the Oscar!* Bill Snyder's cable came several days later. Letters from Hollywood colleagues followed, telling us that Snyder had accepted the award with the following remarks: "Thanks to Gene, Jules, and Al." *Gene who? Jules who? Al who?*

It was Jules Feiffer of course, who wrote the great story, and it was Al Kouzel, from my staff at Gene Deitch Associates, Inc. who drew the layout sketches for the film. Later, when we saw a film of the Oscar ceremony, we realized that Snyder had entered Munro under his own name!

(Copy of the statuette)
© AMPAS

The project had been created, as I related earlier, within my New York studio before Snyder even appeared on the scene. The story adaptation, dialogue soundtrack and graphic preparation had all been done under my direction, at my company, and the film rights had been contracted to me from Jules. Snyder did not even pay me for my direction of the film. I was to get a percentage of the "net profits" (there were none). All he paid for, (and that was a pittance), was for the animation production at Zdenka's studio.

His one and only venture into the creative aspect of the film was an attempt to castrate one of the strongest lines of Feiffer's dialogue. An army officer is addressing a group of new recruits:

"I want to welcome you men to the Army. This is a time of great conflict. I will explain the issues: Our side is in favor of God. The other side isn't. Any questions?"

Snyder was terrified that we were making a satirical reference to God in a cartoon. He was pressuring me to add another o: *"Our side is in favor of good. The other side isn't."* Even if I would have acquiesced to such a cop-out, which I was not prepared to do, I knew that Jules would have considered it a breach of my promise to be completely faithful to his story. Snyder insisted that we at least record the alternate line. (Howard Morris performed all the voices except the voice of 4-year-old Munro, performed by my 3-year-old son Seth, and the voice of a little girl and Munro's mother, performed by my former wife Marie.) I am proud to say that the film retained the original line.

So, for putting up a few bucks Snyder got to leap onto the stage at the Oscar ceremony, and in front of the watching world, pick up an Oscar with his name on it. The original Oscar sat on his night table, while I had to be satisfied with a copy.

But what did it matter? I know whose Oscar it really was; (so, for that

matter, does the Academy. They wrote me that under the rules at that time, they had no choice but to accept the name of whomever entered the film.) In those days I was too preoccupied to even think about it, or to take seriously our chances of actually winning. To Zdenka and me, the real meaning of the Oscar was that it virtually guaranteed we would be together.

Almost immediately, the publicity resulted in our winning a contract from MGM to produce Tom & Jerry cartoons, and from King Features Television to produce Popeye and Krazy Kat cartoons. None of these were what I really wanted to do, but it was work, it would keep me here, and it was great experience for the Czech animators, to have a go at these typical American cartoon characters.

I do feel some guilt for intruding upon the Czech animation culture, which in many ways is more mature and subtle than ours. But the fact is, they enjoyed doing this work, and it did prepare them for what was to come, bringing them into the wider, international aspects of our art and craft.

I do credit Bill Snyder for many things. First and foremost, on a personal level - whether it was his intention or not - he did bring me to Zdenka. And on a professional level, he certainly did have excellent taste in his choice of material to produce. Aside from those books already mentioned, he was the first person to discover and acquire the film rights to J.R.R.Tolkien's "The Hobbit" and "The Lord Of The Rings."

In addition, he backed my "Munro," "Samson Scrap & Delilah," "Nudnik," "Terr'ble Tessie," "Big Sam & Punky," the satiric "Self-Help" projects, and many others, most of which you never heard of, because his big flaw was in having large dreams with small results. He was never able to do anything with the treasury of films we turned out for him, because his negotiating tactics always backfired.

Even after we won him the Oscar and three other nominations, including two nominations in one year - something no other animation director had done before - all he was able to get for us were custom projects with characters owned by others, such as Tom & Jerry, Popeye, And Krazy Kat. He was never able to close a deal for the much better items we created for him, which he himself chose to produce. His phony manner and attempts to overcharge turned off even the most eager distributors.

Imagine having the film rights to The Lord of The Rings in 1963, and letting the property slip through his fingers. With him it was always sharp and tricky deals that always backfired. That was Bill Snyder's tragedy.

Today, Snyder is tragically gone. His son Adam, a much more level-headed person, has taken over his father's company and film library, and has managed to bring our old and nearly forgotten films back to life. He is distributing "Gene Deitch Presents The Nudnik Show," featuring the character I created 35 years ago for Snyder senior and Paramount release. This, along with a tribute to me at New York's Museum of Modern Art in April 1996, was engineered by Adam Snyder, who has gone to great effort to make up for his father's foibles. I thank him for that.

24 – YANKEE, NO!

In my early years in Prague a continuing concern was the political and international events around us, over which of course we had no control. Zdenka now says she was never worried. I was. It seemed to me that we had no control over anything. I was completely at the mercy of Snyder and the Communists. I wasn't sure which was worse.

Many of my American friends and colleagues, perhaps even my family, might well have wondered if I might be, at the very least, a communist sympathizer - while the local authorities, and certain people around us, might well have thought I was a CIA agent!

The hardest thing for people to believe was the simple but unusual truth, *which I was here just to make children's films!* Of course, with people being widely exposed to James Bond movies, all manner of spy movies and books, and the conspiracy theories surrounding the JFK assassination, it was difficult to get across my situation without actually increasing suspicions through endless explanation.

I understood the suspicions. After all, being a children's film animator would seem to be the perfect cover - an innocent sounding occupation, masking a devilishly clever undercover operation! As it occurred to me later, I did come to feel that my very presence here could convey a message to the people who were around me. But in absolute truth, I was just an animation film director, and my coming here had nothing whatever to do with politics or the Cold War. My one and only undercover operation was my love affair with Zdenka. But whether I liked it or not, we were both at the mercy of political and international events.

Many people have told me they thought the worst and most dangerous time for us must have been when we were here during the Soviet-led invasion in 1968. Well that was of course a major crisis, but by then Zdenka and I were married. We at least had a chance to get out together if it came to that.

But it was the 1962 *Cuban Missile Crisis* that frightened me the most. Those were still early days for me here, and I was still feeling that Zdenka and I were on separate ice floes, heading for the rapids. We were still a long way from being married, and had no lifeline that could save us from going over the edge.

I was in Prague when the installation of Soviet missiles in Cuba led to the American blockade of the island, and the government here was playing this action up to the hilt. It was the Communist line to talk peace, peace, peace, but in fact to do everything to thwart it. Slogans such as, "PEACE, MIR, FREIHEIT, PAIX, PEACE FOR THE CHILDREN OF THE WORLD, PEACE ON EARTH, LONG LIVE THE PEACE POLICY OF THE SOVIET UNION!" were written on every wall, and on road signs and banners everywhere. There was a "Peace Square" in Prague, "World Peace" streets in most towns, an annual International "Peace Race," and so on and on.

The implication of all this was that it was the West, and mainly the *American "Imperialists,"* who were the threat to peace. "The blockade of Cuba is the perfect example of this!" they shouted in their media. What was not mentioned at all was why we were blockading Cuba, just something about "trumped-up charges."

Czechoslovakia in those days was full of students and trainee terrorists from other communist, Third World, Arab, and African countries, all those which nurtured anti-American attitudes.

So they hauled out all the Cuban students who were here, and got them to march on the American Embassy. The U.S. embassy happens to be just around the corner from our apartment in the Malá Strana corner of Prague. The marchers were going right past our building, shouting, *"Cuba, si!, Yankee, no!"* over and over. I had no idea how violent they might become. Czechs are not violent people, but I wasn't so sure about Cubans. Everyone in the neighborhood knew an American was living here, and all those "Yankee, no!" shouts on our street were not at all comforting. Zdenka wasn't yet living with me, and for once I was glad she was somewhere else. At least she was safe.

I phoned the American Embassy to get some advice; naively thinking they might want me to hole up there until things simmered down.

"The Embassy is closed," a male voice answered before I could get out more than a couple of words.

"I'd like to come over there and get some advice. I'm a bit concerned about..."

"The Embassy is closed!" - Louder this time. Perhaps he thought I couldn't understand English. He hung up on me. I assumed the guy must have thought I was a Czech, seeking asylum. I figured I'd better nip over there and show them my *bona fides.*

Grabbing my passport, I went out the back passage from our building and crossed Karmelitská Street, then hurried up Tržiště (Market Street), where the American Embassy is located. To my dismay I saw a throng of shouting

Cubans crowded around the Embassy entrance, shouting and waving signs with anti-American slogans. *"Cuba, si!, Yankee, no!!"*

As I nervously approached, I could see that they formed a sort of arc in front of the Embassy door, keeping a slight distance from the actual building. The Czech policeman - who was supposedly guarding the embassy, but was mostly crouched in a little booth just opposite the entrance, photographing everyone who went in or out - simply stood around behind the crowd, not protecting the embassy at all.

I realized I was in a dumb situation, but I had to brazen it out. I gingerly edged my way in front of the hostile, jeering crowd full of shouting, fist-and -sign-waving Cubans. I tried to act as if I didn't see them. There I was, all by myself, tight up against the huge oak doors, (the building is a former palace), surrounded by all these raving robots. It was obvious that there was nothing spontaneous about them. No demonstrations were held in this country without being officially organized. I began to pound my fist on the door. Of course I would be admitted. After all, I was an American citizen, and it was my right to seek protection from my Embassy. *Right?* I pounded some more.

Perhaps they didn't hear me above the din. I was really beating on that door now like a half-wit. *No response.* The man on the phone had been right. The embassy was closed.

Now I was faced with sheepishly slinking off. The crowd continued to sing out their slogans, almost as if they were reading from a score. I had pretended not to notice them, and now they were pretending not to notice me!

As I made my way home through gathering mobs of shouting demonstrators, my tail dragging behind me, I was glad not to be beaten up. But I was also furious. I resolved to return to the embassy the next day, when this ugly charade was over, and demand an explanation,

When I came back, it was not with a slink, but with an attempt at an indignant stride. I demanded to see the Consul. I was after blood. I did not actually pound on the Consul's desk, but tried to give that impression. "How come," I demanded, "an American citizen is locked out of his own embassy when he might be in physical danger from violent anti-American throngs?" I awaited his groveling apology...

"How come you're in this country, anyway?" was the genuinely hostile answer. "If you want to be in this country, that's your business, but you're here at your own risk!"

Boy, was I learning! The American Embassy didn't want me here, and the consul made it abundantly clear that the embassy had no duty to protect me. They likely thought I was a comm-symp, too.

In those days our embassy staff rarely if ever stepped out of their protective doorway. They had ample facilities inside. Actually it is the most beautiful palace in Prague. The garden slopes up to a structure called a 'gloriette,' atop which flies the American flag, the highest in Prague - even higher than the president's atop the Prague castle. This was always an embarrassment to the Communists, who couldn't do anything about it. Any broad view of Prague from the riverfront would show Old Glory fluttering above it! The Americans acquired this property in the young Czechoslovak Republic of the '20s, when the USA was the 'most favored nation' in this country. But now it was a fortress for our diplomatic people, who didn't dare venture out even to see the glories of this eternal city. They had their own grocery store full of Fritos, Crisco, peanut butter, Kleenex, and fresh Western milk daily. They even had their own gas station in there. They definitely did not fraternize with the locals nor consume goods from the local market.

I quickly learned that I was on my own if I was depraved enough to want to live here.

But the embassy did offer me other useful services, besides renewing my passport from time to time. They had an excellent library, and the librarian agreed to take delivery of my International Herald-Tribune, Time and Newsweek subscriptions. I would never have gotten them in the regular mail. What was denied, besides bodily protection, was shopping privileges at their glorious grocery store. I would have braved hostile crowds every week for that!

Well, things did seem to quiet down, and a necessary trip to the States came up. No sooner did I get to New York than the *real* crisis surfaced. Soviet warships were en route to Cuba, carrying more long-range missiles!

As we all know, that was the closest the USA and the Soviet Union actually came to war. Not only could the world have exploded, but also I would never have seen Zdenka again. A ridiculous comparison, perhaps, but don't forget that I was intensely in love. Most Americans were afraid they might be atomized, our cities blown to bits, but I was thinking that I might never see Zdenka again. That was undoubtedly the blackest time of all for me. No one besides Kennedy himself could have felt greater relief than I, when the Soviet ships turned around and went home.

Another dismaying experience with the American Embassy occurred shortly after, when my close friend, actor Allen Swift decided to take his honeymoon in Prague. We had collaborated on many, many animation projects since 1951. I had been writing him how beautiful Prague was, but I also had my own motive: I needed him to record some voices for my new series of TOM & JERRY cartoons we had in production for MGM.

When Allen and his bride Lenore arrived, I gave them a grand walking tour of the old city. By that time I was becoming a knowledgeable guide of the town on my own, having learned much from Lulka and from the many books about Prague I had been studying. On our way down from the castle, having circled across the glorious viewpoint atop the Petřin gardens, we came down past the U.S. Embassy.

At that time, when there were no noisy demonstrations going on out front, the embassy doors were wide open, and there was minimum security. So we walked in, and I pointed out to Allen and Lenore some of the architectural features of the inner courtyard and grounds. An imposing man suddenly appeared through one of the apartment doors, (certain high ranking embassy attachés actually lived right in the embassy compound at that time). He heard Allenasking me a question, and the American voice had attracted his attention.

"Hi there!" he called out. "Would you like to come in and see something of the inside?"

"That would be very nice," replied Allen, and we all started walking toward the doorway.

"You can wait out here, please," he said a bit sternly, looking straight at me.

I was of course surprised, but what the hell, if he wanted to exclude me from the invitation, there was nothing for it but to wait. About two minutes later, the guy came zooming out the door with his right hand stretched out, heading straight for me.

"I want to apologize to you, sir!" he blurted.

"What for?" I said, now completely nonplussed.

"I thought you were a *local!*" he said, in a way that made it sound like "nigger." (What if I had told him I was in love with a "local," and had hopes of marrying her?) Anyway, he invited me in with more copious apologies, obviously more than a little drunk, and started to load us all with the standard cold war line. I knew very well what was rotten here, but I also knew a lot of good people, and knew that the way to be effective here was not the way he and the embassy staff were doing it.

After the long harangue, he led us outside, and as we stood in the entrance, a genuine "local" just happened to walk by us on his way up the street.

"Did you see that? Did you see that?" stage-whispered the embassy dude (if I remembered his name I would tell you).

"What? What?" Allen and I asked simultaneously.

"That man who just went by!"

"What about him?"

Tears almost welled up in his eyes. He had a holy beam lighting his face, which tilted upward, staring in reverence at the Stars and Stripes waving gently above the American embassy entrance.

"They love to walk under that flag," he crooned.

The glaze was barely off his eyes when another passerby approached. This one, with the standard Czech greeting to anyone encountered on a walk, tipped his hat and said "Good day!" as he passed us by.

Again, our embassy stalwart leaned toward us and stage-whispered, "Do you notice how friendly they seem to be? But of course, they're all spies!"

Allen, Lenore and I were nearly gagging when we left this clown, but Allen filled me in later about an even more grotesque scene, which took place before I was invited inside. As they entered, the guy, proud of their supply of goodies, freely imported under the privilege of diplomatic pouch, said, "How would you like a real American beer?"

It was too much. Here in the land where, if nothing else, there existed the finest beer in the world, this twit offered my friends a can of Piel's beer, a former New York brand, and probably the worst brew ever marketed! I sadly knew this, because when I worked in New York I made the Bert & Harry Piel animated TV commercials, and was always embarrassed by how lousy the beer was.[1]

I am happy to say that in recent years we have had a great improvement in the quality of our embassy personnel over the dullards of that era, when none took the trouble to learn the language, nor made any effort to learn what really went on here.

Today, all personnel, from the ambassador down, are required to learn Czech. Even before the revolution, with such ambassadorial couples as William and Wendy Luers, a great cultural symbiosis was established which surely made a contribution to the ultimate victory of democracy. The Luers were brave enough to invite the "criminal" Václav Havel to their official residence frequently, at a time when it could have been dangerous for their diplomatic status. In later years we enjoyed the friendship of Ambassador Adrian Basora and his talented wife Pauline, who continued to build a cultural bond with the Czechs. We were regularly invited to dinners and functions at the residence. I feel I no longer have to be embarrassed by our embassy, as I was that day in 1961 with the Swifts.

Our luckiest ambassador was Shirley Temple Black. The former child movie star happened to be assigned here exactly when the seeds planted by the Luers finally sprouted and bloomed. She was able to be the first American ambassador to invite Václav Havel to the ambassadorial residence, officially, as president, and to revel in the joy of the new democracy. So the former movie star, whom both Zdenka and I had loved, was able to star in a real-life Happy Ending!

For me, the luckiest U.S. ambassador has been John Shattuck. John Shattuck and his wife Ellen Hume Shattuck were civil rights activists, and have carried over their zeal to this assignment. Shattuck travelled throughout the country, spoke some Czech, and organized many cultural events, cementing Czech-American relations. Best of all for me, both he and his wife were happy readers of an earlier edition of this book, and Shattuck himself is a great jazz and blues fan. He organized a special party at the Ambassadorial residence in my honor to celebrate the CD release of my 1949 John Lee Hooker recordings. (See Chapter 57 – Happy Endings.)

Ambassadors come and go. I have seen many in Prague during my 42-year residence so far. A Republican victory in 2000 saw John and Ellen Shattuck's exit, and that was the end of a fine time for me. They are great people. Incidentally, Shattuck was named by Czech-born U.S. Secretary of State Madeline Albright. It's fascinating that there was speculation that she would like to succeed Václav Havel as president of the Czech Republic. She still speaks perfect Czech. With her vast international contacts, she could bring this former "East Bloc" country to the center, and people would no longer need a map to know where it is! But the idea seems to have been a non-starter, as she is no longer a Czech citizen.

---

[1] A sidelight to those Bert & Harry commercials was that we first called them "Harry & Bert." The Piels Brewery received many weirdo letters praising the "Aryan Bert" commercials! The brewery freaked out at that, and nearly canceled the entire ad campaign. It was saved only when we reversed the order of the names. See my animation book at <http://genedeitch.awn.com> for their picture.

25 – Time of Trial

What weighed heaviest on Zdenka's mind now was her son. She was devoted to little David, and would have given up her career to care for him. But of course it was financially imperative for her to work, as it was for nearly all Czech women. She had been able to take advantage of the greatest of all Czech home appliances, the babička, or grandmother.

The babička, I've been told, was the primary essential that kept the entire socialist system from collapse. Without the babička, women with children could not work, and the inefficient socialist system would likely have collapsed long ago. The system needed every possible worker, and every family needed income from as many family members as possible. One salary could not possibly support a family in socialist Czechoslovakia. If a family did not have a babička, then the only other recourse would be to leave small children in a state-run nursery school. The Czechs called them "maternity" schools - but whatever, they were no substitute for a granny.

Zdenka didn't have a real grandmother, or even a mother to help take care of her son while she worked. But a close friend, Svatislav Richter, volunteered his own mother, who happened to live near Zdenka, in the Kobylisy district of Prague. "Babička" Richterová took to David immediately, and she really loved him. This was a great boon for Zdenka, and she was able to continue her career in stride.

Zdenka's son David was just five years old when I arrived, and his life was fated to be radically affected by what was happening between his mother and me. We had to console ourselves with what we believed would be best for him in the long run. But in the short run there was no doubt we were being reckless with his well-being.

Zdenka got her divorce, but in the process lost custody of her child. Her husband, privately an outspoken anti-Communist, stood up in court and declared, "I do not want my son to be raised in a non-socialist household!" That type of hypocrisy was built into the system, and it did not surprise us. That cheap shot won him custody of David. Zdenka's unflinching determination, and her optimistic certainty that she would win back her son in due time, kept her going. She never missed a single hour of her allotted time with David. There were many freezing winter evenings when I sat in my car, waiting, while Zdenka exercised her visitation rights with little David.

Each year Zdenka had the right to take David on a holiday, and I was in the position of being able to take both of them abroad to the seashore. But each year, her former husband went to court to stop us from traveling "West." He was able to play on the accepted dogma that Zdenka and I were planning to escape with his son. Every step of the way, for nearly ten years, he was able to take his revenge by making it as difficult and uncomfortable as possible for Zdenka to be with David, who was also her son.

During all those years of having David in his home, he pumped anti-mother propaganda into the boy's susceptible head. And he never missed a chance to tell Zdenka that she had thrown her life away, that I would leave her, never marry her, that she would be miserable forever, etc. etc.

But just as Zdenka had believed all along, working patiently and biding her time, it all came true. Children don't usually say what they really feel, but when David became 15 - the age when Czech children received their national ID books, and thus became genuine persons in the Czechoslovak Socialist Republic - he immediately began spending his time with us. When he was 18 and free to do as he wished, Zdenka got back her son.

David had a doubly difficult childhood. Every child in the country was raised to be a liar. He or she was taught what could be said at home, what could be said at school, at work, in public, on the phone... To me, that was one of the very worst degradations the system imposed. I hated that. It's no wonder that many people in this country have developed a built-in cynicism. In addition to this, David had to overcome his father's anti-mother propaganda. He not only became estranged from his father, but as with most young people here at that time, estranged from the system that had used him as its pawn. His overwhelming desire was to get out of the cage. But the time would not be ripe for another 10 years...

Zdenka got her divorce two years before I got mine. We could live together, but we still had no legal security. She had no right to travel, and I was hanging on with a business visa, which could be revoked at any time.

What I so much wanted to do was give Zdenka a chance to see the "West" - every Czech's dream in those days. But it was totally impossible, or so it seemed, until we could be married. But could a true American accept the term "impossible?"

26 - "You Can't Get There From Here!"

There's an old joke about a guy asking directions from a local yokel, who splutters and babbles about this way and that, giving out a torrent of confusing and conflicting directions, and who finally cops out by saying, *„Fact is, you can't get there from here!"* Well, in communist Czechoslovakia it was literally true. Virtually every nice place in the world you might like to travel to was blocked by a maze of conflicting rules. The rules everywhere in the Soviet system were based on fear. What it feared most was information. It controlled all the media so completely - press, book-publishing, radio, television, film, everything - so all-smotheringly, that not asingle unofficial word could squeeze through. I'm not referring to opposition words. They were out of the question. But even *neutral* words were not allowed. Words had to be for and against the things the official line was for and against. In all the 30 years I watched the Communist-controlled TV news, I didn't hear a single positive word about America, nor a single teeny-weeny criticism of anything Soviet. It was so totally one-sided as to be laughable. And the people did laugh at it. Through the magic of osmosis, the average Czech was far more informed about world affairs than the average American, who had access to everything.

But the information to be gained by foreign travel was what the Czechs *really* craved. After the war, Zdenka had saved her money for a short holiday in France with one of her girlfriends. She wanted to try out her French, which she had been studying for several years. Just when she was ready to go, February 1948 came, and with it the Communist takeover. The cage slammed shut, and free foreign travel came to an end for Czechs and Slovaks.

Even to travel to Bulgaria, another communist country, Zdenka had to invent a "cousin" to send her an invitation - a woman animator in the studio who had married a Bulgarian engineering student and moved with him to Sofia. So Zdenka was able to get to the Black Sea beaches every summer. That, and occasional trips to Yugoslavia, were the very best she could manage. Her chances to see the West were zip. Travel was the most difficult thing to achieve. That made me all the more determined to make it happen for Zdenka. The Czechoslovak Socialist Republic's constitution guaranteed free travel, as well as a free press. But the hedging that actually denied both was so arcane as to defy all but the most foolhardy to attempt to actually demand them. The twisted Communist logic was this: As the State paid for the citizens' education, it was therefore the duty of citizens to repay the State with their work. Their fear of defections - total lack of confidence in their own propaganda - denied them the benefits that would come to them if citizens would be allowed to freely work abroad - to experience Western business, organizational and technological methods, and to then freely return to their country. That would more than compensate the State for their investment in education! It was indeed fear, a gigantic inferiority complex, and distrust of their own slogans, which made the Communists block foreign travel while all the time pretending to allow it.

For example, every citizen not in prison could get a passport, but the passport by itself was no good. There had to be an *exit visa* attached to the passport, valid only for each specific trip. And Czechs couldn't even hold their own passport. It was kept in a special department by their employer. It was handed to them only just before their departure, and it had to be handed over to the officer at the border as they crossed back into the country.

Official trips to the West were in groups, and generally confined to international scientific or industrial congresses. On such trips, almost always by bus - which was the cheapest and most exhausting way to travel - all the passports were held by the group leader, an obvious secret police agent. The leader presented the group's passports at each of the border points and at the hotels where the group stayed. While in the West, individual members were never allowed to hold their own passports. You also had to leave your national identity book at home. So if you entertained the idea of escaping while abroad, you did so knowing you'd be without any means of identification.

A Czechoslovak citizen had to have a visa to cross every line drawn on the map. So every journey was a complex, depressing, and nerve-shattering experience. No one could be sure he or she would actually make it until the Czechoslovak border was actually crossed. Often, hopeful travelers were paged at the airport or turned back at the road border if for some reason the police wished to withdraw permission at the last moment.

I counted 16 separate hurdles a Czechoslovak had to jump in order to cross the finish line of the state border! Among them were:

• A notarized written invitation by a blood relative, (mother, father, sister, brother, or husband or wife, guaranteeing all of your travelling, living, and medical expenses.

- Approval of your trip by your employer,
- Approval by the Communist Party cell attached to your company,
- Certificate from the central court stating that you had no criminal record nor any legal suit pending against you,
- Proof that you had no debt and owed no alimony,
- Certificate of completion of army service (if you were a man),
- Promissory Note from a State Bank, for the foreign currency you would need. (This was particularly tough to get!)
- Formally filled out application to the Ministry of Interior
- Purchase of a 300 crown tax stamp (expensive for a Czech)
- Auto insurance card, valid for each country would travel to.
- Round trip train or plane ticket.
- Travel health insurance.
- Visas to all countries you would pass through or enter.

Each of these items had to be applied for separately; each entailing long lines and waits.

Once you had all that together, you then you had to go to a State Bank branch and get a customs form on which you would have to list every item of value you were taking with you, such as rings, gold wristwatches, fur coat, cameras, etc. A common trick would be to take out old things, which you would dump, and then bring in a new item of the same type. That didn't work with items that had serial numbers. The border guards would often check cameras carefully. But I know of many musicians who were traveling for concert dates, who would take out cheap, second-hand instruments, and then bring back new ones without having to pay customs duty. Traveling was a continuous game of chance, and always the Czechs had a bag full of tricky tools to help them bend the steel bars of restrictions.

When (if) you returned you had to prepare a written report, listing all places you stayed and all persons you contacted, and of course you had to be careful not to be too ecstatic about your impressions of the West! Even in the late part of the communist period, in the mid-80s, when things were easing up just a bit, Zdenka's niece and her family had a humiliating experience. They had finally been granted permission (wonder of wonders) to vacation in France, but they were forced to strip naked at the border for a body search. Someone in the factory where she and her husband worked, apparently out of jealousy, reported that they planned to remain abroad. What were the border police looking for? Diplomas, employment records, or school report cards - - anything that might indicate they were seeking employment abroad.

Against this challenge, I was determined to give Zdenka a trip to the West. From the very beginning this was my dream of something I could do for her. By 1963, after we had won the Oscar and were bringing a lot of work to the Prague studio, I thought we might have enough clout to pull it off. I asked Zdenka which country she would most like to see. She said, "Italy!"

We were not yet married. This was just the kind of "impossible" challenge Snyder relished! He immediately took charge of the operation. At that time he was at his peak as a valued customer, and he put it to them as a matter affecting their business relationship. He grandly offered a $10,000 bond guaranteeing Zdenka's return. Translation: My job depended on it.

Of course, the whole thing was unnecessary theatrics as far as Zdenka and I were concerned. It may have been difficult for the passport officials to believe - officials who didn't at all believe in their own system - but Zdenka had no intention whatsoever of escaping. "This is my country," she told me many times, "I want to see other countries, but this is my home."

Of course her little son and her father were here, but even so, no protestations of national feeling would cut any ice with those buggers. This one innocent trip to Italy, via Switzerland, had to be approved by the Minister of Culture personally! I thought, "No wonder this country doesn't get anywhere."

I had assumed there must be more important things for a minister of the government to do than concern himself with a vacation trip by two young people. But the fact is, that is exactly the kind of thing that obsessed their teeny-weeny brains.

Amazingly, the trip was approved. Zdenka actually got her passport, complete with exit visa. On the big day, our friend Zdeněk Treybal drove us to the airport. Right up to the moment the flight was called, we had our ears nervously tuned to the airport loudspeakers, imagining: "Passenger Zdenka Najmanová, report to the information counter!" Such a call would have brought our plane crashing to earth before it even took off. But no such announcement came, and we actually flew.

When the plane landed at Zürich airport, I asked Zdenka to stay in the plane while I clambered down the steps to the tarmac first. I wanted to take a picture of her first step into the West. We had a wonderful time... It was our year-early pre-honeymoon. Zdenka saw everything there was to see in Zürich and in all of Italy. When we returned, we heard there had been a management meeting at Krátký Film where someone dashed in shouting, "Gene and Zdenka have returned!" The meeting actually burst into applause.

After that, it was easier for us to travel together. Easier, but by no means easy. Even after we were married, each time I wanted Zdenka to go anywhere with me, I had to sit at my typewriter and write a formal invitation:

"I hereby invite my wife to travel with me on a weekend in Vienna (or wherever). I will be financially responsible for all her travel and hotel expenses as well as any medical costs which she may incur," etc. etc.

This had to be officially translated, notarized, and submitted with other documents, including our marriage certificate, signed permission from the studio, permission from the studio's Communist Party cell, verification that she was free of debt, and so on, ad nauseam.

The exit permit, if granted, would list the exact countries, *and no others,* that she was permitted to visit, and for how many days. With this golden document, we could further apply to each embassy of the listed countries for tourist visas for her. Every trip required at least a month or two of planning and of standing in lines, often for hours, for each needed piece of paper.

One of our more hilarious experiences occurred when we managed to arrange a ship tour of Grecian islands. It was booked through a travel agency in Zurich, but the ship actually left from Venice, Italy, which was to be rea-

September 12, 1963: Ready to take off for Zdenka's first trip to the West.

ched by bus from Zurich. When we got to Zurich we discovered that the Italian embassy in Prague had given Zdenka only a one-time transit visa, which meant that if she used it to get from Switzerland to Italy on the bus, she would have no transit visa to get back, and possibly be stuck in Greece. She wouldn't be allowed to board the ship on its way back to Venice! So we contacted the Italian Embassy in Switzerland and applied for an extra transit visa. „No!" Only the Italian Embassy in Prague could issue visas to Czechoslovak citizens. „You must first return to Prague!"

They didn't realize what they were saying! To return to Czechoslovakia, after once having left on a valid exit visa, would mean having to start all over again with those 16 travel requirements! It could put off our trip to Greece until the following year, IF we could go through it all again!. „Here's an idea," offered the Zurich travel office, not wanting to lose the booking, „You will cross the Italian border around midnight. Just duck down in your seat, and maybe the Italian customs inspectors won't notice you!" We had no choice but to risk it, but it was frayed nerves all the way. However, Italy being Italy, the customs officers just happened to on strike exactly at midnight, when the Swiss bus rolled into the crosspoint! A single over-taxed officer was running from car to car and bus to bus. When he got to us, he just poked is head into the door and yelled, „You all Americans?" „Yes!" chorused the passengers, and we rolled right through. BUT, when we got to the Venice dockside we found that the Italian customs were NOT on strike there, and were checking the passports of all passengers boarding the ship! „We're lost!" said I, but not Zdenka. She noticed that a group of Germans were boarding on another gangplank, and no one was checking them, a special tour group. So little Zdenka quickly insinuated herself into the group, went right on board, and was herded directly into a dining area. She took her seat, attempted a bit of social conversation with a German woman, and enjoyed a nice free lunch. In the meantime, I was still on the dock, unsure whether Zdenka would be discovered and be dismbarked. I waited until the last minute, and then boarded through the regular customs, and was relieved to find Zdenka up there waiting for me. „Let's have lunch. I'm starving," I said. „I've already eaten," said Zdenka, full and pleased with herself.

A similar and even more bizarre incident happened on a later journey, when we were returning to Europe from America on the QE2. The great ship was scheduled to dock at Southampton in Britain, and Zdenka of course did have the proper British transit visa. BUT.

The British being the British, the dockworkers at Southampton had gone on strike, and the ship's captain was radio'd that we were being diverted to Ostende in Belgium. A search of the ship's log revealed that Zdenka did not have a Belgian transit visa. There were frantic radio messages back and forth, with the Belgians proclaiming that the ship would not be allowed to dock with a Czechoslovak national aboard! Here was the mighty Queen of Seas, with a thousand passengers on board, in danger of being restricted to the high seas, all because of little Zdenka! It was only after a series of radio'd pleas through diplomatic channels, and a Belgian customs agent being ferried on board to check out Zdenka's travel documents, that a special exception was granted, and all 1,000 of us were allowed onto dry land. Zdenka and I were convoyed to a train that took us out of Belgium and into Germany, on our way home. This story is absolutely true, and illustrates once more the humiliation a Czech or Slovak had to endure in those days to simply get from here to there.

An ironic turnabout to all this occurred after the November 1989 democratic revolution. The requirements took a new twist - as I found out when I went across town to the passport/visa bureau, (same building/different people/new State Emblem on the wall/same hour-and-a-half line). During 30 years of communism, I'd gone to that bureau each year to apply for a one-year extension to my residence permit; but this time the passport officer looked up at me and said, "Mr. Deitch, your wife is a Czech citizen! You can get a five-year residence extension! All you have to do is have your wife sit down at her typewriter and write: *'I hereby invite my husband to live with me in our flat. I will be financially responsible for his support and for the cost of any medical care he may require..'*"

So we have come full circle. Even with democracy, the bureaucrats are still alive and well!

27 - No Man's Land

In the dark days of the Czechoslovak Communist regime, I was the privileged one. My main condition for staying and working in Prague was that I had to have complete freedom to travel. For this I was issued a unique unlimited exit/entry visa. It was good for six months at a time, continuously renewable. It allowed me to jump into my car at any time, without any announcement or application, and head west. As far as I know, no one else in the country had it, and maybe no one in the entire eastern bloc. During the communist era I crossed the border to the West more than any other person. I never became blasé about that, and I never got over the exhilaration of those iron gates opening for me.

I prepared in advance a stack of filled-out border crossing forms, and for every exit and re-entry I had to get a stamp in my passport. I used up six extra-page U.S passports during those years!

The Czechoslovak Department of Passports and Visas was the essence of Kafka. Once a year I had to get my residence visa renewed, and once every six months - once every three months after the Soviet invasion of 1968 - I had to get my exit/re-entry visa extended. It was that unique exit/re-entry visa that allowed me unlimited travel in and out of the country. I had no trouble in getting the chief of Czechoslovak Filmexport to sign the necessary applications for these. The hassle was in physically obtaining them on mysterious Bartolomějská (Bartholomew) street, the traditional Headquarters of the National Security, (Police).

Václav Havel was once jailed there in an ancient basement cell, (now a tourist hotel!), and there is a famous pub called "Konvikt." The odd exception to the forbidding atmosphere on Bartolomějská Street was the presence of the Jiří Trnka puppet film studio, in a converted ballroom where Beethoven once played. (This is now a special film screening hall.)

But where foreigners had to go to get their "papers" was a dimly lit long hallway, lined on one side with plastic chairs and little tables with stacks of Communist newspapers, and on the other by five thickly padded doors. On each door was a hand-lettered sign, "DON'T KNOCK!" Even if you had the temerity to knock, you wouldn't be heard inside because of the padding. To further insure that no secret murmerings from inside the hidden rooms could be heard, continuous loud music issued from plastic speaker boxes - the national cable-music network equivalent of Muzak.

An unspoken understanding existed as to who was next in line, even though the gathering of supplicants rarely spoke to each other. And we never knew which door would open to admit one more soul. When I finally did get into one of the tiny sanctums, it was a quick business to present my applications - assuming everything was in order - but always I had to return 14 days later to get the actual visa papers and a flurry of rubber stamping in my passport, always happy that I had another three months before I must go through this mindless procedure yet again.

For the citizen/subjects of this country, most applications for exit visas were turned down. After waiting a month for a reply, they would get a registered letter from the passport office with this standard dark notice:

"YOUR APPLICATION FOR PERMISSION TO TRAVEL TO (WHEREVER) HAS BEEN REFUSED ON THE GROUNDS THAT SUCH TRAVEL IS NOT IN THE INTEREST OF THE STATE."

And that would be it. There was no way to prove that a hoped-for holiday on the beaches of France was in the interest of the Czechoslovak State! As for a simple shopping trip to next-door Austria or Germany, forget it! A. Czechoslovak currency was mere paper and bought zip outside the country; and B. (more importantly) the government did not want its citizens to see what was in the shops of the bourgeois countries. (All the local propaganda told them how miserable it was over there.)

The fact was, of course, that everything Czechs wished for was in the West. In those days there was nearly nothing you could count on getting in Prague shops. The Czechs could buy only shoddy, outdated, and uninteresting goods. If you wanted whipped cream for Christmas, you had to order it six weeks in advance, and *maybe* you would get it. In the early '60s there was no butter, *no* cheese, *no* meat. You might say that was healthful, but that was not the attitude here. If you wanted onions, bananas, grapefruit, garlic, oranges, tomatoes, whatever, only to mention a few basic items, the chances were you couldn't find them.

I kept an ongoing shopping list - for us, for friends, for colleagues, for Zdenka's family - and once a week, or once every two weeks in winter, I would get up at 4AM, jump into my car, and drive to the small West German town of Weiden, just 30 kilometers over the border. There I would do all my shopping and be back in Prague in time for dinner.

This is how it was: I would drive about 150 kilometers, (94 miles), over a narrow highway (with some potholes as large as the car), past a dozen drab towns and dozens of drabber villages, and maybe one or two desolate filling stations. Then, as I approached within five kilometers or so of the border, I started to see signs: STATE FRONTIER ZONE. NO ENTRY WITHOUT PERMISSION. NO PHOTOGRAPHY! Anyone living in the small village beyond this point, Rozvadov, had to have permission to live there. This was an area - and an installation - the State did not want its citizens to see.

At the end of the village I came to a small guardhouse, two soldiers with assault guns, and a huge steel beam anchored in massive concrete pylons and set at an angle across the road. The bar swung open *inward,* so there would be no chance of ramming it open. Any vehicle attempting that would not only be smashed, but would be shunted to the side by the beam's angle.

Steel mesh lined the sides of road, and stretching out to infinity at each side of the heavy beam gate was, not one, but *three* rows of high barbed wire fences. So what was on the other side of this gate and those fences? Freedom? No. There were still two more kilometers of Czechoslovakia, and probably a minefield. I certainly never checked that out, but any poor soul who misguidedly thought he could just climb those fences and be *out of here,* was due for disappointment. No doubt that's why few were even allowed near this place.

At the lonely border crossing in those early hours I rarely saw other travelers; sometimes perhaps a diplomat or a businessman. One of the guards would listlessly come to my car, ask for my passport and visa, ask me to open my trunk, and jounce up and down on the back seat, feeling for hidden compartments. If I had been smuggling out a person, that would have been the end of me - and the person.

Satisfied that I was clean, the guard would then slowly plod back to his guardhouse and telephone to the *actual* border, two kilometers ahead, telling them he had three cars or whatever, and then wait for the call back saying it was okay to let us through. Under no circumstances would they release more than six cars at once into the customs area. We could wait maybe 20 minutes at this outpost before the guard's phone would ring.

The huge beam would then be slowly dragged open, and I would be waved through. After the two kilometers of this no man's land, passing a couple of high watchtowers, I would arrive at the actual frontier station.

My passport and visa would be taken again, and the officer would disappear inside the building for an indeterminate period. It could be three-quarters of an hour. They had no computers then, and the phones only worked sporadically.

Next, the customs   officer would ask me what I was taking out and then shuffle through my trunk just to make sure. They also used a mirror gadget, which allowed them to look under the car. And these guys knew me! I was going through this same routine every week. Finally they would give me back my passport and wave me through. Another half kilometer, and I came to the honest-to-God border. There was another guardhouse, a final steel beam gate, and two more young soldiers with sub-machineguns. These two really had to be trusted, because they were just a few yards from West Germany. Incidentally, they, and the two at the first outpost, were usually Slovaks, who didn't care much for Czech and thus could not be easily influenced toward compassion. After receiving a signal from the border policeman, they would swing open the final gate for me. I zoomed through this, then over a small bridge across a tiny creek that formed the actual border, and I was in West Germany...

Later in the afternoon, upon my return, I went through the same routine. This time, when they poked around in my trunk and car interior, they were looking for books or magazines - forbidden. (As I had my subscriptions to Time and the International Herald-Tribune delivered to the US Embassy, I had no need to smuggle in newspapers or magazines.)

They didn't seem to care about anything else I brought in, which were mainly groceries and household items, sometimes even a VCR or an electric drill. I noted quickly enough that the same items sent to me by post or freight would get caught in the customs web, requiring hours of time and explanation, and a letter from Filmexport supporting my need for such an item for my work, etc. But if I brought the very same items in by car, there would be no problems, merely a cursory glance and the question, "Is this for you?" Bringing in things to *sell* was their primary concern.

The great discrepancy between receiving shipments of needed items and bringing them in by hand, could only be explained by the laziness of the border people. Once, one of the studio animators begged me to bring him a radio control unit for flying model airplanes. He could manage building the planes, and even scrounging for the little engines, but the remote control units with the little joysticks did not exist in Czechoslovakia, and it was his dream to have one. It was no problem for me to find such a device in Weiden, which I put in my trunk in plain sight. There were two things I never did: One was try to hide items, and the second was to attempt to bribe customs officers, (or anyone else). Anything they found hidden in any secret places within the car would have meant I was in deep shit.

There were times when I saw a car in front of me being literally taken apart, door panels unscrewed, the works. Somehow they seemed to sense who might be smuggling bibles, pocket computers, quartz wristwatches and the like.

In my case, when the customs man spotted the model airplane controller, he lifted it out of the trunk and eyed it hungrily. "Sorry, Mr. Deitch, but this is a duty item. I will have to write up a protocol, and you'll have to take it to the customs office in Prague and register it." I moaned quietly, realizing how much time and *tsuris* this was going to require. Paying the import duty would be only the least of my problems. The man sighed, lifted the beautifully boxed radio control unit like a sacred object, and started toward the customs building. The he suddenly stopped in his tracks.

It was close to the end of his shift, nearly dinnertime. He stood there a long time, his back to me - weighing his options, I supposed. He would have to go inside, hunt-and-peck his way through a long customs protocol form....

He turned back toward me. "Screw it!" he said. He handed me the gadget and waved me through.

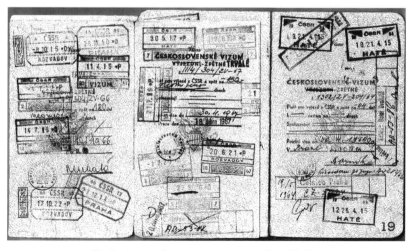

Typical pages from my passport in the mid-60s

28 - The Great Day

I was doing a music recording session with my little Ampex stereo recorder when Zdenka brought the registered letter to the studio. Between takes I opened it and read the awaited news: My divorce had come through! I had paid Marie what little money I had left for her trip to Mexico. "You can at least give me a holiday out of the ordeal," she had said. I agreed. In a situation such as this there is no real way to avoid pain. All concerned - Marie, my sons, Zdenka, her son, and myself - had a price to pay for what Zdenka and I were doing. I was certainly willing to pay my share.

Though Marie was highly suspicious in this regard, and had needlessly hired a high-tech lawyer, I willingly gave her all our possessions, including our Hudson River-view house in Tarrytown, and all that she asked for in alimony and child support. I never missed a payment. That was the least I could do in return for the chance to restart my life.

So now Zdenka and I could at last schedule our wedding. We wanted it to be in the traditional Old Town Hall, a gorgeous Gothic building in the center of the Old Town, dating back to the 14th century. It took a month to book it. November 24, 1964 would be the great day.

Much to our surprise, Zdenka's former husband remarried a month before we did. We assumed that he rushed into a new marriage to show Zdenka that he would be happy, while she would be all alone. To our further surprise, he is still married today; to his surprise, so are we.

Zdenka's big wish was to have mimosas for her wedding bouquet, but they were unheard of here. She remembered seeing some in a Zürich flower shop, so I flew there one day before the wedding in order to get them fresh. I heard that some people here thought I was actually skipping out! It's amazing how hard it is to get people to believe. It was the same with those in New York who had assumed I must have been a Communist to come here. Well, Zdenka believed, and I got back from Zürich in time to have a "night-before" dinner with her.

Zdenka wanted Lulka to be her witness, while I chose our good friend Jiří Brdečka to be best man.1 Our favorite jazz musicians, led by Karel Velebný, agreed to play "our" song, *When I Fall in Love,* during the ceremony.

I designed an invitation, and we gave copies to Zdenka's relatives and to our closest colleagues in the studio. But word soon got around, and nearly everyone in the Prague animation film establishment turned out. It was assumed that the main reason a Czech would be marrying a foreigner would be to get out of the country, so everyone showed up to bid Zdenka farewell! But Zdenka was one of the few Czechs who never considered defecting. She had no love for the Communists, but she took the long view: "Why should I let those crooks drive me out of my own country?"

I too, was off on my assumption of the effect our wedding would have. The night before, when I took Zdenka out to dinner, I told her, "You understand, Zdenka, that when we marry tomorrow you will be thrown out of your job. The Biggies will certainly not tolerate a production manager in the studio who's married to an American representative of the customer." She was ready to face that. But by 1:00 PM the next day - following a 10:00 AM ceremony and lunch with our witnesses - Zdenka was back at her desk in the studio. Proving me pleasantly mistaken, no one had said a word. Zdenka never looked back, and I've been my wife's film customer ever since!

The wedding itself was fascinating. Weddings at the Old Town Hall were churned out like cars on a Model-T assembly line, one every 15 minutes. The groom and principal witnesses and guests all wore little sprigs of myrtle pinned to their lapels with a white bit of ribbon. The cars in the wedding procession were also decorated with ribbons. Zdenka and I arrived in our "Great White Saab," which also added to the spectacle of the event.

The first thing that happened was they took us into a room where an official filled out the marriage license. Then our witnesses, Lulka Kopečná and Jiří Brdečka, and we, signed it. We were then organized into a line to wait our turn. In the meantime, the entire attending crowd was somehow squeezed into the waiting room.

Finally the doors swung open and, as our little jazz quartet began to softly play "When I Fall In Love," we slowly walked in. Zdenka's father, stepmother and sister-in-law were all weeping, (presumably for joy), while everyone else beamed. A deputy of the Prague Mayor officiated, a hefty woman with a tri-colored ribbon and medal of office hanging across her bosom. Over the stained glass window was a large emblem of the Czechoslovak Socialist Republic.

I could not yet understand enough Czech to get everything that was said, but Zdenka, smiling radiantly beneath her bouffant hairdo and clutching her barely surviving mimosa bouquet, gave me a good nudge when the time came for me to say, "I do."

Zdeněk Treybal caught it all on color film, while Jiří Janda recorded it on tape. All in all, a truly great day! From that point on, I knew that anything was possible.

November 1964

[1] Brdečka was one of the leading writers, cartoonists, and animation film directors in Prague, and was someone with whom I could discuss almost anything. He came to our flat each week to talk, watch films on our VCR and take over my week's worth of International HERALD-TRIBUNEs, TIMEs, and NEWSWEEKs. He passed on my newspapers and news magazines to his discreet circle of intellectual friends. In this way I was able to do my bit to get news and information to at least a few people. Jiří Brdečka was a brilliant man, with an ironic and macabre edge to his writing. Even though not a Communist, he had the prestige and language capabilities the authorities could make use of to promote Czech animation. He was one of the very few sent abroad to foreign film festivals, and he himself turned out a great canon of animation and live-action films, magazine articles, and books. Unfortunately, he was a chain smoker, and died of a heart attack at the age of 64. We greatly miss him.

29 – Shop 'Til You Drop

"COMES THE REVOLUTION, YOU SHALL HAVE STRAWBERRIES-AND-CREAM!"

That was said to be Lenin's promise to the proletariat. And you know what? In Communist Czechoslovakia, there really was strawberries-and-cream...once a year. And once a year there were watermelons, and once a year there were bananas. It was terribly exciting. When the big day arrived, people would line up in the squares. A truck would roll up, and these rare treats would be sold directly from the truck to the eager crowds. I must say, those wondrous days made everyone appreciate things we take for granted now.

I saw Antonín Novotný, the country's last Stalinist president, give his 1962 New Year's address on TV. He informed the populace that the government had decided to import lemons instead of oranges that year, "because lemons have more vitamins!" Why, I wondered, is the president of the nation grappling with the question of oranges vs. lemons?

"It's just as well," said Zdenka, "Our government imports the cheapest oranges." She was right about that. When there were oranges, they were from Cuba, and those were a blotchy greenish-gray color, misshapen and unpeel able.

I once told Zdenka I craved some corn on the cob. "What?" she said, "Corn is only for pigs!" Later, when I saw what the locally grown corn looked like, I had to agree.

Shopping for food, or anything else, was a daily trial. How to get what you wanted, how to finagle scarce items, how to make do with what you could get, was an all-consuming passion. If you couldn't get what you needed after work, you simply stole time during working hours, the universally practiced way of shopping here.

Everyone was a shopping scout. "I saw garlic at Můstek!" someone would announce. Your best friends would tip you off.

For most people, the main daily activity was looking for something to buy. Working hours were conveniently arranged from 6AM to 3PM, which allowed time to shop before the stores closed at 6PM. During these hours the babičky were on constant vigil. Retired grannies patrolled the streets, carrying their ubiquitous net shopping bags, ever on the alert for lines of people. Whenever they saw a queue, it was a sure sign that something good and rare was on sale.

There was a story about one such babička, who saw a line of excited shoppers and immediately joined them. One by one, the line slowly advanced, and each lucky customer got a little box. What could it be? The granny's excitement mounted as she neared the counter. At last she got her little box. Her curiosity impelled her to open it immediately, and she pulled out a long strip of material.

"What is it?" she asked the clerk in puzzlement.

"It's shit now, lady," said the clerk dryly, "but it was color film."

When I arrived here there were no self-service stores. Everything was behind counters. God forbid you should handle the merchandise! You had to stand in three separate lines. The first line was at the counter where you asked for what you wanted. The second line was for paying at the cashier cubicle - only one person in each shop was entrusted to handle money. The third line was at the delivery counter, where you actually picked up your purchased items. When they didn't have what you wanted, which was most of the time, the bored clerk would deliver a standard line, "Ask again in 14 days!" This would protect the clerk from your nagging for at least that period of time. The phrase had no other meaning, for it was impossible to order anything. Even the manager of the shop couldn't order anything. He just waited for whatever was delivered, confident that whatever it was would be easily sold.

All goods were "guaranteed," but refunds did not exist. Asking for repairs just meant more lines, delays and frustrations. Further consumer protection was in the previously mentioned "Book of Wishes and Complaints," which hung prominently in every shop and restaurant.

The greatest protection a harassed shop manager had against the annoying demands of shoppers was "INVENTORY." This ubiquitous sign, nearly always displayed at the very shop you were headed for, kept you out and them safely inside, counting whatever it was they had in stock. This could go on for days. And when they finally did reopen, you could not assume they had in the meantime restocked. "Ask in 14 days," was still the bone-dry advice from the sour-faced clerk. He clearly wished he were somewhere else.

On our street was a shop advertising itself as an ironing service. True, there was a huge electric mangle inside, but only rarely was there someone to operate it. Nearly every time I stopped by - sent by Zdenka, and burdened with a huge pile of sheets and pillowcases for ironing - I was greeted by a locked door and one of a series of little hand-printed signs:

"I AM AT THE POST OFFICE," "I AM AT HEADQUARTERS," ""I WILL BE

BACK IN HALF AN HOUR" (hah!), "I'M AT THE DOCTOR," and other highly imaginative notices, apparently rotated each day.

Even if I had the remarkable luck of finding the ironing woman actually present and the door open, I would be greeted by her glum news: "No electricity." Or, "The machine is broken."

On one momentous day I arrived, loaded down with laundry, to find the lights on, the machine humming, and the lady there! It was 11AM, near the usual early lunchtime. She had been open since 10, but I noted on the door that the shop had afternoon hours. I optimistically plunked down my load and asked what time I could pick up the ironed stuff.

"I am sorry," she said dryly, flipping off the machine and not even bothering to look at me, "But I am finished ironing for today."

"But you have afternoon hours," I reminded her. "What will you be doing in the afternoon?"

"I will sit on my butt and stare out the window!" was her hostile reply. She was obviously exasperated with me for bothering her. "I'm not going to heat up my machine for a lousy 10 crowns!"

That was indeed the catch. The price for this elusive service was ridiculously cheap. Ten crowns equaled less than 30 cents. I suggested that I would gladly pay more. She retorted, "Sure, and you'll report me for price gouging!"

Most shops kept a supply of those notices: "NO BATTERIES AVAILABLE," "NO TOILET PAPER," "NO GARLIC." Those handy little signs saved the harassed shopkeepers much annoyance.

A curiosity for me was that many shops sold goods according to the materials they were made of, rather than the use they were intended for. So toilet paper, whenever available, was sold in stationery shops. In rubber shops, you could find automobile mud-guards, beach balls, sink stoppers, shower caps, erasers, and condoms, and in plastic stores would be dashboard parts for cars, toilet seats, coat hangers, toy trucks, dustpans, and bathtub duckies. Wooden coat hangers? Try a lumberyard!

The price of every item you bought was printed on it, or molded right into the product. Any given item, whether bought in the largest Prague department store or in a tiny podunk shop in a remote village, would cost exactly the same. You shopped not according to price, but according to where you could find it. Prices were completely artificial and never changed. They made a big deal out of ensuring that you got the exact *weight or amount* of whatever crud you bought. Consumer information, therefore, consisted solely of quantity and price. Even in restaurants, the liquid measure was engraved on the glasses.

Weight and amount was all any factory needed to produce in order to fulfill its state-required plan. So a nail factory would find it easier to produce just one size of nail. All they had to show was that they produced so many tons of them. What kind, how good, or what size nail, didn't matter. What did matter was that when they "met their plan" all the workers got a bonus! [1]

You wanted a car? Sure. Only a four-year wait. You wanted a telephone? Yours in 18 years - if you were lucky. You'd like your child to have an apartment when he or she becomes an adult? Easy, just sign up the kid shortly after birth, pay a large deposit, and maybe in twenty years he or she will have risen to the top of the list. Twenty years interest on your deposit? Forget it!

Could you live without tissues? Sticky tape? Paper towels? Band-Aids? The Czechs had to. Everyone carried well-used cloth hankies. We had to supply the animation studio with various types of sticky tapes. The technology of adhesives was apparently not on the socialist agenda.

If you wanted your clothes cleaned, you really had to think ahead - like if you neede your suit two weeks from now - and oh yes, don't forget to remove all the buttons from your clothes before entrusting them to the cleaners. If letft on, th buttons would ususally melt!

The technology of *toilet seats* was one of the main indicators of consumer goods desperation. When I arrived in this country, the toilet seats installed in new flats, in the various unspeakable public toilets, and available (sometimes) in shops, were pressed from some thin brittle plastic, apparently recycled from former coat hangers, shoehorns, or jam jar caps. They were a uniform nondescript greenish color, and just barely able to support the average butt. The worst thing was that they were subject to splitting at the most inconvenient of moments, and capable of delivering a scream-inducing and bloody pinch. I am not willing to display my scar for you, but it's there.

A standard joke of the time was about meat markets. It was said that in Masaryk's First Republic there were signs outside the shops that said "BUTCHER," and inside was meat. In the ČSSR there were signs outside saying "MEAT," and inside was a butcher. I remember that during the early '60s, when there really was only a butcher inside meat shops, they became quite adept at arranging pretty potted plants in their shop windows so that at least there was *something* there.

Occasionally I tried to poke at the system, with mixed results. I like cottage cheese, but it was completely unknown here, so I bought a package of it in Germany and brought it back packed in ice. I then sent it to the manager of the Prague dairy producer, suggesting this might be a popular and worthwhile product. I actually received an answer; the manager assuring me they already produced cottage cheese, which he then referred to by its Czech name, *tvaroh*. It turned out to be a solid, gummy form of milk cheese, with no relation at all to what we know as cottage cheese. I just wondered if he actually opened the package and tasted what I sent. Obviously, it would have been too much work, and disruptive of his *plan*, to produce any kind of new product. Risk was foreign to the system. (Today of course, real cottage cheese is widely available, and I like to think that it was I who first introduced it to the Czech marketplace!)

Many foods were still sold in bulk, as packaging was especially primitive. Towards this end, *Rudé Právo*, the official Communist Party daily, played perhaps its only useful role. Along with the huge blocks of butter that were sliced and weighed then wrapped in its large pages, loose goods, such as dried beans, were poured deftly into *Rudé Právo* pages formed into cones. The clerks were very good at making paper cones.

There was always a shortage of something. I remember when all the women were in distress over a total lack of women's panties. Because of the usual bureaucratic production bumbles, there were no feminine underthings to be had anywhere, not even under the usual counters. Clothes for sale here could not be taken seriously by anyone attempting to be fashionably dressed. Even women of modest means had all of their clothes tailor-made. What would have been a luxury for us was a necessity here.

Whenever there was something special available, the lines before the shops suggested that they were giving away gold bricks. One such sensation was the Italian plastic raincoat, popular in the 60s, which could be folded up into a small envelope. People here would kill for one of those, and the few people who could travel to the west, brought back as many of these as they could carry. A hefty profit was assured, selling them to others. Another questionable sensation were the paper sport jackets that had a brief popularity - anything that would give people a chance to sport an item of clothing that would set them apart from the standardized apparel available to the masses.

Shoes were a dismal joke. The uppers resembled painted cardboard, being made of leather more suitable for luggage tags. Foreigners were easily identified by a glance at their shoes.

The toilet paper chase was a constant, and again Rudé Právo proved its usefulness. When available at all, toilet paper rarely came in rolls, but in little packets of very thin "wrapping paper" whose roughness seemed designed to guarantee a life of hemorrhoids. When it later did appear in rolls, it was the same brownish crisp paper. It occurred to me that it might work nicely for roll-your-own cigarettes.

But let's return to the other end of human needs - food. Often, if there was a shortage of one type of item, you had to buy something else that happened to be plentiful in order to get the rarer item. So if you wanted onions, for example, which were usually in short supply, you had to also buy potatoes, which were plentiful. But those potatoes were often so rotten that nearly half of each bagful had to be thrown in the garbage.

One of the most revolting products available was ordinary cooking oil. The greasy glass bottles were generically labeled "Table Oil." I hated to think of it on our table. If you held it up to the light you could see filaments of phlegmy fat floating inside. This stuff would turn you off fried foods forever!

Furniture was all made up of boxes, generally oak veneer on pressboard, with no style whatsoever, bad or good. The standard apartments were also like boxes, and had no clothes closets. Everyone had to have wardrobe cabinets. What were available looked like what you would find in a cheap hotel or college dormitory - plain, unadorned boxes, always with a key. All such cabinets, shelves, etc. were of a universal oak veneer color. Even plain-Jane but attractive Ikea-type pinewood furniture was considered a rarity.

There was no such thing as a double bed. There were only cots. Two could be shoved together. Cots were basic wooden platforms on which were placed three hard, kapok-filled cushions. No spring mattresses. Even slabs of foam rubber were hard to get. Amazingly, this did not deter sexual activity.

There was also no such thing as a pop-up toaster. All the way up to the 1989 revolution only one toaster model was available. It had those little bottom-hinged doors on each side of a heating unit with which you had to flip over the slices at the precise moment of preferred brownness (see any 1935 Sears-Roebuck catalog). It was no wonder that very few Czechs ate toast.

Carpets and floor coverings were all of universally dowdy patterns, and made of shoddy materials. The so-called linoleum was in narrow rolls of some heavy pre-vinyl, rubberoid material, which would not stay flat, but tended to wave and buckle, and thus wear unevenly. So all floors everywhere, whether in shops, institutions or apartments, looked pretty much the same.

The only department store in town to sport elevators was Bílá Labuť, (The White Swan), a relic emporium from the First Republic. Here you lined up for the two available lifts, which had live operators. The elevators did not carry passengers down at all, only up, and only to the top floor. There were no stops in between, and from the top you had to walk downstairs to the floor you actually wanted, even if was the 2nd floor!

This store also had the only escalator in the country, a rickety narrow wooden-step affair (again, up only) to the mezzanine. It worked for a short while after I arrived, but was soon dismantled and removed completely, as no one was capable of maintaining or repairing it.

The most fascinating type of lift for me was the so-called "Paternoster," named for its cabins' resemblance to Catholic confession booths. It was an endless chain of such booths, which were constantly in motion, rolling up one shaft and down another. You had to jump on and off one of the little open-front booths as it approached your floor, quick and deftly, to avoid being scissored as the booth passed the floor above or below you. Yes, on this delightful contraption you could also ride down! I wondered what it was like at the upper and lower turn-around points. It took a lot of convincing to get Zdenka to ride with me all the way to the top. The ancient machine drew us up into total darkness as we were trundled, wobbling, over the upper wheels, then sent down again into the adjacent descending shaft. Zdenka was alarmed that we would be turned upside down as we went over the top! Despite her mighty talents, insights and abilities, she hasn't a clue in the realm of the technical.

Elevators in Prague during the communist era reflected not only the primitive state of everyday technology, but also the regime's attitude towards people. High-rise *paneláky*, over four floors high, required elevators. But what was provided could only be described as a flimsy packing-crate-on-a-cable. It would have swinging inner and outer doors - sliding elevator doors did not exist - and both sets of doors had to be closed securely before the frightening thing could be set in motion. The cabin started and stopped with a sudden lurch - no such thing as slowing to a stop - and the noise of the motors and relays whined and clanked throughout the building. Tenants living near the elevator shafts were treated to this loud clicking and thrumming day and night - that is, when the elevators worked at all. The most common sight on a Czech elevator door was a little sign, always at the ready, which hung on the door. "PORUCHA," it said. (Out of Order)

The local media constantly trumpeted the success of the "Socialist Sector." That puzzled me because as far as I could make out, the "Socialist Sector" included everything except Eduard Čapek's secondhand junk shop behind the Týn church. Čapek was a local legend, as he appeared to have the only private shop allowed to exist in Prague, and in perhaps the entire country. It was an incredible cave of a shop - musty, with the smell of rusty, dusty iron, shelves full of ancient wooden boxes filled with old hinges, stove parts, bits of grill work, dented pots and pans, an occasional bicycle wheel, lanterns... You had to lower your head to miss the myriad of odd metal items hanging from hooks in the vaulted ceiling. It was a marvelous place, frequented by people hoping to replace that special missing or broken part that could not be found in any regular state-run shop. Čapek himself was a crusty coot who knew how to survive with independence. He had fans from all over the world who would never miss a visit to this strange and unique establishment. When he died, his son attempted to keep the shop running, with the name Eduard Čapek in metal letters still imbedded in the wall, over arched, weathered wooden doors that were heavily hung with the oddments of his trade. But the son had to leave this traditional site, now too valuable a location for a junk shop, and set up on nearby Dlouhá Street, where you can still visit it.

Today, of course, there are curious new problems. Nearly everything we could ask for is here to buy. We have McDonald's (48 and counting), KFC, Pizza Hut, and we had K-Mart until the British chain Tesco bought it out. We have endless models of pop-up toasters, and every kitchen gadget known to the planet. Not only are there now elegant automatic elevators, which run smoothly, but they also go down as well as up!

But what to make of the cute, taught-to-smile K-Mart salesgirls who wore large buttons reading, "I AM HERE FOR YOU?" This led to some rather lecherous remarks from male shoppers who, unused to politeness from shop people, still had to catch on to American-style marketing techniques.

---

[1] Everyone in the country had two levels of pay. There was your basic salary, on which you could starve, and then there was the monthly premium, or bonus payment based on various standards of performance set by the party apparatus for each enterprise and each job.

30 - We Help
The Mayor Help Us

The door was sealed by the police! That was the surprise that greeted us when we returned home one evening in early 1967. It wasn't our door, fortunately, but the door of Dr. Stejskal and his family, one floor below us. We knew the Stejskals since the time they had invited us to their two-room apartment to show them color slides from our trips to the States. They had been hypnotized by the lure of America. Our perspective, on the other hand, was somewhat less expansive: Wow, we thought, if we could only have a flat like theirs. *Two whole rooms!*

And now they were gone, their flat empty. When people managed to escape the country, their apartment was sealed immediately to facilitate investigation and to prevent looting. Abandoned personal belongings were subject to government confiscation.

Later we learned that the Stejskals had been clever. Each day they had taken out a painting or other small object wrapped discreetly in newspaper, a piece of furniture "to be reupholstered," even a piano "to be restrung." Everything had been quietly distributed to friends and relatives. The flat was now completely empty, except for a gas refrigerator attached to the kitchen wall.

Acting as any alert Praguers at the time, we instantly applied for the flat, clearly believing that, as we lived in the building, we would be the first in line. Fat chance! *Seventeen* people were already ahead of us. In those days no news traveled faster than news of an empty flat. It was the universal vulture reaction. One of the 17 applicants, we were told, had six children! How all would fit into a two-room flat, we didn't know.

But *I* had *connections.* Not only that, I was bringing dollars into the country with my American film projects, and we had two flats to trade for one. Our application would be a cinch.

Or so we thought...

Before Zdenka and I were married, we each had a "garsoniérre," or one-room studio apartment. Then Zdenka moved into my top floor Malá Strana room, leaving hers unused. All we wanted was the right to trade our two 1-room flats for one 2-room flat. I had letters from Czechoslovak Filmexport supporting my great need for this two-room apartment. Our case advanced from bureau to bureau. "The apartment is yours," I was told repeatedly.

"If the apartment is ours," I asked, "why can't we get the key?" This repeated question drew wry smiles. Was I just too naive to understand? Should I dare to offer a bribe? Or would that kill it?

There was always a hitch. One was that there was still a refrigerator in the apartment. A police-sealed apartment, confiscated from defectors, had to have a complete inventory of its remaining contents, and only when every last item was accounted for - and officially disposed of - could the apartment become free for reassignment. So we *bought* the refrigerator, a hopeless tiny gas model full of moldy food - but no matter. One roadblock after another appeared between the keys and us. I was desperate enough to offer a bribe, even though our claim to the flat was entirely legitimate. But to whom should I pay? The stairway to our desired two rooms was stoutly defended by ascending levels of bureaucrats.

I finally got as high as the Czechoslovak Minister of Culture himself, Jiří Hájek. Flats of this two-roominess were in extremely short supply, and it was not unusual for their allotment to be decided on a *ministerial* level! Hájek, who would become one of Dubček's men during the '68 Prague Spring, told me that the man I had to see was the Lord Mayor of Prague - personally!

I couldn't believe my ears. Was the mayor of the Capital City of Prague involved in private apartment transactions? Was this decision on a par with the government's importation of lemons instead of oranges? Was the Mayor interested in my views on civic management? Did he want me to express an American's opinion of Prague's problems?

Hájek, who obviously knew something, arranged the meeting. So at the appointed date and time I found myself in the city hall sanctuary of the Biggest Animal in town, sitting before his huge mahogany desk, trying to quickly explain why I was there. I needn't have bothered. He knew.

Mayor Černý, it turned out, had a villa, one room of which was rented to an elderly lady whom the Mayor could not legally or quietly expel.[1] Now if this lady could be given our Malá Strana one-room garsoniérre, we would be given the two-roomer downstairs - some other deserving and well-placed person would get Zdenka's Kobylisy one-roomer, *and the Mayor of Prague would have his villa all to himself.*

And so it came to pass in the land of socialist equality. It may be difficult for readers abroad to understand our joy at getting an apartment with two -entire-rooms, plus a bathroom, roomy kitchen, two actual closets, and a little entrance hall. But part of the joy of living in a deprived country was the appreciation one had for every small gain or success. We learned that everything is relative.

We were by this time financially in a position to make our little apartment better furnished than our neighbors', and Zdenka was a first-class interior decorator. Over the years, we obtained color television, a VCR, a satellite dish, a freezer, and a dishwasher all before anyone else. Imagine the status we had with all that pslus two rooms.

We were once visited by a Russian stage designer, whose eyes bugged out when he entered our door. After a grand tour of both rooms, the bathroom, and the kitchen, he asked, looking over his shoulder, "How many people live in this flat with you?" When we assured him that just the two of us lived here, alone, he rose to his feet, spread his arms with a grand Russian gesture, and shouted, "*It is Ameeeeer-r-r-r-ika!*"

Even so, by American standards our flat would be judged tiny digs. And yet for us it's been more than enough. Taped to our door is our family motto, taken from an old Czech proverb: "WITH A GOOD WIFE AND ENOUGH POTATO SOUP, DON'T ASK FOR MORE."

---

[1] The lady, a retired attorney named Dr. Marie Grünfeldová, became our upstairs neighbor and friend. She was the only member of her family to survive the Nazi death camp at Auschwitz. She still had the tattooed number on her arm. One summer day, she told us, she was riding on the Prague tram, wearing a sort-sleeved blouse that revealed her tattoo. Sitting nearby was a German visitor with her young son. The kid stared at Dr. Grünfeldová, then called out to his mother in German, "Why does that lady have a number on her arm?"

The woman flushed. "I don't know," she stuttered. "Be quiet!"

But Dr. Grünfeldová spoke German fluently. "Madam," she said to the woman, "I think you should tell your child the truth. You know perfectly well what this tattoo means!"

31 – Revolting!

"WE WILL BURY YOU!"

So shouted Soviet chief Nikita Khruschev to the West in the mid-sixties. He predicted that within 20 years communism would triumph in the world both materially and spiritually. Unfortunately for him, he got that almost exactly backwards.

Ironically, it was Khruschev himself who first pulled the plug on the sacred Communist ideology, in his not-so-secret speech in the mid-50s denouncing Stalin. There is the possibly apocryphal story that, in that vast meeting hall, a voice from the rear shouted, "Comrade Nikita Sergeyevitch, you were a high ranking Party official under Stalin. If you knew that he was doing such terrible things, why didn't you raise your voice?"

Khruschev turned blood red. *"WHO SAID THAT? WHO HERE DARES TO QUESTION AND ACCUSE THE GENERAL SECRETARY OF THE COMMUNIST PARTY OF THE SOVIET UNION?"*

There was a deadly silence in the hall. Whoever had spoken now only quivered, biting his tongue. After a lengthy pause, Khruschev said:

"There, comrades, you have the answer to the question!"

And of course he was right. It was fear that kept the system glued together - fear of the populace towards their Communist rulers - fear of the rulers toward the populace.

In Czechoslovakia, at that time run by the hardest of hard-line servants of Moscow, the same fear echoed back and forth between the rulers and the ruled. They dared not allow a single word of open discussion. You would think that everyone shared the official opinion, that everyone here was a communist. But I can tell you now that, in my 30 years living in this country during Communist rule, *I never met a single true communist!*.

By that I mean, I met none I felt were believing communists. In spite of all their public platitudes about being "the vanguard of the working class," it was widely known most of the biggies had Swiss bank accounts. This was crystal clear when, after the "Velvet Revolution," the most orthodox communist officials suddenly became the most eager capitalists. They had the inside information as to which industries, factories, etc., were the most promising, and they all came up with enough cash to get themselves in on the ground floor of the new booming Czech market. There is now no more talk of Marxism-Leninism from those communists, but only of stocks, bonds, and tax dodges! Most of the financial scandals in recent years have involved former top communists. They changed their ideology, but not their morals.

In those days they shouted, "Socialism Forever"! The Czech communists believed - or seemed to believe - that their rule was eternal. The dominant slogan, on bilboards, banners, and illuminated rooftop signs, was "With The Soviet Union Forever !". The number one marching song was "Forward Left!" (sic) "Not One Step Backward!" The warning to infidels was that they nust "accept the Socialist Reality!" Even in the rush of the Velvet Revolution they were still shrieking, "the gains (sic) of socialism cannot be reversed". What eventually happened to them was beyond their comprehension.

The Czech Communist Party, which still survives today, is a puzzle to me. They retain the name Communist, but in place of the hammer & sickle, their symbol is 2 cherries on the stem. Don't ask. They no longer speak of Marxism-Leninism, or communism. I have no idea what they are for. There is no way that totalitarian "socialism" can be reinstalled here, without a powerful Soviet Union as backing. But enough misguided citizens still give them the second highest poll rating, about 20%! They are nevertheless still kept out of any participation in the current coalition government. Those disgruntled old-timers who vote for them are in fact throwing their votes away. Go figure.

But in my early days here, I admit I did get to know a couple of naive people who seemed to believe in the utopian idea of socialism, but certainly not any of the really active Party members who actually knew the score. As a rare bird on the scene, and as representative of a steady customer of the Czechoslovak film industry, I was invited to many affairs where high-ranking officials were present. Once I was introduced to a government minister. He didn't tell me, "We will bury you!" or attempt to paint a glorious portrait of what their press called "The inevitable triumph of Socialism?" No.

What he said to me was, "*Oh yes, Mr. Deitch, I have heard about you. Are you having any troubles here? We know things are not as well as they should be. There are many problems, and we have made many mistakes. It is a matter of a generation before we can expect things to be better...,* " and on and on, *apologizing!* He wasn't going to admit to me that the entire system was bullshit, but in essence that's exactly what he was saying. Party members further down the line were far more explicit.

I got to know one of the most famous men in the country at the time, Jan Werich, actor and comic. He had been half of the team, Voskovec and Werich, so famous that all they needed to announce was W+V. WWII, (just as famous a shortening), separated them. George Voskovec found success as a character actor in New York. When I first met Jan Werich he told me, "Our country has an 'and' president!" What he meant was that the president of the country at that time, Antonín Novotný, was always written and spoken of as, *"Comrade Antonín Novotný, First Secretary of the Central Committee of the Communist Party of Czechoslovakia and president of the republic!"* His main title was as head of the Party, the real power. His ceremonial post as president rated only an "and."

A colleague in the animation studio gave me a calendar saved from the year 1952, in the form of a cookbook expressly aimed at women. It gave recipes for lunch and dinner for each day of the year. The blandness and sameness of the suggested meals clearly indicated the limited food choices of the time. And along with the dumplings, goulash and mashed potatoes, was a heavy seasoning of propaganda. In red letters, the days dear to the communists were noted along with the recipes: *"Day of the Czechoslovak Cannoneers,"* *"Murder of Karl Liebknecht and Rosa Luxemburg,"* *"Death of V.I.Lenin,"* *"Day of the Red Army,"* *"Founding of the Paris Commune."* *"Victorious February,"* *(the communist putsch), "The Birth of V.I.Lenin,"* *"Birth of Karl Marx,"* *"Founding of the Communist Party..."* On and on, the glorious days marched among the goulash.

But the fact was that Communist ideology simply didn't go down well in this country. Czechoslovakia was founded on French, British, and American culture. During my stay here, there gradually developed all kinds of American -style jazz bands, and later American country and western music - but there was not a single balalaika band! There were blue jeans and American style T-shirts, and long lines whenever an American movie played, but Russian culture did not resonate here. It existed only in the posters and banners of the Soviet-imposed political system, which were simply ignored.

The Marxist definition of communism was *"From each according to his ability. To each according to his needs."* But even if you believed that, just imagine the bureaucracy needed to decide who needs what, and how to handle the distribution. However benevolent such a system might be designed, it still means that a citizen must be a supplicant, applying to a disbursing authority for whatever was felt to be needed. But how could one prove that their "needs" included a VCR, designer jeans, or a nice car?

For me, this was the question it always came down to, and it was the main reason I never could accept communism as a viable system, even in my youth. Though somewhat of a radical in my early teens and late 20's, my early flirtation with communist ideas lasted just six months. In my wild mental flights, ever dreaming of some kind of fair social system, I tried to devise my own concept. I called it "sharing." For example, I don't believe that oil deposits, gold, gas, diamonds, uranium, or what have you, should necessarily belong to the state that just happens to occupy the territory where those minerals reside. The "God-given" natural resources were laid down eons before people or countries existed, and should thus be shared by the whole world. BUT...*How could it actually be done?* And how could it be done without the bureaucracy once again taking control? The answer, as I quickly began to see, was that it couldn't.

We used to hear much about the bloody Communist atrocities. We heard about political prisoners, tortures, executions, terror. Much of it was true, but it usually involved people who openly attempted to buck the system and challenge its power.

There were other, more everyday things about the system that troubled me. One of these was the fact that whenever I complained about anything here, people would say to me, "But Mr. Deitch, this is *Czechoslovakia!*"

In other words, "What could I expect?" It was a sad indication that Czechs and Slovaks had lost all respect for their own country.

There were many symbolic stabs perpetrated by the Communists that tore at Czech and Slovak hearts. The ancient crest of the Czech nation, unchanged for hundreds of years, is a two-tailed rampant white lion with a crowned head. The Communists removed the crown and placed a five-pointed socialist star over the lion's head. The crown was declared a "provocation," and to fly the Czechoslovak flag by itself was a punishable offense. When I once asked an official why a Soviet flag must invariably fly besides every Czechoslovak flag, he corrected me.

"That is not the Soviet flag," he assured me, "It is the banner of the Czechoslovak Communist Party." The flaw in this argument was that it was *exactly identical in every detail to the Soviet flag.*

Flag display orders were issued on official occasions, and all the flags were put up. Every tenant was supplied with enough twin flags for each window of the flat. There would be hell to pay if your windows were flagless on the given celebratory day. Every entrance of every building also had twin flag holders. Trucks and pushcarts loaded with flags would work their way down each and every street as workers mounted the larger flags over all the doorways. No wonder there was full employment!

And Lord knows the Communist regime appeared to have no sense of humor whatsoever. For proof of this, I suggest reading Milan Kundera's novel The Joke, in which the simple writing of a postcard in jest destroys a man's life. The communists could not tolerate even the slightest joshing; yet they said the most bizarre things with straight faces, while feigning belief in their absurd slogans.

What humor there was, was accidental. One hilarity I ran into showed the hazards of poor translation. I read a leaflet giving the Communist slant on the revolutionary character of Czech history. It told about how in the middle ages, the peasants revolted against the landlords, how workers in the sweatshops of the 19th century revolted against the tyranny of evil bosses, and how Czech workers repeatedly revolted against capitalist tyranny... on and on, finally summing up with this surrealist thought:

"...and so it can be said that the Czechs have always been a revolting people!"

The entire system, I found, was based on an outdated premise set down by Karl Marx: "As the Working Class represents the majority of the population, it is right that they should rule. And as the Communist Party is the Vanguard of the Working Class, it is right that they should rule in the name of the Workers." The main problem with this was that even in those days, the working class, by which they meant factory workers, miners, and agricultural peasants, were already a *minority.* The majority of the people were in the bureaucracy and service sector. What was in power here was a Communist Party whose membership never got beyond about 1,500,000 - the great majority of whom were merely pro-forma members. Only a tiny fraction of these were the actual, active rulers of the country of 15.5 million.

What I came to see was that communism, the "Marxist-Leninist" application, was the greatest system ever devised for gaining and holding power. It was cunningly devised to control virtually every facet of its subjects' lives. There seemed no way out of it.

Being a member of the Party was the only way to get ahead - to be sure your children would be able to attend university, etc. etc. It was not easy to become a Communist. It was a very exclusive club, with many perks, including a network of hidden shops where only Party members had access to goods unavailable to the general public.

By the time communism finally wore itself out, there had been so many twists and turns in the wobbly Party line, and so many layers of phrases and weird terminology, no one at all could believe in it.

The horrors of Nazism and fascism were constantly written and spoken about, but no account ever allowed for any similarities with communism. In this regard, great care was taken that the term "totalitarianism" was never used when damning the Nazis, as it clearly also described Czechoslovak "socialism."

Before this country was dubbed a "Socialist Republic," it was called a "People's Democracy," presumably meaning it belonged to the people, and that it was democratic. What it meant was that the Communist Party was supposedly doing what was best for the People as a whole. That is what "democracy" was proclaimed to mean. The Communists decided what was best for society as a whole, without allowing individual choice or dissent. Recently I heard a wonderful new euphemism come out of Communist North Korea: "voluntary conformity." The Czechoslovak Communists rejoiced in the same delusion.

One major word game concerned Germany. For example, there was a West Germany – ("the revanchist threat to peace") - and there was The German Democratic Republic. *But there was no such place as East Germany!* The people who lived there were not "Germans"... Lord no! "Germans" had brutally occupied Czechoslovakia during World War II. These were completely different "anti-fascist" people, *"citizens of the German Democratic Republic."*

The most fun was watching a football game between an East German team, and, let's say, a Polish team. Pity the poor sportscasters who had to keep up this rapid fire, tongue-twisting commentary:

"...and-now-the-Poles-have-the-ball,-but-here-comes-Schulz, a representative-of-the-German-Democratic-Republic, taking-the-ball-and-being-shielded-by-Siegfried-a-representative-of-the-German-Democratic-Republic But-the-Pole-nearly-fouls-the-representative-of-The-German-Democratic-Republic-and-the

-referee-awards-a-free-kick-to-the-representative-of-the-German-Democratic -Republic, and-it's-a-GOALLLL-for-the-team-of-The-German-Democratic -Republic!!"

I kid you not. That is really the way it was on local TV and radio. The Poles could be called Poles, but the East Germans could not be called Germans. Only the West Germans could. They were Germans all right, but also something called "revanchists." I had never heard the term before, but it indicated that they were the sole German inheritors of Nazi thought, and were a constant threat, seeking revenge for their wartime territorial losses against the "Socialist Camp."

The word game was even more exacting about Berlin. There was a West Berlin, *but no such place as East Berlin.* Once Zdenka and I were there, driving through East Berlin on our way to Odense in western Denmark. Zdenka luckily had permission to travel through West Berlin. But where was it? There were no direction signs. We zigzagged through the shabby, nearly deserted streets of East Berlin, until finally we came to a citizen of the German Democratic Republic who was tinkering with his precious Trabant auto. Struggling with a few words of German (yes, they did speak German there), we asked for directions to Checkpoint Charlie, the famous cross-point to West Berlin.

"Checkpoint Charlie?" His expression seemed to indicate he had never heard of it. He produced a map of East Berlin from his car trunk. We stared at it. All around the perimeter of that part of the city he was confined to, his map showed only *blank yellow areas* - there were no streets shown at all beyond the wall, just that flat yellow color!

But as the label on the map indicated, there was also no such place as East Berlin. Instead, it was "BERLIN, CAPITAL CITY OF THE GERMAN DEMOCRATIC REPUBLIC." So that was it. There was "West Berlin," and there was "Berlin, Capital City of the German Democratic Republic." Finally, through sheer luck, we came upon Checkpoint Charlie. And after the most elaborate border crossing maze ever, we crossed into a place where everything was called by its true name.

I also found out that the Czech post office would not accept a letter addressed to "Berlin, West Germany." It had to be just "West Berlin," period. To them, West Berlin in no way belonged to West Germany. But the letter would actually be routed via West Germany, as were phone calls. There was no way to telephone directly to West Berlin.

To the Communists, facade was everything. The Potemkin Village routine was common. I remember once, when Brezhnev was due to visit, the local authorities quickly (and roughly) painted all the shabby buildings on Nerudová street, the street that led up to the castle - but only as high as the second floor. When Brezhnev was driven along that route in his Vaz limousine, his view out the window would not be any higher!

This kind of Communist flummery continued right up to the very end. During the surge of the November 1989 revolution, Miroslav Štěpán, chief of the Prague Communist Party branch – and the very person who ordered the police to beat the students on November 17 - stood on a factory balcony, to where he had rushed in a last minute attempt to squelch the flames. For the first time in his life, he faced an openly hostile audience.

"If you think," he shouted, reminding me very much of the earlier Khruschev outburst, "that this country can go forward without the Communist Party of Czechoslovakia, you are very much mistaken!"

Luckily for the Czech nation, he was the mistaken one.

"Resign! Resign!" shouted the crowd in reply. And he did.[1]

---

[1] In 1995, Miroslav Štěpán, out of prison for his pre-'89 offenses, established a new, separate Marxist-Leninist Communist Party, and predicted socialism would be re-established by 2002. Stay tuned. "Well, it's only spring 2002 as I write this!"

32 - Funny Money

The actual value of the socialist Czechoslovak crown was, as mentioned earlier, always a mystery. From the "official" rate of seven crowns to the dollar, to the "tourist 100% bonus rate" of 15 to the dollar, to the black market rate of 35 to the dollar, the crown's value depended on where you changed your money. No foreigner in his right mind would accept the "official" rate after being bitten once at a hotel desk. Any alert tourist or businessman was quick to discover the black market rate, which was almost openly offered, often by moneychangers hanging furtively around hotel entrances or in front of Tuzex shops, or through personal contacts, (for those who had them). At this upper rate you could clean out the antique shops, the only places where there were items worth buying, and live it up at the best restaurants. To be a diplomat assigned to Prague in the period of communism was pure heaven. Before every antique shop in Prague you could always see an ambassador's car parked, while his wife shopped inside. Most diplomatic wives divided their time between giving parties and shopping for antiques.

Non-diplomatic foreigners actually living here fell into two distinct categories: "Foreign Foreigners" and "Local Foreigners." A "Foreign Foreigner" could have bank accounts abroad, and bring foreign currency in and out of the country. These were generally businessmen on short stays, and diplomats. "Local Foreigners" were those poor souls who may have had foreign passports, but were employed here, working within the Czechoslovak economy, earning local money, and thus subject to local economic rules. They included political refugees, (some were American Communists), or those married to Czechs or Slovaks and who had opted for local residency. The Czechoslovak money they earned could not be exchanged for Western currency, and could not be taken out of or into the country.

Some, of course, was smuggled out, (at great risk), sold for a low exchange rate, and found its way into some foreign banks, where Germans or Austrians, for example, could buy Czechoslovak currency at the black market rate, and have a cheap holiday in Prague. But "Lenin-forbid", that you should be caught at the border carrying Czechoslovak money!

So the "Local Foreigners" were just as economically stuck here as were the local citizens. I was one of the fortunate few, a genuine "Foreign Foreigner." I was never asked at the border if I had any dollars or deutschmarks, but always if I had any crowns. Of course I had to carry some, if only to buy gas or lunch enroute, or if I had to stay in a Czech hotel for any reason. But I had to leave all my crowns at a bank window at the border station on my way out, get a receipt for them, and then pick them up again upon my return to the country. For this "service," the bank generously deducted a percentage for itself. All of this made it imperative to carry as few Czechoslovak crowns as possible on any journey.

In order to maintain my exclusive status as a "Foreign Foreigner," it was important that I never become a local employee. That was the key to the classification. So I was completely at the mercy of Snyder, and later to other American producers, to maintain my foreign employment. In all my years here I never worked for the Czechs, except as an externist, doing some translations, narration for some Czech cartoon films in English language versions, or an occasional live acting role in a few innocent Czech comedy movies. That was OK, but regular local employment was not. The moment I would take a local job, I would become a "Local Foreigner," with all the financial restrictions that entailed.

In Snyder's financial dealings with Filmexport he soon found out that they could take in dollars, but there was no mechanism whatever in place in any business or bank to pay out dollars. If by chance Snyder was overcharged on a film, there was no way Filmexport could refund the overcharge. They could only deduct the amount from the next film. This ploy surely kept the orders coming!

There were some rather hilarious incidents resulting from this "dollar dichotomy." Once, when Zdenka and I were on a car trip through southern Bohemia, we stopped at a small hotel for the night in the picturesque town of Český Krumlov, now one of the jewels of the Czech Republic, but then shabby and semi-ruin. When we presented our passports at the reception desk, the clerk informed me that I must pay double what Zdenka was paying. "But we're married," I said. "We don't want two rooms, only one. So if my wife's will be the cheaper one, then we'll both sleep in hers."

"Sorry, sir, but that will not be possible," the desk clerk informed us. "Even if you sleep in the same room in the same bed, you must pay double."

"You mean to say that my half of the bed will cost twice as much as my wife's half? I tried to play with him: "Look, we like to sleep cozy. We'll both sleep on the cheaper half of the bed! - Or what if we change sides?"

This did not amuse the clerk at all. "Whichever half you sleep on, sir, that will be the expensive half!"

Even in the new market-economy Czech Republic, there was for a while this curious double standard in pricing. If you went to a Czech restaurant and asked for the menu in English, it may well have had much higher prices than the same menu in Czech. A Czech, checking into a hotel here, would pay only about half as much for a room as a foreigner. Fair? Of course it was fair for the Czech, who couldn't afford tourist prices. And it was a great incentive for hungry foreign residents to learn the language! But at hotels you generally had to show your passport, so even a convincing accent wouldn't help you.

This has finally changed. The Czech crown is now at last a convertible, strong currency, and the old money comedy has come to an end. Witness this recent happening: Doing some shopping on a Sunday, (that in itself was unheard of in communist days - shops weren't even open on Saturday afternoons!), - Zdenka saw a man waving a 100 deutschmark note at some people waiting at a tram stop, asking if anyone would take it in exchange for crowns. "Czech crowns are okay with us!" someone shouted, and the man had to make do with his deutschmarks. (Today, that would be the smae if he were waving Euros!)

In the communist days, as Zdenka said, "if a foreigner offered any D-marks for exchange with Czechoslovak crowns, people would almost tear his arm off!" In those days, money was not only a passion with the people, but also an obsession with the government. Of course all foreigners needed a visa to visit here, and had to apply for one at the Czechoslovak Embassy in their home country. Americans had to mail in their passports if they lived outside of Washington, DC.

If you were *lucky,* the visa and your passport would arrive in about two weeks (there's that old 14 days again!). The visa was a separate paper in two copies, with your essential data inscribed, and two photos attached. You had to announce exactly how many days you intended to stay, and pay a minimum of $15 per day for the visa. When you entered the country, the visa and your passport would be stamped. Then you had to submit them to your hotel - or to the local police if you were staying in a private home. Every time you changed money officially, the transaction was entered on your visa paper. Most important of all, you had to show this paper at the border or airport when you left. If, upon leaving, your visa paper showed no money changed, they would assume you had been changing money illegally on the black market. Once, my friend Lenore Swift threw her visa away, thinking it was a useless receipt, and she was nearly refused exit. I had to give a knowing wink to the customs agent at the airport, and rely on a readily acceptable sexism: *"You know how women are!"*

Zdenka once heard that a really good Soviet film was showing. There were Soviet films everywhere, most of which were boring tractor epics, but this film was said to be really worth seeing. So Zdenka decided to use her maximum influence to get us tickets. She called the box office and said, "This is Deitchová from State Film. I have an important visitor, (It was me!), and I will need two tickets for this afternoon's screening."

After a pause, the movie cashier asked, "You need to see this particular film?"

"Yes," said Zdenka. "We will be there within an hour to pick up the tickets." When we arrived we were astounded by the big welcome. The cashier, the cloakroom attendant, and even the projectionist were delighted to see us. After all, *we were the only customers in the entire theater.* They needed to have a minimum of five people to run the film, otherwise they would have to cancel the showing, and they wouldn't get their bonus, or premium pay. Luckily, at the last moment another couple showed up, the cloakroom woman bought a ticket, and the film was run. It was called "Premium," oddly enough, and it lived up to its billing.

Occasionally we were able to contribute a bit to the micro-economy. In 1970, at the beginning of the second communist 'Dark Age,' Zdenka's former husband once again refused to allow us to take David on holiday to the West. So we decided to go to Slovakia, which at that time was part of this country.

We drove to a gorgeous Slovak valley near the Polish border, to a picturesque village named Ždiar. Some Slovak friends had referred us to a family there named Krasula. We were to stay with them in their log cottage.

All of the cottages in the village of Ždiar were of the traditiional log construction, with the special Slovak touch of blue colored plaster between the logs, and blue and white painted decorations, typical of the area. This was a place of genuine old village charm and atmosphere, and it was a pleasure to see and experience living in it, if only for a couple of weeks.

We were given a rousing welcome by the Krasulas, who installed us in a cozy attic room, with tiny windows looking out over the idyllic valley. We were charmed with all of the details of this bucolic cottage, but noticed that the cow stall in the cellar of the cottage remained empty for several days. We had been looking forward to fresh country milk. The plainly distraught Mrs.

Krasula eventually let us know that her husband had drunk away their cow. They had to sell it to get money to feed their kids.

Just then Mr. Krasula appeared, wobbling a bit, and showing a much bigger belly than we had noticed before. He waddled up to the kitchen table, pulled up his shirt, and a cascade of illegally caught river trout flipped out in a slippery heap. It was clear that he had ways of feeding his family, even without money!

This was charming country stuff, even though the tension between the Krasulas was a bit off-putting. One evening Mrs. Krasula nervously approached us, and asked if we could possibly pay for our stay in advance. She didn't have to say why. It was clear the family was nearly penniless. We still had almost a week to go, but of course we gave her our room & board money immediately.

That night we were awakened by the sound of a clanking chain, accompanied by loud, boozy singing. We peered out our attic window, and saw the joyfully drunk Mr. Krasula, weaving toward the cottage in wide arcs across the moonlit meadow. It was clear that for a time at least, our advance payment was restoring a basic element of well being to the family. The happy Mrs. Krasula came out to meet her husband, as he led home a newly purchased cow.

Soon after the revolution, even Zdenka was trying to do her bit for the economy. One Sunday, coming home from our Chalupa, we were driving over a thruway exit bridge when Zdenka spotted an old man selling plums. "Plums! He's selling plums!"

"I can't stop here," I said, "There's bumper-to-bumper on my tail."

When I turned out onto the main road, I found a stretch of dirt about 50 yards ahead where I could pull over. Zdenka leapt out, ran back and turned out of sight onto the thruway exit bridge.

After a goodly pause I looked up into my rear-view mirror, and I saw the old plum seller energetically pushing his cart toward me, Zdenka striding at his side, carrying bags and talking a blue streak.

"My God!" I thought, "She's buying the whole bleeding wagon load! Where am I going to put all those plums?"

But then the plum man suddenly veered around my car, and shoved his wagon onto the roadside space in front of me. "I told him he could do much more business if he set up his wagon where people could stop," reported Zdenka blandly, once again managing the vital affairs of yet another hapless human.

During the communist era, the only financial success the average Czech could realistically look forward to was the old-age pension. It wasn't much, but it did come remarkably early. For men it was age 60, and for women

53-55, depending on the number of children they had. When you finally got your pension, you were virtually free of the system, finally finished with a boring job in which you were probably powerless to accomplish anything gratifying. If you survived in good health you could travel more freely - (If you stayed out of the country, all the better; the government would no longer have

The long-gone Eduard Čapek iron monger shop behind the Tyn church, said to have been the only private shop in Prague in those days. Čapek had stuff that Czechoslovak Funny-Money couldn't buy in the usual State-run shops.

to pay you your miserable pension!). You could pursue your hobby or move to your cottage. Quite often your income would be supplemented by your children or foreign relatives. The latter would usually invite you to visit, all expenses paid. Retirement was the only really good life!

A young person's ambition often skipped over his or her working life completely, and centered on what he or she would do when on pension. I saw an embarrassing moment on TV during the '60s when a reporter was interviewing some kids at a summer camp. Live interviews were always risky. He asked an 8-year-old boy what he would like to do when he grew up. "When I am on pension," the kid answered without hesitation, "I will travel to Africa and hunt lions!" Trying his luck on another kid, the rattled reporter asked what kind of car he would like to have when he grew up, suggesting one of the socialist country models. *"Chrysler or nothing!"* shouted the lad. Today, he is probably driving one...

For 30 years I got my regular haircut on our block I got my regular haircut for the standard 7 crowns. In the early days I did have a reasonable amount of hair. During that period we got 35 crowns to the dollar, so my haircuts cost less than two bits. Being a big spender, I always gave the young woman barber 10 crowns (all barbers in this country were women). Okay, so that was a big 30 cents total.

Privatization and property restitution after the 1989 Velvet Revolution converted our Mostecká Street barbershop into a thing called The Golden Bun. A big sign in plain English now proclaimed hamburgers and fries. So I had to walk all the way across the bridge, just beyond the Old Town Square, to another barbershop, where they had doubled the price of a cut to 14 crowns. Being more generous than ever, I gave 20 crowns - 70 cents total.

Imagine my dismay one morning to arrive in a brisk sweat to find that this shop too had been shuttered, awaiting conversion to a more tourist-oriented existence. Wandering back, my few remaining locks flapping against the back of my neck, I passed a new elegant friseur for both ladies and gents. I stared at the sign in disbelief. *Forty-nine crowns! Almost a buck seventy-five to cut my hair? What next, for Lord's sake?*

What was next was a male barber - one who charges 150 crowns per head. Now desperate, I sighed, "Okay, let's do it." But no. As the receptionist was quick to inform me, "Milan is fully booked this morning. But he can take you at 2PM."

Milan may still be waiting for me. I don' t dare tell you what the haircut current „hair modeling" prices are!

33 - "Kultura"

Of course there was complete censorship of the press, radio and television. Not a single word of doubt was tolerated regarding the "correctness" of the current Party line, not a single word of tiniest criticism of the Soviet Union, nor, (Lenin-forbid!), even a hint of praise for anything American. The press was totally one-sided because the Communists seemed to believe there was only one side. What was a poor newspaper vendor to do to get customers? Once I was passing through a downtown Prague subway station and heard a newspaper seller shouting like mad. I knew that no really sensational news could be printed, but in his eagerness to sell his supply of papers, this hawker was belting out the only uncensored news his sheet had to offer: *"Read all about it! Tomorrow's weather!"*

But that does not mean there were no interesting things to read, hear and see in the Czechoslovak Socialist Media. State TV had excellent, expensively produced plays, musical and comedy shows, safe but funny; there were even discussion programs about serious matters. A much-appreciated aspect of all these programs was that they were uninterrupted. There was none of the American-style TV interviews where the moderator says, "We only have about 10 seconds before our commercial break; can you tell me in a few words the meaning of life?"

Every show, discussion program, or movie, ran from beginning to end without interruption. Perhaps the downside was that you had no chance to run off for a quick pee, or grab a beer during an interesting movie. One irritant to me was that, before any program, an announcer would come on and explain to you everything you were about to see, just in case you might miss the point. I preferred to just see it, and make up my own mind as to what it was all about.

Aside from the inevitable dramatizations of the lives of Marx, Engels, Lenin, Gottwald, and the rest of their pantheon, there were plenty of beautiful things to see on TV. This extended to various magazines as well, though they were shoddily printed.

One of the better-printed magazines was an illustrated weekly named The *World in Pictures,* and one issue in particular perfectly illustrated the pervasive idiocy of fear-ridden censors. It featured a photo spread of entrances to many Parisian restaurants. One photo showed a doorway on whose glazed section was emblazoned in gold-leaf lettering, "Chez Gustav."

Innocent enough, except that the General Secretary of the Communist Party of Czechoslovakia and President of the Republic was named Gustav Husak. After the entire edition of the magazine had already been printed, the nervous-Nelly magazine censor suddenly was seized with the horrifying notion that the photo of the doorway to the Chez Gustav might be perceived as a veiled mocking of the Communist High Poobah. The entire editorial staff of the magazine was ordered to expunge the name, and they stayed in their offices all night, using heavy grease pencils to black out the blasphemous bistro's name on every single copy of the magazine's print run! We have lovingly saved our copy as a souvenir of this exquisite example of communist cultural lunacy.

Books were plentiful, well enough printed, and very cheap. And there were plenty of good books. Obviously they didn't publish Solzhenitsyn or other heretic tomes, but there was a world of classic and modern literature of excellent quality. While it is true there were no politically stimulating books, there were also no junk books. Now the market here is flooded with merchandising spin-offs. Good books are also plentiful, but they are vastly more expensive than in communist times. I was impressed in those days that in every apartment I visited, whether the home of "intellectuals" or ordinary working-class people, there were always bookshelves full of books.

"What did you expect?" asked Zdenka. "We are a culture nation!"

Culture with a capital k, *kultura*, and it was all very accessible. Concerts, opera, theater, ballet, films, museums - all were very cheap. In order to bring culture to the working class, the authorities would bus in factory workers, and insert them into the National Theater, concert halls, festivals, etc. After the 1989 velvet revolution, when this force-feeding of high culture to the working class ceased, and prices to plays and concerts rose close to world levels, the so-called working class went right for the tabloids and the pervasive American action movies. We went to concerts and theater during the communist era on our own free will... Tickets then, to the top theaters or symphony concerts were no more than $2.50. There are far more theaters per capita in Prague than in New York, and the level of staging, acting, lighting, set design, and overall production is just as high or higher. And Prague audiences were and are the most appreciative I have ever experienced. They applaud on and on, calling forth seemingly endless curtain calls. An integral part of each theatrical production is an elaborate curtain call routine. I lived and worked in New York for ten years and was a regular theatergoer, but in my opinion the theater in Prague, even during the communist era, seemed richer.

As I learned the language, I came to appreciate all of this much more. For a lover of not only classical music, but also traditional jazz, Prague was and is a little piece of cultural heaven for me.

One of the most significant popular musical events took place in 1964, when my old friend Pete Seeger, the great American folk singer and human rights activist came to Prague for a series of concerts. I first met Pete in 1945, when I lived in Hollywood. He came out there with a theater company to perform in the musical play, "Dark of the Moon." After the show, he was brought to our Westbourne Drive bungalow by the stage manager, a habitué of our weekly jazz record sessions. Pete arrived, still in stage makeup, with his wife Toshi. We soon became close friends. He sang and played his songs for my first acetate disc recorder, and he sang our kids to sleep in their cribs.

With my Czech friend, Zbyněk Mácha, a jazz and folk music fan who worked at the Ministry of Culture, we managed to convince the authorities that Pete, who was then being suppressed in America for his left wing views, would be a great person to perform in this country. Pete was eager to do it because he was naturally attracted to socialism. It worked out because Pete and his brood were already on a world tour, and it would not cost much to have him stop in Prague.

By 1964 I had already been here long enough to become disabused of my own earlier socialist leanings, and I cautioned Pete to be careful in his choice of songs. We arranged to have Lulka be his translator on stage, so that the audience would understand what he was saying and singing. She became nervous when he started to do his anti-Vietnam war repertoire. Though the US government is now able to acknowledge that the Vietnam war was a tragic error, back then that was not the case. In 1964, the war was beginning to escalate, making it one of the richer veins of propaganda for the Communist government here. Pete assumed that at last his war protest songs would fall on happy ears. Not so. Pete was loudly booed when he sang them! That was a shock for him. What was official, he discovered, was automatically unpopular.

Otherwise, his concerts in Czechoslovakia were a roaring success, due partly to his performances of standard American country songs, and his brilliant 5-string banjo playing. Pete's banjo rang out the greatest sea change in the history of Czechoslovak popular music. His was the first such instrument heard in this country, and it ignited the wildfire rise of American country music here. Today, you can hear country music groups in Prague that rival Nashville's!

The literal Czech translation of "country music" is *venkovská hudba,* but those words are used only for *Czech* country music. The English word "country" is used here to mean only *American*-style folk music. It is one of the strongest sectors of Czech popular music today. There is even a radio station that exclusively plays American style country music, and it all started with Pete Seeger's visit in 1964! I recorded all of Pete's concerts then, and an edited version of my tapes was issued at the time on the Czech Supraphon label. That LP was studied by all the local musicians.

The latest news is that a complete, uncut version of those now historic 1964 recordings have been issued on a double CD album! The same British CD producer that put out my now legendary John Lee Hooker recordings, (see Chapter 57), asked me, „What else do you have in your Prague cellar?" Pete himself, at 82 years of age in 2001, recorded his personal notes for the album, It's available from Interstate Music Ltd. 20 Endwell Road, Bexhill-on-Sea, East Sussex, England TN40 1EA. Email address: interstatemusic@btconnect.com.

I am delighted that I was at least a go-between in spreading Pete Seeger's musical message, if not his political one. I have the greatest respect and love for Pete as a person and artist. Even at our geographic distance we are still in constant communication by post. One must respect anyone who lives by his beliefs, who never sells out no matter how much pressure and abuse he suffers. Such respect is due Pete Seeger. But oh, how I wish his idealism of socialistic thought was true!

I learned that all those in the West, myself once included, who dreamt of a socialist-based, humanistic society, needed only to come live in this country between 1950 and 1989. The reality would have been quickly evident.

But that did not mean a rich cultural and personal life could not be found here. I feel awkward to say it out loud, but I personally enjoyed my life here throughout all that time. *I had the best of both worlds.* I was able to enjoy the riches of Czech culture without the restrictions of being a Czech citizen. Was that fair? Of course not; it was just dumb luck. But having fallen into it, I did enjoy it, and salved my conscience by trying to discreetly help as many people as I could, by providing some of the little things that make life more pleasant. As I explained earlier, I felt that my just being here, made a certain effective statement.

I am grateful for all I have learned here, and for all of the Czech writers, musicians, artists, and other good friends who helped me learn.

34 - Zdenkish

One of the great benefits of my sojourn in Czechoslovakia was that I had the opportunity to learn a wonderful language. The language was English. Oh yes, I did learn enough Czech to speak, understand, read, and even write a little. I would say that after 42 years, I do speak bad Czech fluently.

But it was *English* that was the revelation. I am a natural-born American, and English is my mother tongue. I spoke it reasonably well when I lived in the States, and I did a lot of writing, but I can't say that I gave the language all that much thought. For instance, it took a while to eventually realize that no *English-speaking country ever went communist or fascist.* Could there be something powerful in our language that intrinsically supports freedom of thought?

But here I was, thrust into a foreign environment where I had to be sure I spoke clearly, so that those with limited English could understand me. Out went all my long-acquired jargon and my less than precise pronunciation. I had to learn to speak like (or is that "as?") a schoolteacher.

When I first came into contact with Czechs who wanted to communicate with me but didn't know English, they always spoke to me in German. At that time, German was the second language here, a leftover from 300 years of Austro-Hungarian rule and six years of life under Nazi occupation. When I indicated I couldn't speak German, they were flabbergasted. It seemed they thought I was mentally defective. "But if you speak English," they said, "surely you must understand German. *English and German are practically the same!"*

Once I'd settled down in Prague, word got around very quickly that "an American film director" was living here - one presumed to be highly educated. To be a film director in this country, one has to graduate from the film -directing academy, which means you had to have a *diploma* to direct films - *and I ain't got no diploma!* My only schooling in film was years of actually doing the job. Nevertheless, it was assumed I was an "educated man."

My phone number got into the hands of a babble of professional translators, turning it into an English-language hotline. I was constantly being called to answer abstruse questions of English structure and syntax, as well as having to explain old and new slang and idioms, such as "laid back," "make a clean breast," "carry a torch," "take a bath" (financially), "beat around the bush," "kit and caboodle," "shavetail," and on and on. And then there was the question of why through, trough, rough, bough, and bought are all pronounced differently... And those were the easy ones!

One classic mispronunciation cemented into Czech usage was the name of my native city, Chicago. Early in my time here I met the famous actor and comic, Jan Werich. He and Jiří Voskovec, (later known as George Voskovec, successful on American stage and screen as a character actor, most notably as one of the jurors in "Twelve Angry Men"), were the top comedy team in this country before the Nazi occupation. Both being Jews, they fled to the United States where they experienced moderate success during the war. When the war was over, both returned, but Voskovec soon went back to New York. Because they had been anti-Nazi, their memory as a team was kept alive here during communist times. They were so famous and well loved that just the initials "V+W" were enough to identify Voskovec & Werich. And though Werich was increasingly shunted aside due to his well-known anti-Communist sentiments, he was still considered "big time," and he did establish a funny way to pronounce Chicago.

From his wartime experience in the Windy City, he, like Bernard Shaw, saw the humor in our illogical English phonetics. "ch" was tch, as in *Charlie chooses chocolate.* A was *ay,* as in *blame Mame.* So Werich joked that Chicago should be pronounced: *"Tchi-KAY-go."* Because Werich was a famous and respected man, who had actually lived in America, his followers assumed *he must be right.* So Chicago was pronounced "Tchikaygo" by one and all - even on radio and television - for forty years! No one seemed to get the joke, nor understand that the "ch" in Chicago was pronounced "sh," because that area of our country was once French. It's my natal town after all, so I felt it my duty to relieve the Czechs of their misconception. I wrote letters to the radio and TV managers, explaining all of the above, and I am happy to say that the toddlin' town is now mostly called by its right name.

It intrigued me how the perception of sounds is controlled by the characteristics of a people's native tongue. Because the Czech language does not have the A sound as in "the bat sat on a flat mat," the average Czech cannot distinguish the difference between English words such as "bad" and "bed." They are likely to say, "bed bed."

There is also in Czech no "u" sound as in "Bloody mother plucker." "Butter the mutt, but cut the hut," comes out of a Czech's mouth as "Botter za mott, bot cot za hot!" "Country" music here is "Contry!"

Probably the most difficult English sound for Czechs is our voiced and unvoiced "th." I made up this exercise for Zdenka: *"Mother and father both thrummed the zither in the bathroom."* The American r, which rarely rolls like the Czech r, was another problem, so I drilled Zdenka with *"Rosie rarely arranged red roses."* Her other biggest problem was distinguishing between v and w. There is no w in the Czech language per se, only for foreign words or names, (such as Werich!), so v and w are pronounced exactly the same, and are frequently mixed up in English. Zdenka used to say "wery vell," for "very well." I figured if my Czech friends could get those three things right they would have English pronunciation practically in their pockets! Needless to say, (and I won't), the Czechs have their own tongue twisters for smart -alecky Americans who have the presumption to try to learn their dearly beloved tongue.

What puzzled me most was that Czechs had no dictionaries! In America, I told them that if a family had only two books in their house, they would be a Bible and a dictionary. In Prague you could buy Czech-English dictionaries, Czech-French, Czech-German, Czech-Russian, Czech-Italian, etc., but I could not find a *Czech-Czech* dictionary! Zdenka said, "Why do I need a dictionary for my own language? I learned to read, write, and speak my language in school. I know what all Czech words mean!" She had me there.

The downright perverse English pronunciation, irregular verbs et al are hard to defend or explain logically. They just have to be learned. And English word order, (dog-bites-man/man-bites-dog), does not work in Czech, where declensions make word order irrelevant. Our unreasonable s-p-e-l-l-i-n-g, was also difficult to explain to Czechs. I realized there was no logic to our language! Czechs tend to apply their own phonetic logic when speaking English. They are used to pronouncing every letter, as in Czech, so they pronounce our words, such as "fruit," as "fru-it."

Czech is a language in which 'no means yes, host means guest, and in which a phrase, "I haven't got no time" is perfectly literate! The double negative is a Slavic norm.

In self defense, and so as not to bring shame upon myself as someone ignorant of his native tongue, I began to seriously study English, surrounding myself with English language tomes, unabridged dictionaries, thesauri, dictionaries of British and American slang terms and colloquial expressions, word-origins, and analytical books on the language, its history and development. In the process, I discovered what a great language we have.

I began to realize that we Americans and Brits are in possession of the linguistic treasure of the world. Logical or not, wherever we go on this planet we will find people who can speak at least some English, and in many places even better than we.

Some European intellectuals decry the "invasion" of English, how English words are corrupting the "purity" of their own tongues. I suppose the French are the most rabid in this regard. What they seem to forget is that nearly 50% of the immense English vocabulary is made up of words borrowed directly from *French*.

The borrowing and integrating of words from other languages is exactly what has enriched ours, giving us a variety of words capable of expressing so many different shades of meaning. We have the world's largest vocabulary, and arguably the world's richest literature.

The Czech language, too - especially after the 1989 democratic revolution - is being enriched at a very rapid rate by new words, mostly English. But there were plenty here already when I first arrived. At first I laughed at this "Czenglish." Here are some typical local clangers:
bekhend = backhand (tennis)
biftek = beefsteak
byznys = business
džem = jam
džez = jazz
džínsy = jeans
džus = juice

dabing = dubbing (as in film voice dubbing)
fotbal = football
gól! = goal!
grep = grapefruit
host = guest
leazing = leasing
lídr = leader
ligy = leagues
mečbol = match ball (tennis)
mítink = meeting
ofsajd = offside
perspektiv = outlook
preservativ = condom
pulovr = pullover (sweater)
respektive = specifically
rostbíf = roastbeef
šek = check (cheque)
šortky = shorts
strečink = stretching (as an exercise)
tým = team

Many other English words are adopted straight-on: sport, stop, input, country (music), playback, program, monitor, video, hamburger, chips, snack bar, fast food, parking, software, etc.

The Czech language is not designed to be easily latched onto by outsiders. It is beautiful, but its grammar is mind numbing. Czechs, on the other hand, are baffled by our spelling. Not much in English is spelled the way it sounds. Czech is highly phonetic, with each letter assigned one sound only. The little marks, áéíýúěščňřž, that dance along the tops of many letters in the Czech alphabet are like musical notations; they change the sounds of the letters and avoid diphthongs. A sound that may take two or three letters to indicate in English, German, or Polish, can make do with one letter in Czech - for instance, "cz," or "ch" written as "č," or "sh," written as "š."

Czech is a compact language. Whereas English only has two words compri" sed of a single letter, "I" and "a." Czech has several: "a" "i" "k" "u" " s" "v" " z" are all complete words in Czech!

160

A means "and" ,i means "and-also", k means "to", s means "with", u means "by" or "at" and z means "from". There are no such things as spelling bees in Czech schools. If you've learned the sound of each letter, and you hear a new Czech word, then you can write it. But in English, for example, there are over twelve different ways to write the sound "sh," as in shoe, sugar, ocean, nation, nausea, ancient, mission, fashion, patience, tissue, glacial, partial, etc. And enough said about enough, rough, through, bough, trough, cough, draught... There's no logical way to explain that sort of thing.

But our language has to do with history and derivation, not logic. So we're in no position to sneer at Czech or any other language. We Americans can barely manage our own tongue. And God help us if we are born with a name other than Jones or Smith. I have had to suffer with Deitch all my life, and have received mail and forms made out to Dietch, Deetch, Doitch, Daitch, Ditch, Dutch, Deutsch, Deutch, Dietrich, Deith, Detritus, Dettich, and Douche.

Americans can hardly handle Zdenka's name at all. She is regularly addressed as Zedenka, Sdencka, Zenda, Zelda, Stenka, and Stinka. But what kind of name is Zdenka anyway? It seems to be pure Slavic, and was once very common here, but is now less in fashion. It might be translated as Sidonia. I'm quite happy to stick with Zdenka, or with the wide array of diminutives the Czechs love to apply to all names. Among family and friends, Zdenka is known variously as Zdena, Zdeni, Zdenička, Zdeninka, Zdendula, or even Zdenininka. All Slavs love babytalk!

Okay, they win on spelling, but they get you with grammar. Every Czech word has a multitude of forms designed to torture the mind of a non-native. It's always amazing to me that even tiny Czech kids manage it so easily. When I arrived here it was my ambition to be able to speak Czech as well as the average six-year-old.

Zdenka already spoke some English when I arrived, otherwise we would never have made it together, as I obviously didn't know a word of Czech. But in the isolation this country suffered, she forged ahead with her own personal approach to English. I came to refer to her speech as pure "Zdenkish." She was never shy about her renditions, and was convinced she could speak English perfectly well.

161

I loved her favorite phrases: To indicate that the coast was clear, a threat expunged, or all was well, she would say: "Everything is in order!" She locked into her own verbal concepts, such as, "You don't supposed to do that!" "How old you are?" and "I will tell you the all."

Her English malapropisms, meanwhile - her "Big Diaper" in the sky, her "skycrappers" in New York, and her "investors from outer space" - were of the highest order, and were always proclaimed with full confidence. I certainly do not quote these clangers with the idea of ridiculing Zdenka's English. I do gently correct her when it's necessary for clarity, but Snyder swore a curse on me if I ever "spoiled" her charming speech. This of course completely overlooks my own hilarious rendition of Czech. Unfortunately, I can't easily make clear to you English-speakers my own "charming" Czech chokers. As with Zdenka, I'm happy to be basically understood.

Czech, like many European tongues, is not just one language, but several. Whenever Zdenka answers the phone I can tell from her first words whether she is speaking to a relative, friend, a studio underling, her boss, or a stranger. In English we can deduce this by tone or feel, but in Czech there are actually several "sub-languages" and a whole set of different words and forms for addressing different classes of people and different sexes.

When I came here, the Czechs were insistent about addressing me with some kind of honorific. A genuine American film director was simply not to be addressed as just plain "Mister." Anyone with any kind of a diploma has a title, and will always be addressed Mr. or Mrs., as in "Mr. Engineer," "Mr. Doctor," "Mr. Supervisor," or "Mr. General Manager." Even if they don't know your position, but assume you are somebody special, it's "Mr. Chief." They couldn't quite accept that I have no diploma for my profession, so those outside my circle of close friends insist on addressing me as "Mr. Director."

Seemingly similar words in another language can often lead to embarrassment. When our dear late friend Bill Bernal came to Prague in the early '60s to work with me on a film project, he too found many surprises here.

On a walk up Nerudová Street on his way to see the castle, his throat was dry, and he was looking to see where he could buy some chewing gum. He was delighted when he spotted a coin machine labeled "GUMA." Okay, so it wasn't

Wrigley's in those days. He stuck in his coin, and then eagerly unwrapped the little packet that fell into his hand. A group of nearby locals could hardly suppress their amusement as Bill unrolled, and held up in puzzlement, a generous-sized condom.

Garbled English is only to be expected in any foreign country, but it is fun to note a few I've encountered here:

A sign offering pigskin wallets made of "pure pork."

A sign on a hotel room TV that said, "If set brakes, inform manager. Do not interfere with yourself!"

A broken elevator in the same hotel with the sign: "ELEVATOR BEING FIXED FOR THE NEXT DAY. MEANTIME WE REGRET YOU WILL BE UNBEARABLE."

In Prague's Old Town Square, a horse-drawn carriage advertised, "TAKE OUR HORSE-DRIVEN CITY TOUR. WE GUARANTEE NO MISCARRIAGES!"

During the summer, river bathers were warned, "Women wearing topless suit will be put in the hands of authorities."

A large department store had this sign: "VISIT OUR BARGAIN BASEMENT, ONE FLIGHT UP."

On our square, a kiosk snack bar was working against its own interests with the sign, "FOOD FAST."

And my favorite old graffiti, I photographed on a wall near us"
"MAKE THE LOVE, DON'T WAR!"

As a footnote to all this wordery, I should add that one of the sweetest things about the Czech language is in the naming of the months. These are very ancient - much older than the Roman names most Western languages use. In Czech, the names of the months are evocative of their seasonal positions and redolent with pagan imagery. Janu is leden, from the word for ice. February is únor, from the floating of breaking ice. March is březen, from the word for animals giving birth. April is duben, from the word for oak, (oak trees bloom at that time). May is květen, flowers. June is červen, from the color red. July is červenec, which language experts say refers to the worms that start to eat the apples. August is srpen, from the word for sickle, (the harvest.) September is září, to glow with color. October is říjen, the rutting season. November is listopad, falling leaves. And December is prosinec, time to kill the pig! I think those are lovely names, though the pig may well have some concern.

And finally, should you bring your pet animals here, even they must learn a new language! And other everyday sounds suddenly make a different sort of noise:

"HAF! HAF!"	=	Bow wow
"MŇAU!"	=	Meow
"BÚÚ!"	=	Moo
"MA-A-A!"	=	Ba-a-a
"KVA! KVA!"	=	Quack quack
"KI-KIRI-KÍÍÍÍ	=	Cock-doodle-doooo!
"BIM BAM!"	=	Ding dong
"PRASK!"	=	Crash!
"HVIST!"	=	Whoosh!

And then there is that little "at sign" @, now universally used in email addresses. Many have likely forgotten its original use in indicating prices per unit. The Czech didn't quite know what to make of it, as their "at" sign was an à with a backward mark over it. So what to call "@" ? It's a "zavináč! - a coiled herring!

35 - Petty Cash

"May we offer you a vodka, beer, or coffee?"

Snyder, my other producers, and I, were customers in this country, ordering films to be produced to our specifications, for distribution in America and world markets. In this sense we were like the buyers of Bohemian glass, cut crystal and myriad industrial goods today. Commercial buyers in countries that normally conduct international business often enjoy the perks of being wined and dined by those who are trying to sell their wares.

Not so in socialist Czechoslovakia. There, the entertaining of customers was limited by tight budgets to the offer of a glass of vodka, a beer, or a cup of káva *turek*. Actually, the vodka and beer were safer than the coffee, as the unwary newcomer was likely to get a mouthful of coffee grounds.

Unlike most business venues, here it was the *customer* who was expected to buy the dinners and bring the gifts. Of course, through these minor - and sometimes major - private "payoffs," goods and services were quite often able to be had at bargain-basement rates. So the usual buyer/seller roles were reversed.

Snyder got a lot of mileage out of presents. His luggage was always stuffed with women's shoes, nylon stockings, perfume, makeup, and fancy underwear intended for managers' wives and secretaries. Had the airport customs officers opened his suitcases, they might have thought he was a transvestite. Ladies' shoes came in - antiques and cheap films went out. He really had it nice.

The concept of petty cash was mostly unheard of in those times. This lack led to a rather absurd situation after the animation studio's space at Bursa was taken over by Czech Television.

We were relocated to a building that also housed the editorial offices of the official Communist Party newspaper, *Rudé právo*, and several of its magazines. The courtyard there had parking spaces for four cars. I aspired to one of those spaces. But the courtyard led to a locker room where guns were stored for the local Communist People's Militia, so the gate from the street had to be kept locked. The problem was, there was only one key. This left the courtyard mostly locked and unused. There was no petty cash available for a new padlock and keys, which cost something like 75 cents. If I bought a new padlock, I was told, I could park in there, and it would also open the way for three other lucky drivers.

With 75 cents' worth of Czech crowns in my pocket, I managed to find a suitable padlock at a hardware store. It came with two keys, both of which the porter of the building was supposed to get. The idea was that each day when I arrived at the studio, I would honk, and he would shuffle out and open the gate for me. I knew this gent was old and fat, so I figured it would be easier if I just had an extra key made for myself. God knows I had no desire to threaten the People's Militia. It was just a simple matter of convenience.

I delivered the new lock and two keys, but from that day on I simply opened the gate with my own key. No one ever said a word. After all, it saved the old porter from having to release his coffee cup and waddle out into the cold.

And so it came to pass that, for 10 years, this "agent of imperialist America" had a key allowing him access to both the Communist Party publishing house and the arms cache of the Czechoslovak People's Militia!

The animation studio's tenure in The Rudé Právo building coincided with the coming to power of Nikita Krustchev in the Soviet Union. A slight easing was in the air, and the editors of one of magazines, knowing an American cartoonnist was in the building, and feeling a bit adventurous, wondered if I would have time to do a weekly "American style" comic strip for them. There were no comic strips here then. Oviously, I wasn't keen about contributing to communist propaganda, but the editor assured me I wouldn't be censored. It was agreed that I wouldn't sign the strips; no point in terrifying any communist muckymucks with an American cartoonist!

I wondered whether I would really have a chance to sneak in some gentle parodies, and thought it over. The payment would be petty cash, but it was a slight effort and a chance for a little fun. I decided to do something ostensibly about little children playing games. Each installment at first gently parodied some of the problems of everyday life in "socialism." A couple of typical episodes are copied here from the original pencil roughs and translated into English. I gradually introduced more pointed gags. When I came up with one about the meat shortage, the editor balked. "The shortage of meat in this country is not funny," he announced,and that was the end of my comic strip.

("Malý Svět" translates as "Small World")

36 – How to Avoid Doing Business

Our friend Allen Swift returned to Prague to visit us in May 1967. Walking through town, he saw some charming little multi-colored glass figurines of musicians in a shop window. He thought they would make terrific gifts for his clients. They were about $25 apiece. He startled the clerk by asking to buy 120 pieces, and wanting to have them shipped to New York. The clerk was put out by this threat to her peace and quiet.

"No, no," she said. "That is not possible."

"Why not?" asked Allen in all innocence.

"No, no, it cannot be done."

"I'll pay for the shipping, whatever it costs."

"No, no - not possible."

"Look, Miss - your country does business with my country. There's got to be a way."

"Well, you can try Glass Export," said the clerk, eager to get back to the magazine she was reading.

"What is Glass Export?" Allen asked me.

I helped him find the address of this one-and-only official glass exporting organization. Now in compulsive/determined mode, Allen hiked up to the dingy office, where he was delighted to find a man who spoke English.

"Good day sir, what can I can do for you?" the man said, doubtless hoping it would be something simple. Allen introduced himself as an American - a magic word that immediately elicited offers of beer, vodka, or a cup of Turkish coffee.

Allen explained that he just wanted to buy 120 of those charming little glass figurines as Christmas gifts for his clients, and he wanted them shipped to New York.

"Ah-hah," said the man, in full understanding. "But you see, that presents a problem."

"Why is that?

"Oh, it can be done, but it will take time."

"Can I get them in time for Christmas?"

"Well, that I cannot promise... You see, we have to establish letters of credit..."

"No, no, no! I will pay you right now!" Allen pulled out his checkbook.

"Well. That certainly simplifies the matter to some extent. But you see, the salesman in charge of this assortment of glass figures is currently in Bavaria. Only he can write up this type of order."

"What? Why can't you take my check, give me a receipt, and inform your salesman when he returns?"

"I am afraid that is not possible. Why don't you return in 14 days? He should be back by then."

"Sir, I am leaving here the day after tomorrow."

"Oh, I am terribly sorry. Are you sure you would not like a glass of beer? Please do take one of our catalogs."

Allen had no recourse but to take the proffered catalog and retreat from the office in total defeat.

Months passed. Allen was back in New York, the entire glass figurine matter gratefully shelved, when out of the blue came a phone call. His secretary informed him that a gentleman was on the line who claimed to be a representative of Czechoslovak Glass Export. Allen naturally assumed it was one of his joking friends who had heard the aforementioned story. But no, the Glass Export salesman was indeed in New York! An appointment was made for him to come to Allen's office, which he did the very next day. Allen was careful not offer the man any coffee, vodka, or beer, but tried earnestly to get right to the core of the matter.

"I know exactly what I want. And I am ready to give you my order, *cash in advance.*"

"There is no rush. Let me leave you our catalog."

"I already have your catalog! It's all marked with exactly what I want: 120 pieces of these little glass musicians! I WANT YOU TO WRITE THE ORDER *R I G H T   N O W!*"

Allen pulled out his checkbook. "Just tell me the total cost," he said, "including the cost of shipping."

"Please, sir. There is no need to write a check now. You will be billed." Finally, the gent wrote out the order and gave Allen a copy. At least now he had something in hand besides the catalog.

The Glass Export salesman left. Time passed. Sometime in November, a crate arrived in New York containing 120 separately boxed glass figurines, as per Allen's order. Each was individually packed in excelsior (the shredded wood used for packing material in those days), and all arrived in perfect condition - along with the bill: The total cost, including shipping, came to two dollars per piece!

It all reminded Allen of the old joke about a company that sells everything at a loss, but makes it up on volume.

"Big Business"
in the communist era.
A skimpy souvenir stand,
set up right before
the doorway of The Ministry
of Commerce,
with three young " Pioneers"
as customers

37 - 1968; Hope Scotched

Years ending in 8 were thought to be fateful for Czechs. In 1848 there was a revolt by students and intellectuals against the harsh 300-year rule of the Austro-Hungarian Hapsburgs. The first Czechoslovak independent republic was proclaimed in 1918; the Munich betrayal was in 1938; the Communist takeover was in 1948; and the "Prague Spring," smashed by the Soviet-led invasion, was in 1968.

In the mid-'60s there began a gradual easing of the hard-line regime. A few little dribbles of interesting news actually began to appear in the local media. It became ever so slightly easier to travel, and shops began to stock some fruits and vegetables. A few exceptional plays and movies appeared. It was a great period for Czech movies. During those years of the Czech "New Wave," Jiří Menzel, Miloš Forman, and other great Czech directors first gained world acclaim. But everyday life for Czechs still wasn't anything all that great.

Then, on January 5, 1968 there suddenly appeared in all the papers - *(and in those days all newspapers printed essentially the same news - I could never quite figure out why they bothered to have more than one paper!)* - the news that someone named Alexander Dubček was named First Secretary of the Communist Party, taking over that function from President Antonín Novotný. "Alexander who?" we all said.

But after that, really strange things began to happen; just little things at first, like an actual photo of Tomáš Garrigue Masaryk appearing in the press, and a few remarks on TV that actually seemed related to reality. Then it began to quickly accelerate. Amazing things were said and written. Independent organizations were allowed to form. The Boy Scouts were revived to challenge the socialist "Pioneers" organization, which had replaced them in the early '50s. All manner of thoughts began to appear in the press, and of course Dubček himself was making incredible speeches. He proclaimed his goal of creating "Socialism with a human face!" What in the world was that?

Foreign journalists were allowed in to try to find out, and soon the world press was raving about Dubček! Dubček! Dubček! We too were caught up in the euphoria, and it all culminated in the first May Day parade in which the people took part freely and joyously. It was all sensational, and the Czechs were so proud to be featured positively in the Western press that they tended to ignore the rumblings coming from the East.

But I'm sure many of you already know about that cyclonic year in Czechoslovakia's history, a year full of hope and dismay, the top story in the world's media. What may be of interest here, is how some of us were personally involved, and how we interacted with the rush of those events.

For Zdenka and myself, the events of 1968 ran parallel with the presence here of American journalist Alan Levy. Levy was, I heard, an award-winning magazine feature writer who had written a book on Elvis Presley and had interviewed Sophia Loren. Miloš Forman had suggested he adapt a show by the famous Czech song and dance team of Jiří Suchý and Jiří Šlitr into an off-Broadway musical. Using an open-ended contract with Life magazine to foot the bill, he managed to get a visa to Czechoslovakia and arrived with his wife and two small daughters in late 1967.

As with most Americans arriving here, he had been referred to us and given our telephone number. It seemed a great thing to me to have another American around, a writer, someone interested in political and world affairs, someone to be able to talk openly with, so we gave him a big welcome. We introduced him to Lulka, who became his interpreter and babysitter, and - wonder of wonders - Zdenka found the family an apartment! Some other Americans we knew were moving away, so we were able to move the Levys in.

To top it off, Zdenka recruited the cleaning woman, Mrs. Bejvlová, from the Klárov animation studio, as the Levys' housekeeper, and our close friend Antonín (Toník) Růžička, who can make or repair anything, as a domestic Mr. Fixit. (Alan was manually undextrous, and reportedly could not change a light bulb on his own.) The American Embassy, friendlier by this time, even agreed to give his family shopping privileges at their commissary, something I could not get for us. (The Levys had two small children - we didn't).

We set them up so that all Alan had to do was write. The children adapted right away, and Alan's wife Valerie, already a teacher of French, very quickly learned Czech, though Alan never quite got his tongue around it.

So there he was, writing along at his musical, with us constantly at his beck and call, when suddenly along came the year with the 8 in it - 1968. Alan had fallen into a journalist's dream: to be in on the ground floor of a major international story. In the suddenly opening atmosphere, he was able to get a journalistic accreditation from Life Magazine, and shot an article to them, "Czechoslovakia Destalinizes," which ran in the March 29th issue of that year. He was watching the suddenly fascinating TV news, with Lulka doing running translations, and was interviewing the new leaders - having a reporter's field day and making hay with it.

Of course, with the titillating prospect that a crack was developing in the Soviet Empire, Prague began filling up with correspondents from all the western world's newspapers and TV networks, all of whom were bunkered in my old dormitory, the Alcron hotel. One day in July I saw a strange sight in the Alcron lobby: There, pressing forward to form a pyramid, were clustered many of the great names of the American media. At the apex, perched on a chair atop a table, was the ample figure of Eva Stíchová, a Czech translator and stringer for Time Magazine. In her hand was a small transistor radio tuned to the local Czech news broadcast - the "authoritative source" for these famous newsmen! Outside, meanwhile, there were plenty of fascinating things going on that these guys were missing.

There was a great difference between what I heard on the international radio - largely information passed on by Stíchová and other Czechs assumed to be in the know - and what I saw on the streets. During those days of continuous banner headlines about Prague, the media were trying to dramatize the situation to the maximum by using the most alarming terms possible.

To me, the most dramatic part of the situation was how normal everyday existence continued to seem, and how quietly the people lined up by the hundreds of thousands to sign the manifesto, "Socialism! Alliance! Sovereignty! Freedom!" (All four words begin with an S in the Czech language.) This was part of Czech slyness. "Socialism" and "Alliance" were clearly put into the manifesto's title, hoping those words would calm the Soviets. They didn't.

The rumbling from the East reached upper decibels by July, as the Warsaw Pact forces began threatening military maneuvers just outside the Czechoslovak borders, and later, inside the borders. The government here had to accept their request to hold war games on Czechoslovak territory "in the name of brotherly solidarity." Still, we lulled ourselves, assuming that after their terrible loss of prestige in Hungary in 1956, the Soviets would certainly not use military force again, especially against such an overwhelmingly popular leader as Dubček, who was after all a Communist, and was doing everything here under the direct leadership of the Communist Party of Czechoslovakia. We were wrong.

The East German "Berliner Zeitung" had screaming headlines, "AMERICAN TANKS & TROOPS HAVE ENTERED PRAGUE!"

174

True... They were a few WW2 tanks from an Austrian movie prop firm, brought in for the filming of "The Bridge At Remagen." The Soviets, after their maneuvers here, added to this synthesized hysteria, by leaving caches if old WW1 American guns in strategic places, where they could easily be found.

On the morning of August 21, 1968, at 4:00 AM, our bedside telephone rang. It was Zdenka Skřípková - a matronly animator at the studio; a close friend who kept a ledger of everyone's birthday, and who was especially protective towards us.

"They're here!!" she said, (predating the "Poltergeist" line by 14 years). "Gene should leave the country immediately!"

Through our sleepy haze we heard planes roaring overhead, and even distant cannon fire. We shot out of bed, got dressed, I grabbed my Nikon, and we ran downstairs to see what we could see.

It's nearly impossible to visit Prague and not become familiar with our street, Mostecká, which leads from the Charles Bridge into Malá Strana. Today it features several currency exchange booths, Bohemia crystal shops, a pizza bar, souvenir shops, boutiques, bistros, and even a McDonald's, all serving the mobs of tourists surging down its short two-block length. But on that morning of August 21, 1968, it featured one long, unbroken line of heavy Soviet battle tanks, parked along the curb so tightly, tread to tread, that I wondered how they could possibly maneuver. Their motors were rumbling, and a heavy pall of black diesel smoke rose up all around them. The gunners atop each tank were dressed in black, looking sullen and confused, and waiting for their next orders. Already people were emerging from the other buildings along the block, shouting in school-learned Russian at the tank crews, "What are you doing here?" "We didn't call you!" "This is a free, brotherly socialist country!" "Go home!"

The tank crews didn't seem to understand. In fact, many weren't even Russian. The Soviets had sent mainly eastern, Mongolian troops on this first wave, perhaps fearing that Russian soldiers would not be willing to shoot fellow Slavs. These guys actually thought they were in West Germany, the advertised enemy, and not in a "friendly" neighbor socialist country!

I took a few photos, but once office hours arrived I made my way to the American Embassy, just around the corner from us. This was the second crisis that prompted me to go there, and I figured this was much more of a threat than a bunch of pre-programmed Cuban students. I had been married to Zdenka for four years by then, and I assumed and expected that we couldn't be permanently separated. So I wasn't so worried as I had been in 1962.

The American Embassy was already planning a convoy of cars headed for Vienna, to depart a couple of days hence, and would evacuate all Americans who wished to get out. I was invited to join. The catch was that it was only for Americans. Zdenka was considered a "local." So that was out. As usual, the atmosphere coming from the US Embassy scene was one of panic and foreboding. "Don't miss this chance to get out!" they warned. I met some people from Life and Time magazines there, and they agreed to get my photos out if I could get the film to them within two days.

What many people in America and elsewhere may not have comprehended from the dramatic 1968 news coverage was that:

A) However tragic these events were for the nation, they played themselves out here as black comedy; and

B) In spite of all the hand wringing and tearful reporting, the American government was secretly *relieved* that the Soviets had made this move to restore the cold-war status quo!

You may find B) hard to believe, but it was immediately apparent, not only from words I heard at the embassy, but from the total inaction of the US government following the invasion.

When we first glimpsed those ugly, strangely immobilized tanks on our street, one of our neighbors shouted to me, "This is good! Now the Americans will *hermetically* seal off the Soviets. They will ostracize them from all world organizations and trade, and force them to retreat!"

He was wrong, of course. Think back to 1968 in European affairs: Czechoslovakia was not the only country in crisis. There were violent student riots in Paris. France and Italy were headed for elections in which their Communist parties stood a good chance of winning. Can you imagine what would have happened if Dubček's "Socialism With a Human Face" had succeeded? The United States had no vital interests in tiny Czechoslovakia, and had practically *given* it to the Soviet Union at the end of the war. But France and Italy? That was a whole different story. The "loss" of France and Italy to a Communist regime would have been a deathblow to America's position in Europe. Dubček and Czechoslovakia were expendable.

Another of my neighbors, meanwhile, was gloomily correct. I said to him, "Of course this is terrible, but even with tanks they can't turn back the clock.

Now that the Czechoslovak people have experienced democracy again, it will be impossible to reimpose a hard-line, closed regime."

Dr. Boris Troníček was a lawyer who had studied for several years in the Soviet Union. "I know them," he said mournfully. "They are ruthless. They must have this country under their control. You will see. *It will be even worse!*" He was right. Dr. Troníček didn't live to see just how bad it did get in the '70s, nor to see the victory of democracy in 1989.

Alan Levy, on the other hand, grasped his big chance. He shelved his musical, and devoted himself to chronicling the drama at hand. I went around Prague taking photos and trying to decide what to do. I was certainly not going to join the embassy convoy, but I knew I had to do something. I put several rolls of undeveloped film into the hands of the Time-Life photographer. I never saw them again. With no idea what kind of revenge might come, I asked that if they were published it should be under the pseudonym "Jean Munro," to protect Zdenka. Actually, they were published under the name of the journalist I gave them to.

The very first thought I had after Zdenka Skřípková phoned us was that without question the Soviet troops would immediately seal the borders, so that getting out would be hopeless. I also assumed they would be checking on all foreigners present, and that I would surely be expelled and Zdenka locked in. That was my number-one fear.

The hard reality was that all mail, phone, and telegraph contact with the outside world was cut off. From the lurid reporting of death and destruction we heard on the short wave radio, I knew that my mother and family, my friends, and Bill Snyder, (who was not here when the invasion came), would certainly be worried sick about us. I felt I had to get out to Vienna just to make contact, and to assure them we were okay. But I was not about to leave the country without Zdenka.

We had received news through the grapevine that, amazingly, the borders were wide open, and that Czech people were leaving by the thousands. But Zdenka's son, her father, and her nieces were all staying, so she didn't want to leave at all. I had to insist.

"Look," I argued, "it'll just be long enough for me to make a few calls, and then we'll come right back!" The man from Time had given me his card, and said I could use their office in Vienna to make all my contacts.

Later I stood on the Charles Bridge, looking gloomily up at the castle from which so many differing regimes had ruled. "Will it now be a Soviet commissar up there?" I thought to myself.

Just then I saw in the distance the half-limping figure of Zdenka's aged father coming across the bridge towards me. None of the trams were running, so he had walked all the way from his distant section of Prague. He was carrying a parcel, a large loaf of good Czech bread. "It's for you, Gene," he said in Czech. "I was afraid there would be no food in your market." This is, for me, an indelible memory. I knew right then that I was really part of the family.

The wondrous fact was that the bakers were still working, though the babičky (grannies) had cleaned out the flour, sugar, eggs, and salt from all the shops. The Czech wartime mentality had never left them. I felt that Zdenka's father really loved me, and that he knew I would take care of his daughter in any situation. Now I needed him to help reassure her. I had to take her to Vienna in tears. To this day she thinks we should not have left.

There were some strange aspects to those invasion days. Before we left, we experienced the bizarre as well as the inspiring. Amazingly, people had seized control of many printing and duplication facilities such as existed at the time, and had managed to get out unofficial editions of all the newspapers, as well as printing thousands of leaflets (many of which I've saved). During those days, everyone was your friend and colleague. If a stranger drove up and handed you an armload of leaflets to distribute, you did it. If you needed volunteers to paint signs, they appeared. It is a truism that terrible times bring people together.

As I wrote in a letter to Allen Swift in New York:

"All shop windows, walls, balconies on all streets, papered, painted, chalked with giant signs defying the occupation forces. The asphalt streets themselves are painted with huge letters in Russian: 'AGGRESSORS!, RUSSIAN FASCISTS!, BETRAYERS!,' "GO HOME!' Signs are everywhere. People spit and jeer at each passing occupation tank or armored vehicle. All street signs and house numbers have been taken down, so as to confuse the Russians. People have even burned their telephone books! After five days of occupation, the Russians have not been able to silence the free radio and newspapers, which still miraculously appear daily! And what's more fantastic, they are so far incapable of putting out a single leaflet or local broadcast of their own. No one will work for them... A spontaneous underground radio network has magically come into being. The daily newspapers still get out, leaflets are printed, collaborator autos are identified on the radio, and

within minutes the license numbers are painted on the streets and posted on buildings. The betrayers are caught. A train carrying Soviet radio jamming and broadcasting equipment was similarly identified and derailed. The incredible fact is that the <u>only</u> information that is getting to the people is through free, loyal sources!"

Symbolic was the spontaneous name change of the "Moskva" restaurant on the main shopping street, Na Příkopě. It was a second floor restaurant with a glass fasade. One huge letter of its name was on each pane: M O S K V A ("Moscow"). With the change of two letters it became, M O R A V A (A province of Czechoslovakia)

I recorded all the "Radio Free Prague" broadcasts until they were silenced; their pleas for U.S. intervention vanishing with them. And in the few days we were still here, I tried to get all around Prague to photograph the action and the signs. Even some of the Soviet tanks had "LONG LIVE DUBČEK!" written on them. Along with all the "IVAN GO HOME" signs, which showed arrows pointing to Moscow, the funniest sign was a large paper banner hung over the State Bank entrance. Two Soviet soldiers with machine guns, who luckily could not read Czech, guarded it. Here is my translation:

"TO PROTECT OUR POOR STATE BANKS
THERE'S NO NEED FOR RUSSIAN TANKS.
THE SHIT THAT LIES ON THESE SAD SHELVES
WE CAN GUARD QUITE WELL OURSELVES.
IT'S ONLY SHIT WITH WHICH WE'RE BLESSED.
OUR RUSSIAN 'BROTHERS' TOOK THE REST!"

Another poster proclaimed: "WE ARE CONDEMNED FOR INTERFERING IN OUR OWN INTERNAL AFFAIRS!"

"One of the most striking images, as I threaded my way through the historic center, was in the Old Town Square. It happened that just before the invasion, an Old Town Square Gallery there had opened an exhibit of Soviet art. A large banner had been hung across the building: "SOVIET ART OF THE 20th CENTURY." Right under this banner on this day was the ironic presence of huge Soviet battle tanks, with inartistic Soviet machine-gunners at the ready.

"What I saw was an almost unimaginable defiance of brute pow-er, with nothing but national unity, pride, spontaneous organization, a spiritual energy, and a naive bravery defying millions of tons of armor."

That is a note from my 1968 diary. In spite of the blackness of the situation, there was always that humor, that typically Czech way of overcoming. It was indeed a high point in the history of this people.

As the short-wave radio reports about Prague, mainly from the BBC (our only free news source), grew more and more turgid, I felt it urgent that I be able to contact my family, friends, and Bill Snyder. On top of all else, my residence visa was about to expire, and there was no way to get it renewed. So, crossing our fingers and holding our breaths, Zdenka and I glumly got into our little Saab and started off for Vienna. The main difficulty with that was that all road signs had been reversed by the Czechs in an effort to confuse the Russians, so we had to ask for proper directions in each village. On my many previous trips to Vienna, I had always relied on road signs! We were quite surprised to find the steel beam gates at the border wide open - the Czech border guards just waved us through! People were pouring out of the country.

It boggled us that this was so easy, but we were happy about it all the same. Amazingly, the borders were never closed during the whole invasion period. Some people drove back and forth several times a day to carry their belongings out! Current estimates are that at least 100,000 people - many of the best, most talented, most capable - emigrated during this period. That was how the Communists ultimately crippled the nation and maintained power. It was only on November 29, 1969, fifteen months after the invasion, that the cage slammed shut again. On that night, soldiers came onto trains, confiscated passports, and ordered the passengers to disembark. All exit visas were summarily canceled.

But in last days of August 1968 we glided right out. We heard later that the Russians didn't even know where all the border crossings were! I presented my card at the Time-Life office in Vienna, and they very kindly gave me access to their telephones and telex. I was able to call my mother and closest family members, and to write a series of letters telling what we had been through, (including that previously quoted letter to Allen Swift), and of our hopes to

180

return to Prague. Incidentally, what I had in the Czech State Bank was definitely more than "shit" to me. That was all my available money at the time. I went to Vienna with just $50 in my pocket.

First thing when we arrived, I telexed Alan Levy, c/o the American Embassy in Prague, our previously agreed contact method:

> we are here. heard radio report as we left morning that border crossing barred to czechs so we continued with faint hopes. but drive absolutely clear. saw no repeat no russian vehicles any kind entire way. road clear. no russians at all at border. they forgot about us said the guard. we were through in two minutes. love, gene zdenka

But then the bad news struck. Zdenka and I started back toward the Czech border, but this time the iron gates going in were shut! "Of course we know you, Mr. Deitch," said one of the guards, "but we have orders not to admit any foreign citizens!"

Zdenka was crushed. I was unable to keep my promise to her. At the same time, I was not prepared to let her return without me. We went back to Vienna, and to the Czechoslovak embassy there. Same story. "But I am a customer of Czechoslovak Filmexport," I said. "I have films in production which I must finish or they cannot be paid for." Of course it was useless. They had no control over the situation, and had to stick to their orders from Prague.

Before I left, even the American Embassy telex had been cut off. They told me that, even if it was restored, they could not grant me access to their telex for personal messages. They were always afraid of risking the embassy's diplomatic immunity. Later the connection was restored, and they relented for Levy. Here are some extracts from his telexes to me, as received at the Time-Life office in Vienna:

> amembassy praha this is alan levy in praha would you please relay this message to mr gene deitch who is waiting out current events in vienna... gene: streets relatively free of russians but suspicions and repressions clearly dawning i advise staying out and monitoring bbc and judging for yourself whether you want to come back i will advise when i have a clearcut opinion but current expectation seems to be a return to worse than novotny era some writers being roughed up but also being given hard currency allotments if theyll just leave so as not

to have many critics around foreign press transients expected to be booted out in less than a week but previously accredited correspondents being told theyre ok for rest of year at least this will leave szulc of ny times and myself as only american journalists here gene also please get in touch with milos forman if you can track down where he is in vienna tell him i am in prague... i am advised that his wife returned from france with their kids on august 20th unlucky girl...

A few days later, I received this telex from Levy:

gene it is still not safe for zdenka to return while tanks are somewhat disappearing and safety is much better border and other security seems to be getting tightened by russians i have evacuated valerie and girls to bad godesberg west germany... i will let everybody know whenever prague is livable again virginia weissinger is sleeping in your apartment occasionally and tending your canary... in our neighborhood they are taking census of who is there and who isnt i think it is better that your apartment be occupied...

Later, he wrote:

cartoon studio contacted filmexport which contacted czech embassy in vienna to arrange to have you readmitted to czechoslovakia...

None of this yet worked, so we had to cast about for something to do until the border opened again for me. Zdenka was in tears. It was dismaying. Equally dismaying was the letter I received in Vienna from Bill Snyder:

```
Mr. Gene Deitch
August 27, 1968
c/o Time-Life Inc.
Gonzagagasse 2/1/5
Vienna, Austria

Dear Gene:

The fact that you left Prague for Vienna is a personal
choice about which I have no comment. It is ironic though that on
the day I had your cable I was trying to get a flight to Prague
```

just because I wanted to be a part of the heroic history that those people are writing...

I will produce in Prague with or without your direction.

You may consider yourself relieved from any further responsibility on these films...

Please tell Zdenka that I send my very best and that I think of her always.

Sincerely,
William L. Snyder

I wonder if I should have expected anything different from him? I tried to answer:

"August 30, 1968

Dear Bill,

In our present depressed circumstances it was a shock to receive your snarling letter of the 27th - especially so, because I got the letter exactly as I returned to the Time office after having been turned back at the Czech border again this morning.

Of course, I have no choice but to accept your decision to cut me off, but I must say you are misinformed on all counts.

As far as your dashing in to join the heroic people's fight, you should realize that this is no game, but a dead serious tragic reality. The last thing these people need is an outsider making a daring provocation to the Russians. That's just what they are waiting for. The beauty and purity of this situation is that they knew exactly what to do and what not to do. In their physical defeat they won the spiritual victory.
But even this aside, there is no way for you to get in there. It

183

isn't a question of your swindling yourself a plane seat. There were none, are none, and will be no planes for at least two months. The Russians ruined the Prague airport landing system...

Anyway, no Americans are allowed in for any reason. My first concern was for my wife... The U.S. embassy urged my departure, but my own reason was clear: My residence visa expires in five days. The passport office is occupied, and it is absolutely impossible to get a visa extension. Did you think I would leave there without Zdenka???

Your letter didn't even contain the phrase, "happy you are safe," even at the height of world-wide reporting about the death and destruction in Prague...

You will have a difficult time continuing your production here for a while. Half the studio has left the country..."

I went on to list all of the people he knew who were now in Vienna, etc. etc. But I think Zdenka said it best in her letter to Bill (transcribed here from her handwritten original):

"September 1, 1968

Dear Bill,

When I read your letter I was very very sad. We went through a lot of things, and the moment when we were leaving our flat, the radio announced that all Czechoslovak border crossings has been closed. I left everything in our flat, including running frigerator, and I handed key to the Jewish lady, Dr. Grünfeldová, who was urging us to leave. She knew why.

Don't you realise my heart is broken? My dear son and old father are there, all my people.

This once in my life I had the courage to leave everything and go with Gene, and I feel that I must stay beside him. It is a great difference if such a decision is made by me or a Russian. I am the last one who would ask for asylum, and wish to stay outside my country. But I want to return with Gene, to know we could work there and live in peace. What we need now are friends who will give us their hand and feelings, that around us are good people, not bombastic words about heroism. That has no meaning.

I am terribly sad that you are not one of those, because you are the first one about we talk that you'll be terrify what happen with us.

I had a great hope that Gene would be able to cross the border, but when he was turn back it was terrible for me..."

Only the first page of that letter has survived, but you should now have some idea of the conflicting thoughts all around us. Vienna was a boiling pot of rumors, exchanged every day as dislocated Czechs met each morning beside the opera building.

The overriding fact of that time was that no one really knew anything. In retrospect it is easy to say that we should have stayed there and just tried to continue our work. My feelings then were, "better safe than sorry." I wrote letters from Vienna to many former colleagues, all basically the same. Here is an excerpt from a typical one, addressed to John Halas, a British animation studio owner:

```
"We would like to return to Prague if possible, but
naturally I cannot do that until I am absolutely sure
that I will be able to get Zdenka out again. She is
still a Czechoslovak citizen. Unlike civilized Britain,
our great USA does not grant dual citizenship or American
passports to "Alien" wives not resident within the
States... She did not and does not want to be anything
but a Czech. She feels, now more than ever, proud of her
country...

Because I took pictures of the invasion for LIFE magazine,
the TIME-LIFE bureau here in Vienna has kindly offered
their offices as a temporary mail and cable address for
me..."
```

In one letter, to my oldest American friend, writer Bill Bernal, I wrote a paragraph I do feel was prophetic:

"The Russians, I believe, have made a fatal blunder. Hitler too tried to crush the Czechs, and it proved to be the first misstep that led to his destruction. We must only hope that this time the result will be quicker. Czechoslovakia is a fateful nation indeed. As long as it sits where it is, I suppose it will always be someone's temptation to possess. Someone noted that the map of Czechoslovakia resembles the form of a reclining woman. I suppose that is what brings out the desire to rape."

Well, it took longer than I hoped, but many historians do now believe that the invasion of this country was indeed the fatal first step leading to the downfall of the Soviet Union. It was, as I also wrote to others, "the most crude, blundering, ill-conceived occupation in history."

We received dozens of encouraging letters of relief that we were safe, and many offers of work. One especially heartwarming offer, ironic from today's perspective, was from our good friend Želimir Matko, manager of the animation studio in Zagreb, then part of Yugoslavia:

"INVITE YOU AND ZDENKA TO ZAGREB ON UNLIMITED PERIOD WHENEVER YOU WISH STOP READY TO DISCUSS ALL PROPOSITIONS STOP LETTER FOLLOWS BEST REGARDS MATKO ZAGREBFILM"

But Bill Snyder did finally relent, coming up with a live-action film project we could join for a couple of weeks in Norway. That was a beautiful diversion, shooting background scenes for Song of Norway in the northwest fjord country.

By the time that was finished, Czechoslovak Filmexport was in a position to invite me back. It was with great joy that we returned to Prague after only three weeks in "exile" - even though we knew that the country's darkest days still lay ahead.

1968 - These Soviet invaders couldn't read Czech. They set up their blasters right before a gallery announcing an exhibit of Soviet art!

38 - "Normalization"

Bill Snyder, in his delayed effort at heroic struggle, finally made it back to Prague in mid-1969. As police tried to control a demonstration outside the Alcron hotel, Snyder rushed out to join the fray and promptly got his fanny whacked with a police nightstick. He displayed his black and blue welt proudly, lowering his pants on every possible occasion until it sadly faded away. Snyder himself, once the Prince of Prague, faded away shortly afterwards. After 1969 he never again returned to the spired city.

Time. Time lost. Twenty more years of hard-line communism. Dubček raised the people's hopes, but he lacked the strength to deliver on his promise. His overwhelming popularity in early 1968 dissolved into dismay when he capitulated to the Russians. There was only one real hero in 1968, one who is sadly un-noted in the outside world's history books. That was Dr. František Kriegel. When all the top leaders were kidnapped by the Soviet Army and whisked off to Moscow as hostages in the first days of the invasion, Kriegel was the only one who steadfastly refused to sign the protocol legalizing the invasion. For his stubbornness, he suffered total non-person banishment, and died not long afterward.

I was a tad correct when I hopefully expressed my belief to Dr. Troníček that the hardliners could not roll back the 1968 "partial" freedoms. They remained on hold for 20 years. After Dubček and his government were released and brought back to Prague, they continued nominally in power until April 1969, wistfully proclaiming that the "January '68 reforms would continue." In reality, what they did was successively vanish. Bit by bit a regime of "normalization" was put in place. That was the reigning euphemism for the next twenty years: *"Normalization."*

The first step was taken when the parliament was pressured into passing a law allowing the "temporary" stationing of Soviet troops on Czechoslovak soil. That was the second great euphemism. I used to get laughs by telling people that I was working in Prague "temporarily."

Alexander Dubček was pushed out only gradually. It was clear from the moment he returned from Moscow that it was all over, but the charade was maintained for a remarkably long time. Even when he had to relinquish his power base as First Secretary of the Communist Party, he was given the post of Speaker of the Parliament. Then he was removed from view as Ambassador to Turkey, and finally recalled, excommunicated from the Party.

Alan Levy, from Day One of the invasion, was forging ahead with his own document of the events, which was eventually published under the title ROWBOAT TO PRAGUE.[1] Throughout the writing he asked us to keep copies of each chapter, while any visitors he had were given other copies to smuggle out. But when Alan's own mother was caught at the border with one set of copies in late 1970, Alan and his family were expelled from the country. They spent the next 20 years in "exile" in Vienna. Unfortunately, Alan named almost everyone in his book, including us. Zdenka and I are in there throughout. This gave me plenty of concern that we might be expelled, and that other Czechs who were named would suffer. I felt it was really unforgivable, considering the forecasts he'd made in his own telexes to me when we were in Vienna. Amazingly, we never did have any fallout from it, but that doesn't diminish the recklessness of naming people in this country at that time, especially when it is clear in the book that we were all rooting for the "counter-revolutionary" reforms, as they came to be dubbed. (I am naming real people in this book, but am writing in a time of freedom, and no one named in this book will suffer from it...I hope!)

Dubček, a Slovak, was exiled to the woods of Slovakia as a minor official in the forestry service. His name (which means, ironically, "little oak tree") was not mentioned in the media again for the next twenty years. He did not become a dissident. He issued no statements. He did not cooperate with dissidents. He did not sign Charter 77, He did not surface at all until late 1989, when it was clear the regime was about to crack. He then bravely visited Václav Havel in his Prague apartment, after which a photo of him appeared in several Western magazines. Though not the oak his name indicated, he did bloom again, only to be cut down later in a bizzare road accident. His tragedy played out like a Greek drama.

Cut down sooner was the prime villain, Leonid Brezhnev. When he died in 1982 all comedy film screenings in the country were cancelled by the State. That was OK with the Czechs; a good laugh was had all around anyway.

During the 70's and most of the 80's, Czechoslovakia once again sunk from world attention. One Christmas during that period, on a visit to California, we spent a weekend at Lake Tahoe. On a frosty morning walk, Zdenka was fascinated to see a man using a small snowplow to clear his driveway.

"We could use something like that!" she said to the owner of the machine as he paused to rest. "In my country we have only great monster machines, but nothing private."

"You have an interesting accent," said the man. "Where do you come from?"
"Can you guess?" said Zdenka.
"Russia?"
No. A little to the west."
"Germany?"
"No, just in between," said Zdenka, giving the maximum hint.
The man scratched his head, thought for a while, then said: "But there's nothing in between!"
So vanished Czechoslovakia. That's been the country's fate for centuries.

After the revolution, Alan Levy returned to Prague, where he became editor-in-chief of *The Prague Post,* the leading English language newspaper here. He told me it was his „dream job". Ing 1995 he was named Author of the Year by The American Society of Journalists and Authors for his book, *The Wiesenthal File.* His book, *Rowboat To Prague* was reissued under the title, *So Many Heroes.*

39 - Getting On With It

When we returned to Prague in mid-September of 1968, Vojan Masník, still the head of the animation studio, assured me that we could continue our work as usual. And we did. A sidelight was that a film I had in production at the time of the invasion was about violence, and the futility of aggression and revenge. It was titled "The Giants." I was thinking about the never-ending conflict between Israelis and Palestinians, with the giant United States backing the Israelis, and the giant Soviet Union backing the Palestinians.

Fearing I might not be able to finish the film in Prague, I took all the preliminary layout drawings with me to Vienna. As it turned out, I was able to finish the film here, and it became a much more sensational hit in this country than I could really understand. When I attended Prague theater screenings of the film and observed audience reactions, it was clear that it was being interpreted in an entirely different way than I had intended. People saw in it a "masked meaning" about the brutality of the Soviet invasion. When the hardliners took control again in April, my film was banned - not because of its actual content, but because of the way audiences perceived it!

Zdenka tried to find out the official reason my film was banned, and was finally told that it had been labeled "*objectivist.*" That was a new word for me.

A scene from „The Giants", my banned film - 1968

I knew about objective, but what in the world was *"objectivist?"* It soon became clear. The Communists always had everything neatly labeled as "correct" and "incorrect." There were "imperialist aggressors" and there were "camps of peace." They were not interested in exploring both sides of anything, nor any shades of meaning. My film pointedly did not show either side as the aggressor, and thus in the Communist view was not instructive to the audience; it left the audience *room for interpretation...* it was "objectivist!"

The fact that I had a film banned for twenty years became a point of pride for me. After the 1989 restoration of democracy, I received, together with the band of other, more important film directors of previously banned films, a certificate of apology and a token compensation for lost royalties.

But back in 1969, we were still letting our adrenaline calm down, which we did by trying to lose ourselves in our work. Amazingly, the twenty dark years ahead were, professionally speaking, the most rewarding for us. As Snyder faded out, Morton Schindel of the Connecticut organization Weston Woods popped in, and we spent 25 years producing films adapted from the finest children's picture books. This was not a get-rich-quick market, but it was rewarding because we did not have to live by catering to the Saturday morning kiddie-junk market. Under the label Weston Woods, our films have been distributed to schools and libraries, and on Children's Circle Video to "informed parents" in the home market. They have won over 100 top prizes in festivals around the world. I made film adaptations of Maurice Sendak's classics, "Where The Wild Things Are," and "In The Night Kitchen," Isaac Bashevis Singer's "Zlateh The Goat," four books by Tomi Ungerer, and of dozens of books by the greatest authors and illustrators of children's picture books. It was my most gratifying period in animation film work. Since that time Weston Woods has become a part of Scholastic, Inc., but continues to operate under its own identity.

When showing our films to groups of children during lectures, I was often asked, "Mr. Deitch, how can I get to do what you are doing?" I had to answer: "Get yourself into a place where you don't have to make a lot of money." Which is, I suppose, one of the factors that kept us here. During the dark days of the 70s and 80s Zdenka and I were able to take our satisfactions in the quality of the work we were able to do, while living in what amounted to a "low-rent zone." One thing you *could* say for the Communists was that they kept the cost of living bearable - though this was truer for foreigners than for Czechs.

One thing that constantly amazed me was how eager people were, including prospective clients, to visit me. When I had my animation studio on the West Side of Manhattan, It was a struggle to lure East Side (Madison Avenue) advertising agency clients to come those few blocks. But when they heard I was in Prague they were eager to business-class it over the ocean to the darkest East. Most old friends, relatives, colleagues, and vague acquaintances assumed I was wasting away with loneliness, and they heroically applied for visas to visit me.

One of the most successful films we made for Weston Woods was our adaptation of Maurice Sendak's masterpiece, "Where The Wild Things Are." To show the alienation between the little boy Max and his parents, I wanted to indicate that his parents were listening to thirties swing music in another room, leaving Max feeling isolated. Zdenka found me the perfect composer for this in Dr. Emil Ludvík, then an ostracized dissident, but once the leader of a popular swing band. He had the perfect tapes to loan us, actually recorded in the swing era.

©1963 by Maurice Sendak

These are the world-famous "Wild Things" characters created by Maurice Sendak. The adaptation of "Where The Wild Things Are" was one of our most successful animation films for Weston Woods Studios, Inc. (1974)

At the time of the 1968 Prague Spring, Ludvík had quickly come forward and opened a Prague branch of the Institute for Human Rights. This of course was crushed by the Soviet invasion, but every year thereafter we received a New Year's greeting from him, in the form of his calling card, with the line, "Chairman of the Institute for Human Rights," neatly but lightly crossed out! Today, I am happy to report, Ludvík is among the most respected old-time former dissidents, and is chairman of The Masaryk Democratic Movement. Zdenka and I are charter members. We are happy to see Emil Ludvík alive and well.

This is not a photo montage! Alan Levy actually donned a wet-suit and waded into the icy winter waters of the Vltava, so that I could take this photo of him for the cover of his book, "Rowboat to Prague," later issued as "So Many Heroes." After the revolution Alan returned to Prague, where he became editor-in-chief of The Prague Post, the leading English language newspaper here. He told me it was the dream job of his life. In 1995 he was named Author of the Year by the American Society of Journalists and Authors for his book, "The Wiesenthal File." (1968)

40 - Chalupa

So how did we cope spiritually during this second Dark Age? We succumbed to the Czech institution of the *chalupa* (*ch* as in *loch*). That is the Czech word for a cottage. Nearly every Czech family has some kind of old cottage, cabin, or small house somewhere in the countryside. Everyday city life was dull and despairing - most Czechs felt restricted, their work fruitless. The real meaning of life was on weekends in the family *chalupa*. There, in one's own private patch, fulfillment could be had in the never-ending work of building, repairing, restoring, gardening, eating and drinking. This was the one and only private escape from socialism legally available, and everyone who could possibly afford it, took it. We were no exception. We had been constantly invited to visit other people's cottages, but Zdenka pined for her own. They were getting harder to find.

In 1970 we were in England visiting a former colleague, Milena Nováková, who had escaped there with her husband two years earlier. She had enjoyed her childhood in her family's old cottage in the Sudetenland, and begged us to take it over before it fell into the clutches of some Communist apparatchik once her parents died.

You may know that the Sudetenland is in northern Bohemia, but unfortunately the name means *Southland* in German, and that is how Hitler thought of it: South Germany. So he annexed it after the infamous 1938 Munich pact, and thus started down the path toward World War II. After the war, when the territory was restored to the Czechs, most of the Germans - who had made up the majority of the population in those parts, and who had largely welcomed Hitler's takeover - were expelled. The expulsion of 3,000,000 Germans after the liberation from Nazi occupation is a subject of dispute to this day between the Czech Republic and Germany, but the Czechs consider it history. The Sudeten German organizations in Germany today, which agitated for years for the return of German property in the Czech lands, conveniently forgot that German Nazis had plans to expel all Czechs, and grab the entire country for Germany. Czechs generally feel no need to apologize for throwing out the Germans.

At any rate, the reality was that the former Sudetenland became a wasteland after the war. The Czechoslovak government tried to encourage people to move there by giving away land and empty houses. It became possible to pick up a charming cottage for next to nothing. The catch was that few people owned cars, and the region was far from Prague.

The aged parents in question had nearly lost the cottage. They had earlier registered it in their daughter's name in order to ensure her inheritance. But when Milena escaped to England, the cottage was subject to confiscation. It would certainly fall into the hands of a Communist official, and the parents would be evicted.

Fortunately, Milena's parents had a good friend working at the National Committee branch in their northeastern town of Jablonec-nad-Nisou, (Jablonec-on-the-Nisa), who was able to get into the files and deftly delete the daughter's name. This made it possible for the parents to sell the cottage to us. We made a private contract with them, giving them the right to visit it as long as they lived.

So by the fall of 1971, we had our own cottage. It was then about 175 years old, basically a log cabin with additions built on over the years. It was originally built and owned by a family of German glass workers. In that part of the country, people did small farming in the summer time, and made glass buttons and little bottles in the winter time - genuine cottage industry.

Horse and wagon drivers from the nearby glass furnaces would deliver colored glass rods and cast-iron molds to the people, and later pick up the finished items. We found many of these glass rods and iron forms in and around our cottage.

One sunny Sunday in the mid-'70s, we noticed a big white Mercedes-Benz driving slowly past our place. Our cottage is about 50 yards above the road. The car turned around in a neighbor's driveway, and came slowly back. It stopped, and a well-dressed woman got out and walked up the hill toward us. She was German, and spoke some English. "My aunt and uncle owned this place before the war," she said, "and I spent my entire young girlhood here." She was very pleasant and we invited her in, showing her around, pointing out how we were trying to restore the place while preserving its original style and character. There were no bitter words from her, and we had a friendly correspondence afterwards. We couldn't know what she really felt - it was still deep in the communist era, and former German property rights were not open to discussion.

Nowadays, no one in this country wants to open that can of worms. The post-Communist government set the date for property restitution at February 25, 1948, the date the Communist Party took power and subsequently nationalized all private property. Anything confiscated after that date has been restored to the original owners or their descendants. The new government would like to restore property to the Jews, who lost everything during the war, but if they set the date early enough for that, the Germans would also be able to claim back their property, and that includes a lot more than our *chalupa!*

Becoming weekend "country people," we found, added a whole new dimension to our lives, and working on our cottage became a passion, certainly for Zdenka. It also brought us into contact with good and plain people with a no-nonsense grasp of life. On my first meeting with a local neighbor, he engaged me in typical Czech small talk: "Glad to meet you, Mr. Deitch. Have you had your first heart attack yet? I've had three already!" he said proudly. The huge Czech intake of beer, sausage and cigarettes made heart attacks an accepted fact of life.

As Czech people gradually acquired cars, they were able to buy cottages and cabins further from Prague. And while prices began to rise for the choice places in attractive locations, especially those with available water and electricity, most cottages remained reasonably affordable, (even though the work needed on them often surpassed the purchase cost.) A country cottage is basically a project that is never completed; a continuous battle between you, the termites and wall mold. No matter how much work you do on the place, there is always more. A large problem was finding materials. Wood, bricks, cement, steel girders, tools, lawnmowers, what-have-you, were nearly impossible to buy. Building materials were like gold. But many people worked in factories and large socialist enterprises where these items *did* exist.

A reigning slogan in those days was, "He who doesn't steal from the State, steals from his family." So everything in fact was available. All it took were the right friends and a talent for discreet purloinery.

Not only did nationalized socialist bricks and cement find their way into private cottages, but it was even possible for airplane factory workers to turn out simple electric lawnmowers on "night shifts." So weekend country folk did manage. And of course we all became amateur woodworkers, carpenters, painters, gardeners, tree planters, plumbers, and toilet builders.

The typical Czech man disdains safety. Several neighbors near our chalupa have lost fingers in electric tool accidents. One close friend lost his right ring finger to an electric planer - and he's an eye surgeon! Virtually every circular saw that I have seen here, most of them put together by the users themselves, are without any safety cover over the whirling blade. Most of these are large table saws for cutting firewood and construction timber. I have also never seen anyone wear protective goggles. Czechs also resisted car safety belts until they became absolutely required by law. For a few years, belts were only required for country driving, not in the city. Every time I drove back from the countryside with a Czech driver he would undo his safety belt the instant we crossed the city limit sign. God forbid an acquaintance should see him belted up, sissy-style, while driving in the city!

In the early days at our mountain cottage, I had to learn to do the necessary work with the tools and materials at hand. At one end of the house, an attached storage barn had collapsed, and a former interior gable was now an exterior gable. It was ancient dry wood, and needed painting to be somewhat presentable until we could build a new decorative facing.

I spent hours standing on a high ladder painting that gable. The problem was that each coat of paint I applied sunk into the ancient wood and completely disappeared the following week. Each weekend for much of the summer season, I repainted that blotter-like gable, until finally there was visible paint remaining on the surface.

One neighbor, a doctor named Oskar Andrýsek, is an empty field away. It happened that one of our studio colleagues visited Dr. Andrýsek in Prague, and during their conversation she spoke of her work in the animation studio. "You don't happen to know the Deitches, do you?" asked the doctor, "They're also in animation film."

"Of course," said our colleague, a camera operator. "Zdenka Deitchová is my chief, and Gene is the director of a film I am now shooting."

"Well, those Deitches are neighbors near our weekend mountain cottage," said Dr. Andrýsek, "and I must say they are a strange pair! I looked over at their place last weekend, and I saw a large fallen tree steadily moving across their yard! I got out my binoculars, and saw that on the leading end of the tree was a *tiny woman*, dragging that huge tree toward a woodpile. The next day she was chopping the tree into logs, and burning the branches!"

"And all this time," he continued, "that *Mr.* Deitch was standing on top of a tall ladder, painting the same spot on their gable over and over again... *Weird!*"

When we bought it, the most dramatic feature of our *chalupa* was an immense maple tree, said to be 200 years old, which loomed up just inches from the front of the house. In October, when its leaves all turned golden yellow, it was a sight to see, a golden beacon to distinguish our cottage from any others in the surrounding hills. Valley neighbors called our house, "At the Maple Tree."

Our chalupa and our Glorious Maple Tree in its prime – about 1980

In its earlier years it had been struck by lightning and its trunk split, but it survived and healed, looking like Siamese-twin trees of giant stature. We loved that tree for its grandeur and the status it gave our cottage, but cursed it in November when it blessed us with millions of yellow leaves, ankle deep over our entire property, needing to be raked and burned.

Still, we worried about the old tree, as it was definitely showing signs of decay. We consulted with a local woodsman about banding its awesome girth with an iron ring.

Late that year, 1985, after days of continuous icy drizzle and wind, I was inside the cottage painting the wall facing the front. I was lamenting the wet weather, and was just thinking I should call Zdenka to come inside. She was as usual defying the elements, and was working in the front garden, right under the tree. Just as I dipped my brush into the pea-green paint I heard a *"whoo-oosh,"* and caught a blur of motion through the window.

There was a heart-stopping instant before the door opened, and Zdenka walked in. "I suddenly had a feeling I should come inside," she said, just a shade off her usual steadfast self.

We dashed outside, and the sight we now saw informed us both that, had Zdenka delayed an instant more, all I would have found of her would have been her little red rubber boots. Miraculously, the immense tree had not only missed Zdenka, but also our cottage and even all of Zdenka's prized foliage. It had fallen precisely between everything, pulling down our electric power line, crashing through our perimeter fence, and extending halfway into our neighbor's yard.

Its forward branches had been driven deep into the ground, and the mammoth trunk had pounded out a form-fitting trough along its entire length. Had it fallen just a few degrees toward the cottage, it would have surely rendered it in two. Its great weight would have easily crushed our roof and us along with it. The old split had left part of the trunk still standing, enough to reveal its inner rot, which the noble giant had modestly hidden from us. It was nerve-shattering to contemplate.

The fallen tree was, for all practical purposes, now immovable. All we were able to do was call a woodsman and have him chain-saw the trunk into firewood-thick slices. For the following three years, we continued to chop up the slices, until our front lawn was finally cleared and our wood storeroom was crammed with what appeared to be a lifetime supply. Ten years later, we had in fact not yet burned it all.

We grieved over the loss of our beloved tree, which gave us much to think about. It even inspired in me this short piece:

1985 - THE GIANT OLD MAPLE TREE BEFORE OUR COUNTRY COTTAGE HAS FALLEN

Aside from old age and inner rot, which eventually brings us all down, the immediate cause of the tree's fall was five days of steady rain and wind. Water had seeped into the hidden hollows of the trunk...

Like the tree, we can tan our skins, dress in the gaudy colors of youth, and wave about, but we must tremble before each high wind that blows in.

41 - Balloonatic

Vratislav Hlavatý is the sweetest sort of wild man. He is an eccentric graphic artist who designed many of Zdenka's films, and also two films and a book with me. He is big on exotic/erotic. We became friends, and friends call him "Vratya." In his art, in his multi-faceted love life, and in his extra-curricular activities, Vratya relishes dangerous living. He never let the communist system restrain his fun.

His fun was flying in home-made balloons and hang gliders, or any other thrilling, life-and-limb-threatening stunts he could dream up. Once we visited Vratya in the hospital after a fall from a hang glider shattered his liver. He recovered. A magical event was when the wind blew his balloon right over our mountain cottage, filling the sky above us, and landing right in our back yard. No one in the area had ever seen such a thing. "The Deitches are being visited by a balloon!" All came running. This was the only time a balloon had ever landed in the mountain village of Horní Maxov.

"Don't smoke! Don't smoke!" shouted Hlavatý as he clambered from the grounded basket, as the sagging balloon swayed immensely over his head. Why? Because the balloon was filled with *natural gas*! In the communist times, there were no hot air balloons, and natural gas, however dangerous, was the only available medium to float a balloon.

Balloon flying was strictly controlled by the regime; it was too obvious a way of floating over the borders to the West. As with everything he did, Vratya Hlavatý got around the communist restrictions by forming a ballooning club within the Army's SVAZARM umbrella hobby organization - the same device Jiří Janda used to form his hifi club. SVAZARM controlled all hobbies, from ham radio, right down to stamp collecting, to make sure nothing went on that was any kind of threat to the regime.

One crisp autumn Sunday in 1969 Vratya invited us to a balloon launching by his club. We drove our new SAAB Monte Carlo down to Tabor, the ancient Hussite town in southern Bohemia. Just outside the town was one of the main Czechoslovak Army camps. The name Tabor means "camp," and there has always been one there since the time of the Hussite wars of 1419-1435.

Near the camp was a large grassy meadow, an ideal balloon launch site. Seven carloads of members, sandbags and balloon parts arrived and were deployed in an arc near the center. Everything was there except the gas. A tank truck of natural gas was on its way, but late. In the meantime a large circle of sandbags was laid out, and the extremely heavy, carefully folded and rolled up balloon itself was dragged out of one of the cars. It was amazing how it had been wedged inside! It took nearly all of the members to drag it to the center of the circle, and to carefully unfold it. From another car came the great net of thick nylon rope, which had to be laid carefully over the pancake-flat balloon. The sandbags were then carefully attached to the edges. They would have to be each shifted down the net, row by row, as the balloon rose.

A windsock was set up, and it was flapping in furious reproach to our activities. Close to the circle of sandbags was a large wicker basket. Inside it was a sleeping balloonist. Inside the cars were disconsolate club members and their wives and girl friends, waiting for the gas, sheltering from the wind, hoping for it to subside.

"It's no real problem to fly in this wind," said Hlavatý, "but it is a battle to get the damned basket attached!" So we all sat in our cars, eating sandwiches and drinking soda pop, waiting and watching the highway and the windsock.

But waiting was not what fanatic activists like Hlavatý and his bunch liked to do. "Let's have a car rally!" he shouted. Unquestioningly, we all started our cars and trailed out across the meadow and onto an abandoned Army airstrip!

"It's Sunday. Nothing will be landing today," announced Vratya reassuringly.

To get the good times rolling, Hlavatý set his little Fiat 600 going in a circle the width of the runway. He tied the steering wheel to the clutch pedal, and laid a brick on the accelerator. With the little car circling on its own, Hlavatý crawled out the window, hanging on by his legs, with his arms outstretched.

Then he climbed out and onto the roof and jumped, hitting the ground running, chasing after his car, diving into a side window, undoing the rope holding the steering wheel, and finishing off with a wild skidding exhibition on the adjacent slippery grass meadow!

Next was an attempt to guide a blindfolded driver through an obstacle course of our cars set up along the runway, using the balloon's two-way radio for guidance. Amazingly, none of our cars got dented. I was the faintest of heart, as my car was the only one that was brand-new.

By this time, the teen-age mentality of the enterprise had us all revved up, so when Hlavatý called for an auto race down the length of the runway, we all cheered. "Let's do it like at Monte Carlo," someone shouted. So we men all spread-eagled ourselves on the tarmac fifty paces behind our cars, which were lined up at the runway's touchdown mark.

Lying flat on our bellies, with arms outstretched, we each clutched our car keys, and waited for one of the girls to give the start signal. There went 45-year-old me, puffing like a maniac to get to my car, find the goddamn keyhole, and grind the gears. I was the slowest runner, but I had the fastest car, so I won the race.

Finally, the gas truck was spotted as it approached along the highway. A great cheer arose from the intrepid balloonists, and we all drove determinedly back to the launching site. The wind was if anything even more fierce than before, but the balloonatics were not to be put off on this precious weekend day. A long thick canvas hose was unrolled from the gas truck. One of the members dragged it over to the great circle and under the mass of crumpled cloth - the balloon to be - and

somehow attached it to the unseen inflation valve.

A signal was given and the gas hydrant turned on. There was a terrifying (to me) roar, and the huge bag started to rise. The sight and sound attracted dozens of local people, running our way onto this isolated meadow. In one of those situations of unspoken communion, all of these strangers seemed to know just what to do to help, and a real spontaneous happening was in play. Everyone was running around the

great circle, hooking and unhooking sandbags from the network of rope that covered the entire balloon. As the balloon rose, the sandbags had to be unhooked from the successive rising net-levels of rope, and affixed to the lo-

wer net levels. So there was a frantic mass of people, all trying to keep the sandbags on the ground as the net rose.

The balloon itself was sewn together from rubberized cotton sheets, the segments taped over at the seams with ordinary wide, flesh-colored medical adhesive tape. Near the top was one large triangle of cloth, which was not sewn, but held in place only by the tape. This, I learned from shouting over the roar of gas, was attached to a long cord hanging down inside the balloon and extending out the mouth. By yanking on this cord, the triangle patch could be pulled loose, allowing the gas to quickly escape.

This was for use during the last second before touching down, to quickly deflate the balloon, and prevent it from dragging off the basket and passengers. It also was a safety device during a filling emergency. Filling, I was informed, is the only really dangerous part of ballooning, so I shouldn't worry!

There was little Zdenka, hanging like mad onto a rope, as the immense balloon, now rolling and waving in the strong wind, was hauling her up and down. "Let go! Let go!" I shouted fruitlessly, racing after her as the balloon bounced up and down, skimming erratically over the meadow. She actually imagined that her near weightless body was viable ballast to the immense balloon! The wind was so strong that all were being dragged this way and that as the wind shifted and intensified. It was more than clear that it would be impossible to get the basket attached.

Suddenly the filling hose yanked out, and the safety cord was pulled up inside the balloon and lost! Without hesitation, Hlavatý dived inside the gas-filled balloon, held his breath, and blindly groped for the lost cord! The balloon was rubbing fiercely against its restraining rope net. What was that they had said about static electricity being the main danger?
One spark could have set off a cataclysmic poof that would instantly consume all of the oxygen in that entire meadow, and all of us along with it. In overdue course, Vratya emerged, clutching the cord and gasping for breath. "Man, it stinks in there," he remarked coolly. He gave a mighty yank, and the gas streamed from the triangular opening. He was dismayed at having to do that. I was relieved. And it did stink.
The mighty balloon flapped insanely in its dying collapse. It seemed to be having convulsions. In now what was nearly a gale, the balloon was torn from its restraining net. It turned in on itself, and the triangular opening fell face-downward, preventing the complete escape of the gas. If the balloon should break loose now, it could possibly be blown into the nearby army camp. As if things weren't bad enough, all we needed was to be making a gas attack on the Czechoslovak People's Army!
Everyone was scrambling and tripping over the thrashing net, jumping onto the balloon, trying to hold it down and to force out the remaining gas.

Somewhere, inside the billowing, enveloping folds, we caught sight of Hlavatý, rolling around with a young girl in jeans, laughing and shouting, "No smoking! No smoking! There was a final rip, and the confusion of cloth folds and nylon cords sighed to the ground. "It's nothing, said Hlavatý as he emerged. "We'll have it patched up in an hour!"

Today Vratislav Hlavatý has a company supplying modern, sophisticated hot air balloons for tourism and film work, and also continues his work as an illustrator and animation film designer.

42 - Lubbock had The Answers!

Thought control existed on both sides of the cold war. In the fall of 1978 Zdenka and I were sent on a lecture tour, arranged by our client Weston Woods. We spoke and showed our children's films in assembly halls of 12 universities across the United States. One of our biggest welcomes was in the broiling hot Bible Belt, at the Lubbock Christian College, in Lubbock, Texas. Why were they so glad to have us?

Well, they seemed to like our films and our approach to adapting children's picture books to animated films, but it was *after* our lecture that their higher purpose became clear. They told us that they had a special library of interviews with honored guests, and they invited us for such a taped video interview.

Why not? We agreed, and sat down before their cameras. Then they handed us a *script*. I was surprised, and one glance at it set my alarm bells ringing. The written questions were not about our films, but about the political situation in Czechoslovakia, mainly about the Dubček reforms and the subsequent Soviet-led invasion. And right there, along side the questions, *were our answers, all printed out for us!*

How could they presume to know how I would answer the questions?

It was the 10th anniversary of the 1968 tragedy, and could have been an interesting and useful private discussion. But I was there with Zdenka. Should such a tape of us exist at that time - and who knew what they planned to do with it? - we would have both been zapped without having accomplished anything. The then Communist regime had papered over the 1968 invasion as an act of "brotherly help." At the 10th anniversary, the country was still deep in the dark period of so-called "Normalization."

Our interviewer was a student named Joey Cope. I asked him this: "Joey, you've no doubt heard of how political trials were staged in the communist countries, in which the accused were given scripts to read in court. How do you see that as being different from what you are doing here?" I told him that I was not a political analyst, but I knew that the subject was much more complex than the simple "Evil Empire" responses his script called for. Anyway, I was there to talk about children's films, and that was the only type of interview we could participate in. We did it, and it went very well.

But the event upset me, and I asked to see the Director of the University.

He was Dr. C. L. Kay, a pudgy patriot of such intensity that he displayed (by my actual count) 57 American flags in his office! Not only were there huge twin banners behind his desk, but actual *bouquets* of small flags displayed on tables, ledges, and affixed to the walls! How could my claim to be a loyal American citizen stand up to his? I wasn't even wearing an American flag lapel pin such as adorned the good doctor's suit!

I thanked him for his hospitality, and hoped he would understand my position regarding the interview. After returning home I put my views in writing. I still have a copy of the letter:

```
"Dr. C.L. Kay                                    19 October 1978

Lubbock Christian College
Lubbock, Texas 79407 USA

Dear Dr. Kay,

Though I did send you a quick picture postcard, I want to
also write you more formally to thank you for your welcome and
kind considerations during our visit to your university. Nowhere
was the level of hospitality or response to our work more gratify-
ing that at LCC.

I especially appreciate your understanding during the one diffi-
cult moment that we did have. As I told you, I would be happy to
have had a man-to-man discussion with you on any subject which in-
terested you, regarding my experiences, but you did understand
that with Zdenka and me both as guests, the occasion was not ap-
propriate for a video recording.

I do hope that young Joey learned a lesson in the two-edged nature
of propaganda, I am in no way an apologist for anything going on
here, but I have read enough, and remember enough
to know that whatever we think about it, we cannot escape the
knowledge that our own [American] mistakes and reluctance
to help at critical moments has significantly contributed
to the reality which now exists [in Czechoslovakia].
```

We [Americans] have always had our priorities, and they never extended this far.

Rather than make dramatic but futile proclamations, I have found
that by just being here, doing my work in peace,
demonstrating that cultural cooperation is possible and
mutually advantageous, that I am also delivering a message.

Once again, I thank you for the opportunity of speaking to
your students, and please also convey my special thanks to Dr.
Green, a gentleman who must certainly be a great asset
to your school.

Zdenka and I hope to meet you all again, and in the meantime we
hope that our films will be useful to your curriculum.

With best regards, (Gene Deitch)

    The student, Joey Cope, abashed, or on orders from Dr. Kay, sent the
following letter to our client. Cope does not mention the expected answers,
which were part of the original script presented to me.

LUBBOCK CHRISTIAN COLLEGE

5601 WEST 19TH STREET / LUBBOCK, TEXAS 79407 / TELEPHONE 806/792 3221

October 11, 1978
Mr. Morton Schindel
Weston Woods
Weston, Connecticut 06883

Dear Mr. Schindel:

This is to inform you that a video tape dub of my interview with
Mr. Gene Deitch has been mailed to you under separate cover.
The interview has been invaluable to our teachers and is a welcome
addition to our video tape library.

The original design of the interview centered on matters of political science, due to the fact that that sub-ject matter is an
integral part of our curriculum. However, prior to the interview,
Mr. Deitch stated that he was a filmmaker and not a "political
scien-tist." Thus, the resulting interview
concerned only matters of Mr. Deitch's life in regard to his
films. And, at Mr. Deitch's request, I destroyed all notes and questions that were prepared for the original interview.

The resulting interview, as mentioned earlier, has been
invaluable to us. Mr. Deitch's comments on his life and
philosophies of animation and film produc-tion make a
delightful program. I thought you might enjoy it also.

Sincerely,

Joey Cope

Joey Cope

43 - Czech-up

Czech socialized medicine made an immediate positive impression on me. You may imagine the state of my nervous system upon my first arrival in Prague. The presumed danger, the foreignness, the simple jet lag, to say nothing of the tensions around my New York studio and my home life in America - all had played on the twitching mechanisms of my face. Everyone who remembers me from those early days surely noticed my strange grimaces and eye tics.

Zdenka takes credit for smoothing my face over the years, but in my first days here everyone thought I was a nervous wreck. The effect I felt at that ime was extreme enervation. So Zdenka took me to the studio clinic for my first experience with Czech medicine. There was a woman doctor who took a very serious attitude towards me. The novel experience of dealing with genuine American flesh was not taken lightly. At the end of her probing and listening, she pronounced her prescription:

"What you need sir, is plenty of strong coffee and red wine!"

As someone with low blood pressure, I have followed that prescription scrupulously ever since!

At that time, all drug prescriptions cost the same - one crown, or approximately a nickel. The catch was, they didn't have any modern drugs. I had to go to Germany for most medicines, where they cost considerably more.

For health care in Prague, I found I was required to go to a special clinic, exclusively for foreigners, where I came into the hands of a laconic physician I called "good ol' Dr. Nohejl." (Pronounced "No-hale")

When I first visited Dr. Nohejl at the foreigners section of the Prague Polyclinic, and was glumly reporting my various strange symptoms - lack of energy, back pains, twinges, etc. etc., he looked at me coolly and said:

"Mr. Deitch, we all have to die sometime!"

He then gave me a box of white pills and called to his nurse, "Next!"

Another time, after I'd listed all my indispositions, he retorted:

"Mr. Deitch, you should only know about my pains!"

I was under 40 then. Now I'm in my mid-70s, and I feel a lot better. How could I not, with Dr. Nohejl bucking me up all those years?

In 1987 I was in his office for my irregular/regular check-up, clutching my little bottle of urine. I was feeling just fine, except for a slight dry throat

I picked up from one of our holiday visitors breathing for hours in our winter-sealed flat. I had the routine blood tests, and at the drawing of blood, the lady with the needle said, "You look pale, would you like to lie down?"

"Why should I want to lie down?" I asked. "I feel fine."

"Well, men are usually much more cowardly than women at blood tests, and are frequently apt to faint." At this challenge to my courage I strode out in my most manly fashion, and went for the EKG. There, the lady operator told me I looked great! She was obviously out of place in this pessimistic polyclinic.

But things were back to normal when I went back to Dr. Nohejl's office for his report of the results.

"I am sorry, Mr. Deitch, but I must tell you... *(pause)*... that your EKG is completely normal." He said this with a tinge of regret showing through his smile. A great kidder, that Dr. Nohejl.

Earlier, I mentioned to Dr. Nohejl my satisfaction that at long last Czechoslovakia was mounting some anti-smoking actions, and that next year, 1988, had been designated "The Year of Non-Smokers." The government had promised to put through many of the same laws we'd had in America for years already. (It didn't.)

I told him how depressing it was for me to see so many young people, especially young girls, smoking, and how difficult it was to go to any gathering in this town without getting not only your lungs but your clothes impregnated with fag stink.

"It's all humbug," declared the good doctor. "The air we breathe in Prague is worse than cigarette smoke. You won't live any longer here by not smoking!"

"What?" I gasped. "*You, a doctor, are making propaganda for smoking?* I could report you to the National Committee!"

It was clearly a mock threat, but it immediately dawned on me that Doc Nohejl must be one of those multitudes of fatalist, fagged-out doctors who themselves smoke. Ironically, only moments before he had asked me the routine question he has asked at every one of my semi-annual checkups for the previous 25 years: "Do you smoke?"

I can't even count the number of times people here have told me, "My uncle (aunt, grandfather, grandmother, cousin) smoked a pack of cigarettes and drank a half-bottle of vodka every day of his/her life, and lived to the age of 96." This is the standard Czech licensing legend, and even doctors appeared to have such stalwart relatives as examples, to support their habits.

Well, let's look at it this way: So far I have survived both the Prague air-supply and Dr. Nohejl, who is sadly no longer with us.

There was a time, however, when the good doctor was almost certain I wouldn't make it. No doubt you've heard the expression, *"Merry Christmas and a Happy New Year!"* Well, it was neither merry nor happy for me the year I spent my holidays in the hospital - 16 days, from December 21, 1984 to January 6, 1985.

One day I was suddenly stricken with intense stomach pains, and was in need of a hopeful word from Dr. Nohejl. While I sat there, sick as a dog, my stomach boiling, he called Zdenka on the phone. "Your husband is gravely ill," he intoned. As I reported later to my friends and family, that was the worst day of my life.

I have been amazingly lucky with health my whole life, never having been seriously ill, never having smoked, drinking only wine or beer with meals, eating carefully, and being blessed with a perfect heart and low blood pressure. But there was still my turgid brain: always nervous, always believing that the best way to avoid evil was to worry about it in advance: communism / uncertainty / possible lack of projects / animation production problems / tension / stress: ULCER! (Though today we're told ulcers come not from stress, but from a bug. Go figure.)

At first I thought I was experiencing only a really super version of that crummy-tummy I'd learned to live with for the past several years. A simple ulcer I could live with. My reasoning: everybody's got something, I'm getting older, so this is my particular cross to bear. But my ulcer had already healed, and in so doing had shriveled my duodenum to the point where no food was getting through. My stomach had become immensely bloated, until I was literally vomiting gas and ghastly fluid. Nothing would relieve the pain.

I had hoped to manage through the holidays, but in such condition there was nothing for it but to check into the Prague General Hospital, which I did on December 21.

There, I had to face gastroscopy, X-rays, a horrible rubber tube up my nostril and down my stomach to keep it drained (devilishly uncomfortable, but it did relieve the pressure and thus the pain), and intravenous feeding. There were all manner of tests, doctors and nurses fluttering about, and then on December 27 I underwent abdominal surgery.

Zdenka visited me every day in the hospital, helping me get through it. An operation had been one of my standard worries, and having it suddenly thrust upon me here in Czechoslovakia could have easily flipped me out totally. But the amazing thing was - at least it was amazing to me - when the moment came, I was completely cool and accepting. I really felt I was in good, caring hands. The hospital was ancient and beat up, but I was impressed with the quality of the personnel. I don't think I could have gotten better doctors or better care anywhere. The place was far from deluxe, but the staff was. The greatest fear I felt was when I returned to the hospital a month later, for a post-operative checkup, and saw how crummy that place actually looked! *"I laid my life on the table in this place?!?"*

The bright side to that was the bill for the complete works - operation, doctors, medicine, and hospital stay for 16 days: $1,600. And I received a marvelous Christmas present: a new life! I count January 1, 1985 as another new beginning, ranking with the day in 1959 when I first arrived in Prague and met Zdenka.

I also learned some great lessons in that hospital, not the least of which was contained in the first question the doctor asked on each daily visit:

"Good day, Mr. Deitch. Are you farting okay?"

Each day since my operation, and it is over 15 years now, Zdenka gets up at 6AM and makes me a pot of soup from the ground up; each day a different type. She is definitely the Soup Queen! Then she dashes off to her waiting driver at 7:30 in a whirl of instructions for the day. I generally work at home, and of course have my own household duties.

At the end of each day we are both pretty well zonked. One evening there was this bit of dialogue between us:

Me: "Dunno why I feel so sleepy all the time..."

Zdenka: "You're lazy."

Me: "But just told me that you feel sleepy too!"

Zdenka: *"I'm tired."*

44 - Mysterious Prague

Joseph Wechsberg wrote an evocative book in 1971 entitled, *Prague, the Mystical City*. It recounts the long history of weirdness that has enthralled this place. This is the city of the Golem, the alchemists, the cabalists, the astrologers, the soothsayers, Franz Kafka, The Good Soldier Švejk, Faust, and all manner of mystics, Bohemian ghosts, and magic.

We can attest to all that, because we ourselves have been caught up in the magic, and have lived through some amazing manifestations thereof.

Zdenka loves to quote the line, "There are more things between heaven and Earth than we can know..." In fact, the Czechs dearly *love* unexplained and unexplainable things. I have yet to find a Czech who does *not* believe in UFOs. Every convoluted theory about the Kennedy assassination has its advocates here. Erich von Däniken's book and documentary films about spacemen visiting the Aztecs, etc. were swallowed whole here. Astrology columns, magazines, and hot-lines pour out widely varied horoscope predictions daily. Legends, ghosts, and mysteries of every sort haunt the town.

A lot of it has its roots in old pre-Christian Slavic religious practices. Earliest rites were based on the principle that the natural world is inhabited and directed by beneficial and harmful spirits of nature. Later, these mysterious forces were anthropomorphized into divinities with special powers and functions. Byelobog, the White God, and Chernobog, the Black God - representing the forces of good and evil - reflected the Slavic belief in the dualistic nature of the universe.

All of this has filtered down into modern Prague, and if you walk the narrow winding streets of Prague at night - even though the gas lamps are now electrified - you can't help but feel it. The magic of the past is everywhere you look.

Let me tell you our story of Alexander Marshack and the Astounding Book Gift:

We met Alexander Marshack and his wife Elaine in the mid-seventies through Allen Swift. Alex is a self-starter who has done many things. As a photographer on assignment for LIFE magazine, he became fascinated with the subject of archaeology. With no institutional training, he became one of the world's experts on the beginnings of notation; the precursor to writing and art.

Silhouettes above our street, Mostecká ulice, "Bridge Street"

He was able to prove that humans had begun to make marks on bones, to indicate seasons, moon phases, locations, etc., at least 35,000 years in the past. He also deduced that humans at that time had a culture and economy developed enough to support professional artists. Highly competent painting and drawing was done nearly a mile deep inside pitch-dark caves. His work was featured in National Geographic and other scientific journals.

In 1974 Alexander Marshack went to the Soviet Union to examine some relics of early human notation. He also came to Brno in Czechoslovakia, where the city museum had some bones that had been lying in a drawer for over a hundred years, labeled simply: "decorated bones." With stereo-microscopic examination, he proved that the "decorations" were in fact notations of water supply, seasons, hunting locations - the first "writing."

Alex and Elaine stopped in Prague to pay us a visit, phoning ahead to let us know they would be here for breakfast. As they walked from their hotel, over the Charles Bridge, and toward our flat in Malá Strana, they realized they had "no gift for Gene and Zdenka," and decided to look for something for us. They noticed a long line in front of our local bookstore. Having just come from the Soviet Union, they remembered that a colleague there had told them that whenever a Russian sees a queue in front of a shop, he or she immediately gets in line, for there will undoubtedly be something rare, something hard -to-get. And a line before a *bookstore* might well mean a book with some political significance has been published.

The 1968 turmoil in Czechoslovakia was still a strong memory. The Marshacks decided that this could be just the gift for us - a book that everyone was lining up for, first thing in the morning! It happened to be a Thursday morning, and what the Marshacks did not know was that new books came out regularly each Thursday. And as all books in this country had limited press runs, due to paper shortages and limited printing facilities, there was a line before all bookshops *every* Thursday morning! There was no special reason for the line on this particular Thursday. Not knowing this, and in anticipation of something rare, the Marshacks immediately got in the line.

They waited until the shop opened, and ever so slowly neared the stack of the desired new book, each copy having been previously wrapped. Obviously, Alex and Elaine had no idea what the book was, but they were convinced it must be something special and hard to get! Even if they had opened the package and read the cover they would not have known what the book was about. Alex may have been able to read marks on 35,000 year-old bones, but he could not read Czech. The book's title was TUŠENÍ SOUVISLOSTI, "Premonition of Relationships." It was written by the Czech author, Ludvík Souček.

Well, when they arrived at our flat, they presented us with this still wrapped book, and recounted their reasons for buying it. Of course that produced a great laugh, and we had to tell them there was a line before the bookshop *every* Thursday morning. Still, we certainly did appreciate their good-heartedness and patience for standing in line and buying it for us.

We had much to talk about, and in fact didn't get around to looking at the book itself until after the Marshacks left. The book's author specialized in writing about strange and hard-to-explain phenomena. The picture on the cover didn't indicate anything too specific, but leafing through the book we saw that it was about many archeological curiosities of history, and on page 58, to our amazement, *there began the story of the strange bones deciphered by Alexander Marshack!*

When we next met Alex and Elaine, in New York we told them of this astonishing coincidence. They could hardly believe it, but we had the book with us to prove it! We still have it. As with Ludvík Šváb, the Prague Dixieland guitarist and his dog-eared copies of The Record Changer magazine, Prague's magic had struck again!

But sometimes the magic was of a darker hue, and in one case led to personal tragedy.

I have written much in this book about the failings of communism, but as I've said, in my early twenties I was briefly attracted to the idea, and could once be described as a flaming liberal. Among other influences, I met Pete Seeger in 1945. He and his wife Toshi were regular visitors to our house whenever they were in LA. I made many home recordings of him as he sang for our children and for us. I was much inspired by his dedication to social justice and the power of song. We are still dear friends, and though in the intervening 55 years plus we have had vastly differing experiences, I am still inspired by his unflagging dedication to what he believes.

During those indigent, struggling, early years of my marriage to Marie Deitch, we had devised a cheap social/political activity. Every Friday night in our little Hollywood bungalow, we held an open house "Kaffee Klatsch & Jazz Record Session." Marie cooked up wieners and beans, and we collected 50 cents from each attendee for a current political cause, such as campaign contributions for Henry Wallace and Adlai Stevenson. The word spread among local traditional jazz fans, who all seemed to have the same political leanings, and each week many people came whom we did not previously know. We made many good long-standing friends this way, while others drifted off along their separate ways.

One of those was a young man named Arthur Field. Thirty years later, in 1975, the following tiny classified ad appeared in the New York VILLAGE VOICE newspaper:

> I have returned to New York and wish to
> contact my old friends Marie & Gene Deitch.
> Professor Arthur Field (phone number)

My son Kim, at that time a struggling young cartoonist bunking in the Village, just happened to read that ad, and informed Arthur Field of my address and new relationship. What were the odds, I wonder now, of Kim seeing that fateful ad?

Arthur wrote me, saying he would love to come to Prague for a visit. On that visit, Zdenka, forever the matchmaker, saw in Arthur a handsome, still young university professor who could no doubt use a beautiful Czech wife. She had just the one for him - Ivana Jilovcová, the svelte, dark-haired daughter of one of the studio animators. They really did fall in love, and were eventually married in a lavish Prague ceremony. I was Best Man. Art proclaimed that it was the -happiest day of his life, and that he would be forever grateful to Zdenka for introducing him to Ivana. Once married, she was free to emigrate, and the happy couple moved to Art's spacious New York apartment. They experienced a year of wedded bliss. Then, during a vacation trip in a rented VW microbus, Ivana was driving while Art slept in the back. Suddenly, incredibly, a rear wheel fell off. The side door slid open, and Arthur was thrown out of the car and killed.

Ivana was devastated and totally bereft. Without Art's calm management of their lives, her life became rudderless. She was easy prey for those in Art's family who disputed her inheritance. She was all too easy to exploit for her inexperience.

Eventually she found a new relationship and moved back to Prague. We see her now at our regular season symphony concerts, a faded flower who must forever mourn her brief idyllic interlude.

Whether or not Art would be alive today had my son not seen the ad, or whether Art had not visited Prague, or whether Zdenka had not set him up with Ivana, none of us will ever know. It's just one more mystery to arise from this city's enchanted aura.

Some mysteries can be explained, but are mysteries all the same to those who encounter them. Take the case of the Risen Rabbit:

A colleague in the animation studio told us of a friend who has a huge dog and very nervous neighbors. The neighbors, joining the wave of free enterprise which followed 1989's "Velvet Revolution," invested in a pedigreed Angora breeding rabbit. It cost them 400 German deutschmarks, a fortune for a Czech, but it was their key to a new business. Before they could get started with their breeding program, however, tragedy struck in the form of their neighbor's dog, who one day dragged the dead and bedraggled prize rabbit proudly home to its master and mistress.

The friend and his wife were horrified at the prospect of imminent war with their neighbors, not to mention the 400 DM they would have to repay. Frantically they washed the mangled and muddy corpse, shampooed and blow-dried the Angora fur. And in the middle of the night, they stealthily replaced the body in the neighbors' backyard hutch, hoping against hope that they would think their prize rabbit had died a natural death, and thus not shoot their dog.

The following day, the neighbors approached them, ashen with shock."Our Angora rabbit died two days ago," they whispered fearfully... "We buried it in our back yard, but this morning we found its body miraculously clean and back in its hutch."

Would honesty have been the best policy? Our colleague's friends are still wrestling with the problem of if, how, or when to finally tell their bewildered neighbors the truth, before they decide to take up rabbit worship.[1]

[1] This incident has been reprinted with various attributions, but our collegaue, Jan Stibral steadfastly insists on its truth, involving his own neighbor. (1993)

Many visitors don't realize that the mighty Charles Bridge was nearly washed away – well, seriously damaged - in the great flood of 1890

45 – David

Some of David's friends might have thought he was the luckiest guy in the republic, having a dollared American for a stepfather. In fact, it meant trouble with a capital T. He was thrown out of law school, lost a good job, and had a zero career outlook. And when he had to serve his required two years in the Army of the Czechoslovak Socialist Republic in the mid-'70s, he faced more than the usual hassles of military life: *he had me as a stepfather!*

Every time a Czech applied for anything in Communist Czechoslovakia, it required filling out a questionnaire. The most important questions were: "Do you have any relatives living abroad? Do you have any relatives of foreign nationality?"

Misstatements on these forms were grounds for summary dismissal. Of course they didn't even need to ask; they already knew everything. But you had to write it down anyway, and when David listed his stepfather as an American, he was shown the door. In the cases where he tried ignoring the question altogether, he was thrown out of good jobs.

There were a few positive things I could do for him. I could buy special things he wanted, I could get him an occasional trip abroad when he became more independent of his father, and I might one day help get him out of the country and into the USA, complete with immigrant visa and precious green card. That's what he desired most, but of course that had to be done at the right time, and with the greatest care. It would have to be done step by step, and in such a way so as not to damage Zdenka, nor destroy my own residency privileges in this country, threatening my livlihood.

But before I get into that, first let me go back to when David was first called up to military service. In those days every young man of 18 years in reasonable health had to serve two long years in the Czechoslovak army. In its 74 years of existence, the Czechoslovak army never once fired a shot in anger; never once defended the country, neither against the Nazi nor Soviet invasions. The Czechs are dedicated to survival, coping, and eventually outfoxing and outlasting their aggressors. Czechoslovak soldiers, in their rumpled uniforms and scuffed cheap shoes, amusingly represented what may well be the most unmilitaristic people on earth.

The army, at the time of David's induction, was mainly an organization for discipline and propaganda. Two critical years were taken from young men's lives; held up their launching of family and career. For this imposition, they were paid about $7 per month in pocket money.

One day in 1975 we were in the embarrassing position of having to borrow this money from the shallow pockets of our young soldier. Zdenka, Lulka, and I were on our way back from a few days in Budapest. Hungarian TV had filmed a documentary about our work, and I had some blocked money there, so we had to go there to spend it. As a "brother communist" city, Budapest was one of the few places Czechs could visit with little difficulty. But even among socialist countries, money was not freely exchangeable. Czechs were allowed to take a small amount of Czech crowns on foreign trips. I was not. On our way back I was pulled over for speeding, and the two ladies had to pay my fine on the spot. We were running low on gas, and realized we could not make it to Prague on what was in the tank.

"Look," said Zdenka. "We could make it to David's army camp. Maybe we can borrow enough from him to buy some gas."

We were not driving my old marshmallow Saab. We were driving our brand-new banana-yellow Mercedes-Benz 4-door limousine, my own personal indulgence to celebrate our growing success.

"You can't drive this thing up to an army camp," said Zdenka. "You'll have to park a good distance away, and I'll walk."

We had detoured to the town of Jaroměř, and the camp was dead ahead. I quickly pulled over in the shade of a large tree, and Zdenka got out and nipped up to the camp entrance. I could see her waving her arms to the guard, who was intimidated enough to let her go right in.

Then suddenly I saw a group of army officers striding toward me. "Christ, they've spotted me." I winced: "*American in Mercedes, spying on Czechoslovak Army!*" As they marched closer, I desperately tried to think of what I would tell them. "We're just here to borrow gasoline money from one of your soldiers!" Sure - that sounds reasonable! As the group reached my car I decided my best ploy was to say nothing at all. The maximum: *name, rank, and serial number.*

"Sir," said the ranking officer, smartly saluting. "We wonder if you wouldn't mind showing us your motor?" I blinked, then happily jumped out of the car to raise the hood. Once again I realized that, after beer and sex, the most important thing to a Czech male - and that included army officers - was the love of a fine automobile.

A month later, when David's personnel records reached his camp, the stigmatic fact that he had an American stepfather reached the commandant. Suddenly, things were not so jolly. David went from being somehow related to a Mercedes-Benz, directly to the shitlist. It was totally unacceptable to have a soldier in their midst who might well be a spy for the Americans. He might even disclose their most highly guarded secrets, such as the damp and dingy barracks, the greasy food, the fetid latrines, and the rusted tanks. But joking aside, being thrown out of the army was not at all the happy ending to this situation as one might think. Every Czech had to carry a little citizen's passbook in which was written the holder's entire record. All personal details, all jobs, every infraction, was entered. To have a black mark in that book for being expelled from the army would lock David out of any chance for university or decent job.

But Zdenka was as unfazed by this as by anything else that blocked her way. With her canny Czech understanding of how things really worked here, she sprang into action. Whereas fear generally prevented people from bucking the regime in any way, and most people simply resigned themselves to coping with the way things were, Zdenka always knew how to beat them at their own game. In her view, no situation is completely hopeless.

She traveled from Prague to the Jaroměř military camp where David was sheltered, and demanded a meeting with the commandant.

Absolutely flustered by this unseemly intrusion into the military enclaves, the Colonel greeted her brusquely. But Zdenka leaned confidently over his desk, and quietly gave him the word:

"Comrade Colonel," she said, "I understand that my son is in trouble here because of my husband. But I want you to know that my husband's presence in this country has been approved on the highest level." (Well, I did have a business residence visa...) "Comrade, if you persist in making problems for my son it might reflect badly on you..."

The officer sprang to his feet. He kissed Zdenka's hand. Then he ushered her out of his office with a beaming smile of assurance.

What he did not do was check out her story. He never made a phone call. He knew the golden rule of survival in the Communist regime: Better not to ask!

David went on to become a sergeant, and after his two years, left the army with a certificate of honor.

This is not the Certifikate of Honor, but a sign that hung prominently in David's army barracks.

It says:

"KEEP YOUR MOUTH SHUT

Don't speak with anyone
you dont know well about anything you see or hear

Don't speak openly
at public places about the work you are doing in the Army. Enemies are listening everywhere

Don't write
to your relatives or friends about your unit. Be wary in all your conversations, on the telephone or in letters

Follow this exactly
or you will be guilty of revealing State or military secrets, and put in danger our socialistic motherland and the interests of its army"

MLČ

Nemluv nikdy
před tím, koho dobře neznáš, co jsi viděl nebo slyšel, a hlavně, kde jsi přidělen.

Nebav se otevřeně
na veřejných místech o práci, kterou vykonáváš. Nepřítel naslouchá všude.

Nepiš
svým příbuzným a známým domů o své jednotce, buď opatrný při všech rozhovorech, i telefonických, a hlavně v korespondenci.

Řiď se přesně
tímto nařízením, jinak vyzrazuješ státní i vojenské tajemství a tím vydáváš v nebezpečí naší socialistickou vlast a zájmy armády.

Color Folio From
Chapter 59 – Your
Secret Prague
Guide Book

All photos by Gene Deitch.

Look closely at the
sculpture of St. Rocus
on the "Golden Well"
house on Karlova Street,
and you will see that his
loyal pooch has bitten
off the saint's testicles
to ensure his chastity.
See the blood running
down Rocus' leg?
See the little dog-gie's
puffed-up cheeks?
Now that is truly a
dedicated doggie!

This imposing monument to Austro-Hungarian emperor, Franz-Joseph, on the Smetana bank of the Vltava River is totally devoid of the late emperor's statue... Gone with the winds of change!

This mischievous maedieval dude, pushing his hand up the skirt of a medieval lady can be seen discreetly displayed on a corner of the Old Town Bridge Tower on the Charles Bridge.

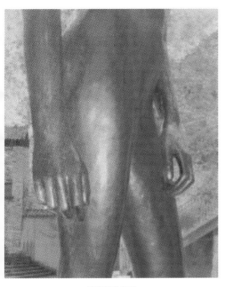 

BEFORE   *AFTER*

See: The Mystery of The Bronze Penis in Chapter 59!

The communists were not big on good taste.
I made this shot on May Day in 1964.

This crucifix is unique in the world.
The story in Chapter 59.

Our Mostecká Street, but only this deserted at 6AM Sunday morning!

When I step out of our door each morning on Mostecka St.
the towers of St. Nicholas loom imposingly on my left
And it's even more impressive flodlit at night!

The shrine of the washerwomen of Prague. Note the wringers at the sides of the image of the Virgin. I took this shot before the Spring flowers were put out, but the little light glows all the time.

This is already the third generation of the famous "Lennon Wall" across from the French embassy In the Malá Strana. When the wall becomes overclogged with stuff, it's painted over and started anew.

This is the wacko "Dancing Building" on the Rašin Embankment. Some say it doesn't fit into Prague architecture, but the truth is that Prague architecture has always been wacko....

What about the most Famous tower in Prague, the St. Vitus Cathedral crowning the Prague Castle? It's the only cathedral in the world whose tower abruptly changes from gothic to baroque on its way to heaven! You can see that in one straight line the gothic ends. The Hapsburg Catholics "modernized" the 400 – year-dormant church by finishing off the tower in their favorite-baroque style.

46 - Escape!

David is now an American citizen, but his mama, Zdenka, is not. Again, flabbergasting all who thought she was marrying me to get out of the country and become an American, she has never wanted to leave permanently. She wanted the freedom to travel, but also the freedom to return. Those who escaped could not return. Returned escapees went to prison. David was ready to accept a legal one-way ticket if only he could get out. In this country he was up against a stone wall. As I was partly the cause of his anguish, I felt I had to do what I could to help him...

In the 1960s, when David was still a boy, and as the country's liberalization slowly built up steam towards 1968, we were able to have David travel with us. His father would try to block it each year, but Zdenka doggedly took him to court to demand her holiday rights with David. Once he was an adult, it was easier for a while. We were able to help him get a trip to America on his own, and here is where I let myself in for years of recriminations from Mama Zdenka: I insisted on a promise from David that he return exactly when his exit visa expired.

This was during the second "Dark Age," in the late 1970s. My feelings were always, [1] to protect Zdenka, (if her son escaped, she would be denied travel, and maybe worse), [2] to protect my own residency rights, and [3] to protect my clients' work. Contracts were signed. Films were in production. All three elements were interconnected, and as much as we wanted to help David get the freedom he craved, I felt he had to be patient until we could devise a plan to do it in such a way that would not incriminate us. We couldn't risk a smoking gun.

Obtaining travel permission often rested on one's behavior during previous trips. If you returned on time and didn't make contact abroad with "imperialist circles," your next exit visa would be easier to obtain. The Communists assumed that those wanting to flee would do it on their first trip abroad, never being sure they would have another chance. So my strategy was to have David go to America, and *return.*

David and Zdenka held the standard Czech feeling that one should take whatever opportunity is at hand. Zdenka proclaimed that she was not afraid of the consequences. I was. The trip to America for David had been obtained on my application, and on my assurance that he would return. I had to read the riot act to David over the phone to New York, where he was staying with Allen Swift. Allen was in sympathy with my concerns, and had phoned to tell me that David really wanted to stay. I insisted that he return not one day later than the expiration date on his visa, and that we would immediately plan another trip for him.

He did return, and in due time he applied on his own for himself and his girlfriend for two weeks in Yugoslavia. A month later, (only a legitimate family funeral could gain faster approval), his girl got her exit visa, but David received the standard registered bad-news letter from the Passport Department. It was that dark old message again:

"YOUR REQUESTED JOURNEY IS DENIED ON THE
GROUNDS THAT SUCH TRAVEL IS NOT IN THE INTEREST
OF THE STATE."

Of all potential responses, that was the worst. How in the world could a person prove a desired vacation trip is "in the interest of the State?" The additional line, "There is no appeal from this decision," was hardly even necessary. It was clearly a total "No!"

But why? On what grounds? He'd been a good boy, (at my insistence), and had returned promptly from his last trip. So why the rejection? What we didn't know was that they were putting together their own mean little plan to entrap us. Worse for David was that his girlfriend did not return! She phoned us to say she was sure we could "easily get David out." She was wrong.

Only much later did we hear the following background information pertaining to David's refused visa - information we could never have guessed, and which put my original plan onto the scrap heap:

David, who was full of speculative ideas on how to make money, had once heard that computer keyboards could be sold in Prague for astronomical sums. In those days of no computers here, some clever technicians were able to make a sort of computer, but not the keyboards. It was like Janda's stereo all over again! So if David could bring in a computer keyboard, he could realize enough money from selling it to start a nice savings account. But unfortunately the guys David sold the keyboard to were engaged in smuggling a lot of such items, and were caught. The trail inevitably led to David. It was not a serious offense, but David had to explain how he brought the keyboard in. The way the Communists worked was to save evidence of minor infractions

- in this case the non-payment of a small import duty on the keyboard - in case they someday needed to pull you in for a political infraction. They never admitted that they had political prisoners. All prisoners, they claimed, were "criminals." The fact is that David brought in the keyboard legally, in his backpack. He declared it on the customs paper as he entered, but it was 2AM when he crossed the border, and the customs agents did not bother to look at it. So David had no proof that he brought it in legally. Okay, so that was a minor flap. The next one was a pisser.

David was the captain of an amateur softball team. It was successful enough that they were able to play teams that came in from other countries. One such team was from West Germany, which included a couple of Americans. One of the American members of the team was a US Army Captain from one of our West German installations. He came to Prague in civilian dress of course. When he arrived at customs, he gave David's name as the person he was here to visit. He did not know David, but had simply gotten David's name as captain of the softball team. Neither did David know him, nor did he know he was an American soldier. The softball games were played, the Captain went home, and that was that.

But now the plot sickens. After the third standard "Not-in-the interest-of-the -State" turndown for an exit visa, David received a visit that made everything crystal clear. (By this time David had his own flat, which he had gotten from a friend who married an American woman and legally left the country.) David's visitor was a Secret Police agent. He started out real friendly-like:

"We know you have had some difficulty in getting permission to travel. I believe I can help you."

David had no love for the Secret Police, but he listened.

"The fact is, there are some serious charges against you. We have good reason to believe that you contacted an American Army Captain when you were in America, and arranged for him to come into our country disguised as a baseball player, but with the real purpose of spying on the State."

David was stunned. How could they put 2 and 2 together and get 6? How in the world could he convincingly disprove such hogwash?

"But don't worry," continued the fink. "We can find a way to solve this problem. We can help you if you'll help us..."

And here came the stinger:

"Your stepfather is an American. I am sure that he could get you a job working in the American Embassy..."

227

That was enough for David. He threw the scumbag out of his apartment. As he left, the agent delivered this parting shot:

"You can kiss foreign travel goodbye!"

That was actually the culminating moment of weeks of continuous harassment, which had included constant phone calls and unannounced visits to David's apartment. At the time, David was attending law school and was preparing for his final dissertation. But the constant bullying made it impossible for him to concentrate. He felt the Secret Police were trying to force him to fail at Law School, and to in fact force him to want to emigrate, while at the same time making it impossible for him to do so.

So that was it. Things now seemed totally impossible, and of course it was all my fault for not letting David stay when he was in America.

I was in the doghouse, but what Zdenka didn't quite understand was that David had been to America on a tourist visa. Anyone who visited the US on a tourist visa could not apply for asylum. I had already been to Vienna, where there is an office of the US Department of Immigration, and I had applied for a full-fledged immigration visa for David. As a result of another one of the stunning coincidences punctuating our lives, Zdenka and I happened to get married just five days before David's 10th birthday. We of course hadn't given that a thought at the time, but it turned out to be vital. According to U.S. Immigration requirements, I had to be married to David's mother before his 10th birthday for him to be considered to be my legal stepson. As such, he had the right to residency in America!

The catch now was, how to get him there? I had all the papers prepared to get him *into* America; now Zdenka went into action to get him *out* of Czechoslovakia. She demanded a meeting with the responsible parties at the department of Passports and Visas. As with the army commandant, this was something the average Czech would not dream of even trying. Messing with these guys could ruin your life for all time!

But at this point there was no other option. A year had gone by since David's girlfriend had left. She was now way ahead of him in adapting to American life and learning English.

Zdenka wrote letter after letter before her persistence finally resulted in an invitation for an interview. An inner office of the Department of Passport and Visas was rarely open to an ordinary citizen. There were two people in the room; the usual method. One simply stood in the corner and said nothing. Zdenka did not plead. She attacked.

228

"How could you possibly try to damage my husband by suggesting he plant my son as a spy in the American Embassy? My husband is doing important work here, work that brings millions of dollars into our country, (a delightful exaggeration), and you are trying to ruin that! --You are acting against the interests of the State! And you are refusing my son the opportunity to travel if he does not comply with your irresponsible request!"

These guys were set back on their heels by this onslaught, delivered with vehemence and tears. They were more used to supplicants on their knees. Without saying one word in reference to spying at the American Embassy, they quickly switched to the question of travel. Zdenka thinks that at this point they realized their line of action was going to get them nowhere but Trouble Town, and that perhaps the best all-around solution for them would be to just get rid of this kid.

But that's only hypothetical. What the guy actually said was:

"Please, Mrs. Deitchová, we have nothing against your son traveling."

"What? Then why are you constantly denying his requests?"

"It's just a matter of a few crowns duty he didn't pay for importing a computer keyboard."

"So why didn't you just say that, instead of constantly writing that his request was not in the interest of the State? All my son wanted to do was to visit for one week his aged grandmother in a sanitarium in Zurich!"

(No answer to that either. The Grandmother bit was the centerpiece of our plan. Trips to the West were mainly granted only on invitations from blood relatives. David didn't have a real grandmother in the West. The granny in question was actually my mother. She was not in Zürich, but she could be...)

"If that is the case, then we must have a notarized letter of invitation from his grandmother..." Zdenka immediately realized that the man was handing it to us on a silver platter. I phoned my mother. She wrote the necessary pro forma letter, and I had it notarized.

Our problem now was that time was running out. The basic statement we had made to the passport police was that we were *all* going to see my mother. The Zürich location for our imaginary meeting was just an off-hand choice, because my mother did in fact go there nearly every year with my stepfather, but usually later in the year. This was May 1984, and the reason time was important was that Zdenka's own exit visa was good only until May 15. She had applied for it earlier, when we thought David would get the permission to travel.

The exit visa the Passport Police had promised for David took a month to actually arrive. An interesting tip-off as to what was really happening came when David received notice that his exit visa was ready, and he went to the police station to pick it up. He had applied only for a week, but the issuing officer said, "We can give you a month, or even longer, if you wish." David kept his cool, and didn't grab at this bait. "A week is all I can take away from my job," he said. "A week will be enough." (Honk if you get it! One day would've been enough!)

Another cliffhanger element added to the tension. David had broken his two front teeth in a fall, and didn't want to enter the West front-toothless. His new teeth were delayed because the dental laboratory in Prague had a power outage. So David wanted to wait a couple of days to get his teeth. My feeling was that after all we had gone through to get his exit visa, and with Zdenka's visa expiring in three days, to hell with the teeth. "We can get your teeth fixed in Vienna," I insisted. "We can't miss this window of opportunity!"

And of course Vienna, not Zürich, was our actual goal. Vienna was where David's U.S. immigration papers were waiting! Nonetheless, having set up this charade, we had to go through with it. It was vital that David have a Swiss tourist visa in his passport to match the Swiss permission on his official exit visa. He could only have an Austrian transit visa. So our route would take us out of Czechoslovakia via a southwestern border crossing to Austria, as if we were on our way to Switzerland. Then, once across the border, we would turn east and head for Vienna. Insane, but the whole business was insane. If only we had known then that just four-and-a-half years later all of these idiot travel restrictions would vanish!

But we didn't, and we were going through all the usual uncertainty and exhausting procedures that Czechs had to go through for each and every trip abroad. It meant that I had to line up at the Swiss embassy to get David's Swiss visa, while David stood in line at the Austrian embassy to get his transit visa. Zdenka, meanwhile, was standing in line at the German embassy for her own visa to Germany - another facet of our plan which I haven't mentioned yet, but which will soon become clear.

The reason I had to personally apply for David's Swiss visa was because, at that time, the Swiss demanded you show them *actual Swiss money* in an amount they deemed necessary for the number of days you were requesting. If you couldn't show them the Swiss banknotes or other hard currency equivalent, you didn't get the visa. Fortunately, I had enough cash with me.

We were all in a sweat, but we got all the necessary papers ready just one day before Zdenka's Czech exit-visa expired. The local tooth factory was still smacking empty gums, so I said, "We're going *now!*"

When we approached the southwest Czech border cross point to Austria, a village called Dolní Dvořiště, David fell silent. It was never to be ruled out that an order could be waiting there, canceling the exit permission. The border cop took all of our passports and disappeared into his bunker. There was the usual interminable wait. I looked at David, who just stared straight ahead. Zdenka was noticeably working her fingers. I was sweating. Finally the guy emerged and asked if we were carrying any Czech currency or gifts. "No," we shook our heads. "Nothing..."

Even after we were waved to proceed, it seemed an endless couple of kilometers until we reached the actual border and the Austrian customs building. When we did, David immediately started breathing again. *We were out!*

We took David to a dental lab in Vienna recommended by our friends there, and David had his tooth impressions made. The teeth would not be ready for three days, so David had to stretch his "transit visa." His magic papers, allowing immigration to the United States were ready. We gave him money for his flight to San Francisco, where my youngest brother lives. We bade him farewell and good luck, and Zdenka and I left for Zürich. Why? Because Zdenka needed a Swiss stamp in her passport in case we had to show that she really went there. But why the visa to Germany?

By chance, I had been invited to speak at one of the American schools attached to our army units in Germany, and that gave us an airtight solution to protect ourselves from being accused of masterminding an escape. This was our "official" story:

"We all three went to Zürich, where we had a wonderful visit with my mother, David's "grandmother," who was so happy to see him! Zdenka and I then had to proceed to Germany for the lecture, but unfortunately, there hadn't been time in Prague to get David a German visa, so we gave him train fare back to Prague and told him we would see him there in two days."

David telephoned his father that he had decided not to return. When we returned to Prague, his father phoned us with the news. We were "shocked!" David had "betrayed" us!

By law, his father had to report to the police that his son had illegally emigrated. So the police questioned him - not us! Nothing further happened to the father, but after all the trouble he had given Zdenka over the years, we didn't shrink from this small revenge. The son he took away from her was now out of his reach, but within hers.

Zdenka "wept" when she told her Communist studio boss about how her son left her, and he duly comforted her. We never had any fallout from the operation.

When it was discovered that he had fled, David was tried in absentia and sentenced to three years in prison. That, of course, concerned him not, and today it's just an ironic joke of the past. He could not visit his country again until after the "Velvet Revolution." Now he comes and goes as often as he likes.

The dangerous and risky 1985 escape is a story we can now tell in safety!

47 - Fanynka,
Our Witch-of-The-Wash

"Fanynka," (Fanny), was how we knew her. Her name was Františka Šepková. This snaggle-toothed wreck of indeterminate age was your image of a Bag Woman. Dressed in layers of well-worn, motley fabric, she arrived at our door in the mid-60s, carrying all of her worldly possessions in cloth bags slung around her neck. "There are thieves in my house and thieves in the banks," she informed us. "I don't trust any of them!"

Fanynka came to us on good recommendation from our good friend Zdenka Skřípková, as a wacko but clean and hard-working washwoman. In the Czechoslovakia of the 60s there was no such a thing produced as an automatic clotheswasher. One could be obtained from Tuzex, or I could have brought one from Germany, but there was the matter of repair, spare parts, a dryer, and an ironer. Our tiny flat could not hold such an array of equipment, and Zdenka nor I had the time to man them. What there was was a communal wash room in the attic of our building, with a monster clothes-boiling tub fed with live steam, a centrifuge for expelling most of the wash water, and a large electric mangle for ironing bedsheets and tablecloths.

Fanynka was one who could master this environment, and so she became our bi-monthly washerwoman, and indeed, housecleaner. When our doorbell rang on her appointed days, I could hear her already beginning to expound outside the closed door. When we opened it, her continuous monolog merely became louder.

"Madam," she greeted Zdenka, "Madam, I hope you will have a proper lunch prepared for me today. Last time, the chicken was without taste, and the soup was sour!" Fanynka was a fussy harridan. She demanded the finest Hungarian salami and Pilsner beer, and complained loudly if by chance we neglected to lay in a supply of these rare commodities.

She adressed me as "Mr. Engineer." I tried to explain to her that I had no title, and was just and ordinary joe. But no, I was her client, and a title was thus required! She insisted on telling us about the "noble" families she worked for, and I suppose she told them how noble we were. "Mr. Engineer, there were some strange spots on your shorts. You should be more careful!"

But that was only a minor embarrassment. Once, after a particularly idyllic holiday in Paris, Zdenka and I returned just before Fanynka's appointed day. We dumped all of our dirty clothes into our hamper. After finishing the wash, Fanynka cackled in mock consternation as she descended from her attic travail. *"Mr. Engineer, your pajama bottoms are missing! Did you forget them in Paris?"* This was delivered in short phrases, punctuated with a rollicking laugh as she hobbled down the stairway. My "missing pajama bottoms" became her favorite topic of hilarity for months to come.

Bluntness was her way, but as outrageous as she was, we became thoroughly attached to her, and she to us. When Zdenka had her 50th birthday, Fanynka arrived in tears, throwing her arms around Zdenka in great pity. "Madame," she sobbed, "It's terrible! *After 50 it's downhill all the way!"*

Fanynka was too rare to be thrown out. She even did windows, for Lord's sake! Domestic help was even harder to come by than an automatic washer. We not only tolerated Fanynka, we lived in fear that she might abandon us.

Should I ever dare to invade her steamy sanctuary in the attic, as she did the wash, she never failed to have a few dozen rapidly stated complaints. It was worth it just to take in the sight of her, in the steamy mists, with a long stick poking and stirring the boiling pre-wash, and to hear the rumble of the great galvanized wash barrel rocking back and forth, powered by an immense old electric motor, with the piping-hot water gushing and sloshing around the clothes inside. When the wash cycle ended, Fanynka released the water, and it rushed out onto the concrete floor, gurgling into drains spaced around the room. She stood in her rubber boots on wooden pallets laid out over most of the floor area.

When she was doing bedsheets, she employed the most unusual clothes drying equipment I had yet seen. Across from the washroom itself was a small area that had painted steel rails coming out across the ceiling. There were four 6-foot-high vertical drawers set into the opposite wall. When the handles were pulled, the drawers rolled out on the rails, revealing long smooth wooden bars. The sheets were hung over these bars, and then the drawers were pushed in. Fanynka had previously requested the house superintendent to turn on the heat to radiators in the 9x10 foot compartment within. This rising heat dried the sheets.

After the washing, she would come down into our apartment, taking over the kitchen, to do the regular ironing, all the while regaling us with one wild tale after another. When Fanynka was here, Zdenka and I had no chance to talk with each other.

The attic washroom, as it was in Fanynka's day

After is was redone as my workroom where I wrote this book 1995

For all her raggedy-auntie image, Fanynka soon revealed herself to us in tales of her wild youth. She came from the east of the country, and spoke fluent Hungarian and German. It became more than clear from her tales that she had done quite well for herself with the German occupation soldiers during the war! "Madame, a girl had to get along in those days!" she told Zdenka.

Even though her appearances completely upset my workdays, we became very fond of Fanynka. We visited her in the hospital when she had to have a hernia operation, and as she became older and arthritic, no longer able to do the vigorous work she had done before, we tried to find out if she had relatives, or a place to go in retirement. She never did reveal exactly where she lived, but from her description we imagined the worst. She did have a sister in Moravia, and eventually she left us. She sent us postcards from time to time, but after a few years the postcards stopped. We were unable to trace her.

When she was gone, the moldering attic washroom fell into disuse. Other tenants had gradually acquired their own washing machines. We, who could have afforded one the soonest, were the last to acquire one. With Fanynka, we were the last tenants to use the old washroom. During building repairs, workman used it as a place to change their clothes, and to sit and drink beer. After the revolution, it dawned on me that here was our one and only chance for expansion. I had commandeered our dining room table for my animation work and for my computer, and Zdenka and I also worked in the kitchen.

I had long dreamed of a little studio space, and I suddenly realized that the grungy old washroom could be it!

Just after the revolution, there was that short, golden time of disorganization, when things could be done. One of David's old girl friends was working in the still State-run organization that controlled apartments, and she was able to get me the lease on the space, providing I would remodel it at my own expense.

When I went up the stairs to look at it, I wasn't so sure. It was filthy. Cobwebs, old shoes, filthy overalls, empty beer bottles, and countless cigarette butts only represented a minor problem to get rid of. But what of the reinforced concrete sinks, the monstrous galvanized washing machine, centrifuge, and the mangle? The drain holes in the floor? Our old friend Toník Růžička, who did so much on our chalupa, worked the miracles, and the former dark and desolate utility room is now my white-walled, cork-floored ashram, where I do my film storyboard work, and where I am writing this book.

The only memories of its former function are the white-painted stubs of the steampipes and faucet handles, which I left as a reminder. Looking around this room now, just one flight up from our apartment living quarters, and seeing the computer, scanner, printer, copying machine, drawing desk, the shelves full of hundreds of children's books, the pictures on the walls, it would be hard for anyone to see what it was. But of course I know... Goodbye, Fanynka, wherever you are!

"Fanynka," Our Witch-Of-The-Wash! Cca.1976

48 - Gypsy!

"Gypsy Queen!" "My Little Gypsy Sweetheart!"
"When the Gypsy Plays His Magic Violin!" "It's Just the Gypsy In My Soul!"

These were the romanticized images of Gypsies I brought to Prague from my American culture. It was a shock to me when I heard my first anti-Gypsy joke. An English-speaking Czech pinned me with this one on my very first visit. Though delivered with tongue well planted in cheek, I sensed it expressed his true feelings. It reflected the official Communist line condemning the evils of America, but with a real Czech stinger at the end:

"Mr. Deitch, we have heard many terrible things about how you Americans are lynching Negroes in the South. That is horrible and despicable, a terrible, beastly, and inhuman thing... Now, if they were *Gypsies*, we could understand!"

Both in communist times, and after the revolution, I saw hate-filled graffiti scrawls: "GYPSIES TO THE GAS CHAMBER!", "GYPSIES OUT!", "CZECHIA FOR WHITES!" It was impossible for me to plead Gypsy tolerance to Czechs (and this included Zdenka) without alienating myself in the process.

I was raised in the Hollywood area. From my earliest school days my classmates included kids of Japanese, Chinese, Mexican, African, Jewish, Italian, Irish, Arab... all manner of ethnic origin. Prejudice about race never even occurred to me. I was so naive about it that I had never heard the term "Jim Crow," and never even knew there was racial segregation in the South until my late teens! Once I did learn of it, I became a campaigner for equal rights for blacks, something I suffered for during the McCarthy period.

I have lived through times when Americans of African or partial African descent were offended by the label "black," and wanted to be called "Negro" or even "colored." Then they did want to be called black. The latest preference, of course, is "African-American." But to me this seems like a bad idea.

I would not want to be labeled "Jewish-American," or "European-American," or any other isolating label. At the very least, all of us who were born or naturalized as citizens of the United States of America should simply be called "Americans." If anyone asks me what I am, I like to announce that I am an "Earthling." Further, if it is found to be biologically necessary for us to hate another group, I would be willing to hate Martians.

"DEATH TO ALL MARTIANS!" "OUT WITH ALL MARTIAN SCUM!" "MARTIANS GO HOME!" I would go for that if it would help bring us Earthlings together.

As I observe our troubled planet, it seems to me that presumed cultural and religious differences are the bases of hatred, as opposed to racial differences alone. I feel I could relate to anyone of any race per se, but would inevitably be put off by an intense advocate of any specific way of thinking, (now called "fundamentalism"). In this country and other Central European countries, the problem of the Gypsies is a cultural impasse.

Whereas our Americans of dark skin or of differing ethnic origin have traditionally struggled to integrate, the Gypsies generally do not. They seem to defy all efforts to be brought into the mainstream. A vicious circle keeps them as perpetual outsiders. Many cannot get decent jobs because they are dirty, ragged, and uneducated. They cannot be well dressed, because they have little income. Many are not well educated because parents don't send them to school, but teach them how to steal or beg. They are bitter because they are hated, but they want to keep themselves separate. They want to maintain their own culture, and revel in their own ways. The Czechs cannot understand them, and do not want to understand them. The division between white Czechs (and Slovaks) and Gypsies is truly an iron curtain.

"90% of all crime is committed by Gypsies!"

"They destroy and spit on everything we try to give them!"

"Even when the Communist government built special housing for them, and an apartment was given to a Gypsy family, within days fifty of their relatives and several goats moved in."

"They tore up the floorboards and made fires in the middle of the rooms!"

"Gypsy women have one child after another, and live perpetually on welfare."

"They are smelly, vulgar thieves, pickpockets and slackers!"

Those are ravings I heard here over and over. Does any of it sound familiar? Our *chalupa* has been robbed several times. Each time the police told us it was "probably Gypsies." It turned out the perpetrators were white. In one case the police were unable to arrest the robbers, even though they were caught with the stolen goods. *"If we confront them with an accusation, they will tell us that they bought the stuff from some Gypsies, and we could not prove otherwise."* (Prove-shmoove; the police readily believed it...)

In another incident, we hired a couple of Gypsies to dig a trench and install a drainage channel at the bottom of our driveway. A police patrol car stopped and demanded to see their papers, questioning them sharply as to what they were doing there, later asking us if we knew what we were doing.

Those workers never approached or entered our cottage, but two weeks later our cottage was robbed. On the following weekend, the local police chief drove up, came into our cottage, and gave us hell. *"You brought this robbery on yourselves because you hired those Gypsies!"* he said. And before he left, this minion of the law uttered these words: *"In my opinion, the only good Gypsy is a dead Gypsy!"* Imagine a cop like that under cross-examination at an American trial! As it turned out, the robbers were caught, and once again they were white.

Because nearly every white Czech believes integrating with Gypsies is impossible, and because most Gypsies do not *want* to be integrated, the situation does seem to be intractable.

The lesson I have drawn from this, and from the devastation in the former Yugoslavia, is that it is not really *race* that divides us. We are indeed all Earthlings. The actual divisive factor of intolerance and conflict is culture, religion, and superstition.

Look at Bosnia and Kosovo: The Serbs and the Moslems of the Baltics *are all Slavs.* There is no racial or color difference between them at all. They are the same breed, the same nationality. Only *religion* divides them. Look at the Israelis and Palestinians. Look at the Protestant and Catholic Irish. They also are of the same ethnic origin. Religion, superstition, and historical conflict divide them.

Why did many American whites hate Negroes? *"They sang and danced to wild rhythms."* *"They were living with apes."* *"They stuck bones through their noses, painted their bodies, and conducted orgiastic rituals."* What about Jews? *"They killed Jesus."* *"They drank children's blood."* *"They controlled all governments."* *"They had weird, wailing rituals."* And the Muslims? *"They deify a man."* *"They are not afraid to die."* *"They have weird, wailing rituals."* The Catholics? *"They deify a man."* *"They believe in miracles."* *"They have weird, wailing rituals."*... And so on.

240

And now our white kids tattoo their bodies, stick rings through their ears, noses, lips, tongues, and belly buttons, and participate in weird and wailing rituals at rock concerts...

Why is it that our American government grants tax exemption to religions, when anyone can set up a religion, become rich enough to fortify and isolate himself from other religions, and create more and more levels of divisiveness? Our U. S. constitution grants freedom of religion, but I cannot find where it grants tax exemption. Did I miss something?

The hatred and mistrust of Gypsies here is not specifically religious, but cultural and superstitious. *"They can read palms, and tell fortunes, and have secret wailing rituals!"*

From the beginning I felt Czechs were the most racist people I knew of. In truth, some Czech Gypsies *do* steal, *do* become black marketeers, do milk welfare, do pick pockets... What is not asked is *why?* What is not mentioned is that what Gypsies steal is small change. The real, world-class, big bucks stealing in this country is done by squeaky clean white guys in power suits and ties.

A breakthrough was the election of a brilliant 24-year-old Gypsy woman, Monika Horáková, to the Czech parliament. She has the idea to put forth a bill to create a Ministry for Minorities, but she realizes that she will have a hard slog. She acknowledges that one barrier to Gypsy integration is their cultural habit, as she says, *"to live each day fully, and not think of tomorrow. But we are a minority. If we want to be integrated we must accept the principles of the majority. If we don't we will look like fools!"*

I wish her great success, but I would not like to see all cultural and religious differences eradicated. It is precisely the cultural and racial variety of humankind that makes all of us interesting. The only answer is *tolerance* and *appreciation* of these differences. Education is the only way to straighten this particular vicious circle. In the meantime, a "Gypsy Appreciation Week" in this country would be a tough sell!

In more recent times a tremendous international gasp was heard when white residents on a street name Matiční in the North Bohemian town of Ustí nad Labem, erected a fence to ostensibly separate themselves from noisy Gypsy neighbors. The international media decried this as racist wall building at a time when we were all celebrating the destruction of the Berlin Wall. This made ironic headlines in the world press, which did this country's reputation no good whatsoever. However, in truth it was really not a wall on Matiční

Street, but a *fence*, which was not solid, but had openings along it through which people could freely pass. Nevertheless, it had to come down, and it did. The real irony was that the countries that most loudly condemned the "wall," simultaneously threatened to impose visa requirements for all Czech citizens, for the clear purpose of keeping Gypsies out of their own countries! (Many Czech Gypsies had been trying to seek asylum in various European countries.) The "wall" came down but soon a racist Internet game went up. "Struggle for the rights of the white race" is the subtitle of a computer game where you try to shoot Gypsy heads that pop up behind a wall. The Czech police have a hard time trying to find the creators of this evil game and to find a way to prosecute and jail them.

Even without these demented hate driven activists, the fact is that no one wants the Gypsies. The Czech white population by and large does not consider Gypsies to be Czechs. They see them as "foreign residents," even though they are bona fide Czech citizens, and have resided in this country for hundreds of years. Many Czechs call them "black," or even "black pigs." The hatred seems irreconcilable. If I attempt to argue in the Gypsy's favor, I get the inevitable challenge: "Would you want to live in the same building with them?" No. Not under present circumstances, but the question assumes an unchangeable fact of life, and I don't for a minute believe there is no solution whatever. I am not in favor of walls or fences. It takes two to tango, and without a willingness to meet and discuss, and to seek mutual ways of understanding, then there is no living together.

Education is at the core. We are not born haters. We are taught to hate. If we can be taught to hate I believe we can be taught tolerance. It will be a long process, as with the seemingly intractable hatreds between Catholic and Protestant Irish, and Jews and Arabs of Israel. White and Gypsy Czechs at least are not at war. There are not decades of mass bloodshed to overcome. At least that. Somehow they must be led to co-existence.

This is not a "Gypsy Shack," but was actually our "temporary" animation studio on the muddy Barrandov movie studio back lot. We worked in there for 10 years while awaiting the construction of the new, modern animation building, which was (wait for it!), actually being worked on by a group of Gypsies! So help me... (They did a good job. The new building is fine.)

49 - Gentle Rebellion

Real rebellion still had to wait, but there were many delicious little pinpricks possible to irritate the communist thugs in charge.

The most painful for the authorities occurred just after Dubček was toppled. Emil Zátopek, the world famous multiple Olympic gold medallist - one of the heroes of Czechoslovak pride - was so bitter at the invasion that he decided to humiliate the government by becoming a garbage collector. He was actually fired from this lowly job, because people all along his route kept helping him collect garbage and shouting encouragement!

My own favorite bug-up-the-rear for the communists involved a little wooden direction sign with Russian lettering saying, "SMICHOV." Smíchov is a district of Prague that borders our Malá Strana section. Embedded in a wall in a quiet Malá Strana square was this little sign, just a piece of board, about a foot and a half long and pointed on one end. It was a crude direction sign for the Soviet tanks, which belatedly liberated Prague in May 1945. The Communist government had this little direction sign embedded in the wall as a remembrance of the liberation, but after the 1968 Soviet-led invasion, the sign completely lost its original meaning. As a symbol of the occupation, it became a constant target for defacement. Every morning during that period, I would take my walk past that sign to see the latest desecration. One morning the Cyrillic letters would be completely painted out in black, and the next morning, lo! There was the sign, fresh and new again! One morning theentire sign would be ripped out of the wall, and within a day or two it was magically restored.

This cat-and-mouse game went on for years. Whatever defacement the unfortunate little sign suffered, a fresh duplicate always soon replaced it. I began to imagine that somewhere in Prague there must be a warehouse full of spare "Smichov" signs, or perhaps a crew of little elves in Soviet uniforms sawing up boards, painting them blue, and neatly painting on the white Cyrillic lettering. The city government, no doubt on orders from higher up, devoted endless patience and facilities to keep this obscure little sign in good shape. Its constant "desecration" was obviously a matter of great embarrassment to them, and very likely the Soviet embassy was not amused. Step by step the protection of the sign was escalated. For a while a policeman was assigned on all-night watch. But he must have snoozed, and I suppose he was reprimanded - for even on his watch the lettering had been hastily scratched out.

Then technology was employed. A video camera was mounted on an opposite wall. This time, not only did the sign disappear, but the camera too! A new sign was then enclosed in a glass case. I can't remember how many times I saw broken glass on the street, and black spray-paint obliterating the lettering. The last step was to put electronic sensors on the glass, such as those on jewelry store windows. In this case, the persistent defacers simply painted over the glass with thick green paint. Finally, the 1989 democratic revolution came, and now nobody cares about the sign any more. The people won. The little frame, and its final little defaced sign, can still be seen at the corner of Míšenská street, leading into U lužického semináře square.

Another example of persistent painting is the now famous Lennon wall. This is in the Maltese Square, just opposite the French embassy, also in Malá Strana. It was traditional for young people to write their love poems on that wall - all very innocent. But after John Lennon's murder, someone noticed a small, former opening in the wall, and painted it to resemble a gravestone. They lettered John Lennon's name and his dates of birth and death, put flowers there, and kept a candle burning.

The authorities never liked anything they couldn't understand, and when other lettering appeared on the wall, quoting some of Lennon's song lyrics, such as "GIVE PEACE A CHANCE," and signing Lennon's name, they cracked down. After all, the Communists had a patent on peace, and Lennon sounded like Lenin! They were sure it was a provocation. So once again the war of paint began. Every morning a posse of painters from the National Committee would appear and paint out everything that had been lettered on the wall the previous night. Which meant I had two comedies to watch on my morning walks. In this case, the city finally covered the entire wall with billboards, which were always plastered with the usual official slogans.

After the revolution, the boardings were pulled down, and a huge, full-color painting of John Lennon's face became the centerpiece of a wall completely full of Lennonabilia graffiti. It has been widely photographed - a good thing, because age and weather - not politics - had taken their toll. There was not much left of Lennon's face in recent times. Finally, the Maltese embassy has undertaken to restore it. But this has required the entire wall to be resurfaced and painted white. The Mexican student who painted Lennon's face had long gone away. New artists attempted to recreate the wall, and once again it became a jumble of words in tribute to Lennon, painted by hundreds of visitors... It's fine, but of course it's not the original, no longer illegal, and no longer so devilishly charming.

I took part in the next pinprick, but the Communists never found out about it so it became only our own private joke. Living in our building was the chief engineer of the Prague subway project, The Metro, which began construction in the late '60s. He had a Hungarian name - Szekely. As the one thing that worked, the Metro system was to become the Communist regime's greatest accomplishment. As the project chief and I were neighbors, one day he asked me if I would like to see the tunnel. There were rumors that there was more than a metro tunnel being installed, so of course no one except those on the work crew was allowed down there. My neighbor thought it would be a delicious joke to take an American "where none had gone before!"

So one day I was given a hard hat, and Engineer Szekely told me not to say a word as I walked through the tunnel. We entered by going down the incline that would soon hold the escalator at the Malostranská station in Klárov Square. This is the exact spot where the original animation studio had been, where Snyder first met Zdenka. That building had at last fulfilled its destiny as a "temporary structure," and was now gone. The tunnel itself was in the final stages of track laying, and there was great pressure to finish in time for the announced opening. This was the centerpiece of the authorities' hope to restore a modicum of approval from the disaffected population of Prague.

The tunnel continued under the Vltava River, heading toward the downtown center. About halfway through, I heard a loud, persistent honking, and saw a flashing red light. Engineer Szekely put his hand on my shoulder, indicating I should stop, and again signaled me to remain silent. Suddenly a huge round structure that had lain against the sidewall of the tunnel began to slowly arc inward on curved rails . It was in fact a giant door, the size of the tunnel itself, swinging shut. So that was the tunnel's secret! A great amount of extra money and effort was being put into a security bomb shelter. But for whom? Perhaps another indication of Communist paranoia. These sealing-off doors were placed at regular intervals along the entire length of the tunnel, their existence was never mentioned in any of the media. The regime obviously did not want anyone to know about them, especially an American. If I ever mentioned what I saw, it would not only cook my goose, but also that of the Chief Engineer who brought me down there as his little slap at the Communists. Szekely later emigrated to the West.

So I added another First-of-Little-Significance to my Prague saga: I was the first and only American to walk across Prague, from Klárov Square to the National Museum...underground!

The famous "Pink Tank" was a more visible statement than the defacing of the obscure little Smichov direction sign in Malá Strana. The tank was actually in Smichov, perched on a pedestal - highly visible. It was supposed to be the first Soviet tank to enter Prague during the May 1945 liberation. A young art student with a bucket of paint climbed up the pedestal one night and painted the entire tank a bright pink. This was actually after the revolution, but it still showed the people's contempt for anything Russian - even a tank that took part in their liberation from the Nazis. The pink tank drew tremendous crowds, and it finally had to be removed, including the pedestal. There is now only a patch of grass where it once stood.

There were hundreds of tinier acts of defiance throughout the entire '70s and '80s, leading up to the ultimate revolution. Mainly there was a pervasive cynicism and a collapse of any work ethic. Gorbachev's ascension to power in the Soviet Union made it easier to express dissent. Whatever we may think of Gorbachev today, the Czechs feel that he made possible their eventual liberation. The collapse of the Soviet Union was surely not his goal, but he, like Dubček, tried to do the impossible: "reform" socialism. I came to realize that socialism must be totalitarian. Once a single word of dissent or a single compromise is allowed, the whole thing collapses - which is exactly what happened. The invasion of 1968 was the Soviets' maximum effort to stifle change, and it inevitably became the beginning of their end.

The subtlest rebellion of all was the creation of the personage "Jára da Cimrman." This was a fictitious personality that predated Woody Allen's Zelig. It was the Czech's laughing-up-the-sleeve retort to their schooling here, which taught them that the Russians invented everything. The schoolbooks sought to prove that it was a Russian who really invented the telephone, the electric light, the phonograph, television - everything! So a few very bright comics started putting on pseudo-lectures about a "little known Czech eminence," with the Czechified name "Cimrman," phonetically derived from the German name, Zimmerman.

Bit by bit they created his entire life story, chose a remote village as his birthplace, and laced their lectures with projected slides of obscure 19th-century photos showing weird gadgets and experiments. It turned out that it was Cimrman who really invented everything; only he had the bad luck to arrive at the patent office just moments after Edison got there.

Photos of "Cimrman" were always fuzzy and indistinct. A few rusty cans of film were "discovered" in an ancient barn - the very first motion pictures, produced of course by Cimrman. Even copies of theatrical scripts were "found," and a "Jara da Cimrman Theater" was established. It runs to this day. Cimrman was also "proved" to have invented jazz, thus leading to wacky concerts. Ultimately, even a feature film of his life was produced here. Cimrman became a comic industry. At first the authorities were edgy, but being Communists they never really caught on to the gag that Cimrman was a parody of Lenin and the all-wise, all-clever, all-genius Soviets. The main creators of this widespread mythology were Zdeněk Svěrák,[1] Jan Smoljak, and our great friend, jazzman Karel Velebný, the very one who played at our wedding.

Sometimes there were just tiny-but-fun acts. One day I was walking down Prague's main drag, Václavské náměstí, (Wenceslas Square), when I heard unbelievable words booming over the entire square from a record store's loudspeakers:

"LIVIN' IN AMERICA! LIVIN' IN THE LAND OF THE FREE!"

These words were joyously sung, over and over again, at peak volume. Pedestrians seemed not to notice, or at least they pretended they didn't understand the simple but potent English lyrics. Whoever was inside that shop playing that record surely must have known what the words meant - but they apparently counted on the fact that most Czech Communist policemen were innocent of any language besides their own.

I've saved the best joke for the last: The Communist Party newspaper Rudé právo had a section where readers could send in announcements of birthdays, wedding anniversaries, memorial notices of deceased relatives and comrades, etc. Some friends of Václav Havel sent in a birthday message for "Ferdinand Vaněk," the protagonist in Havel's anti-communist play, "Audience." The photo submitted was of course Havel himself. Because Havel was a non-person, who was not allowed to be mentioned in the press, nor, Lenin-forbid, his photo to be published, the editors of the paper had no idea of what he looked like. The announcement was duly published in this official communist journal, and all the dissidents had a great laugh!

■ Dne 10. října 1989 se dožívá 70 let EMILIE MAŠKOVÁ z Prahy 4. Mnoho zdraví do dalších let přeje syn s rodinou.
41078-C

■ Dne 5. 10. 1989 oslavil narozeniny FERDINAND VANĚK z Malého Hrádku. Za jeho namáhavou práci, kterou ve svém životě vykonával a vykonává, mu děkují a do dalších let hodně zdraví a dalších pracovních úspěchů mu přejí jeho spolupracovníci a přátelé. 41329-C

■ Dne oslaví 66. soudruh ... URBAN z Mos dák z Olšan, ... Kladno. Za lásku ... obětavost děkují a do dalších let pevné zdraví a životní elán přejí manželka a dcery s rodinami. 910-C

■ Dne 11. 10. 1989 vzpomeneme 1. výročí úmrtí mého manžela, tatínka a dědečka JOSEFA DVOŘÁKA z Prahy 6. Stále vzpomínají manželka a děti s rodinami. 40381-C

■ Před 2 lety, 7. října, zemřela naše LUCIE WEGEROVÁ na následky tragické nehody na Palackého náměstí, která se stala 17. září 1987. Vzpomeňte s námi. Rodiče a bratr. 40980-C

■ ... 85 let ... nositel stát. kých a spole Rozloučení s ve velké ob rodinu Zuz

■ . Dne smutných hého man: dědečka z Lysé n. vzpomínají nami a p: menou

From the October 7, 1989 edition of Rudé právo, the Communist Party newspaper. The home village of "Ferdinand Vaněk" is really the address of Václav Havel's country cottage. The editors were real dummies not to catch this! The text says, "For his difficult work, which he has accomplished and will accomplish in his life, his friends and co-workers thank him, and wish him in his future years much good health and further success in his work."

[1] Zdenek Svěrák was the writer and star of the Oscar-winning Czech film, "Kolya", and also wrote the later film, "Dark Blue World".

50 - Jokes

One of the things that was lost after the Velvet Revolution was the steady stream of biting anti-Communist jokes. What jokes there are now about Václav Havel are very gentle, but in the communist era any new bit of gossip or news would instantly inspire and spread wicked jokes through "the people's telegraph." Our friends always wrote the jokes cryptically in their little notebooks (if lost and identified, there could be hell to pay). Many are not translatable or understandable to anyone outside the country, but I've saved a few that I think do reveal the Czech mind. Here is a typical one that comments on the Czech "what's the use" attitude during the communist era:

An American, a Soviet, and a Czech engineer meet at the site of a magnificent waterfall.

"What a great location!" says the American. "I can see a spectacular hotel built right on the side of the waterfall, with helicopter rides, a fantastic shopping center built around the whirlpool below, and an immense parking lot on the mesa, with glass elevators running up and down alongside the falls!"

"No," says the Soviet engineer. "We would construct an immense power plant to harness the energy of these falls, and bring electricity to millions of working people! And what about you, Comrade Czech? What would be your plan?"

The Czech looks at the daunting cascade of water and says, "I think I'll just piss in it."

....

There were always jokes underlining hatred for the Soviets:

Two Czechs are musing over their country's dismal situation. "I have a great solution," one says. "We could declare war on China!"

"Are you mad?" says the second guy. "We couldn't possibly win a war against a tremendous country like China!"

"You're right," says the first guy, "but they would have to march all the way across the Soviet Union to reach us. As soon as they got to our border we could declare peace, and then they'd have to march all the way back across the Soviet Union to get home!"

....

A variation, again playing on the Soviet fear of China:

One of Brezhnev's deputies comes rushing into his office in a sweat.

"Comrade!" he shouts. "There are over a hundred people in Red Square, and they are all *eating!*"

"So?" says Brezhnev impatiently. "We have no law against eating in Red Square! Don't disturb me with such nonsense."

A half-hour later, the underling runs in again, more agitated than before.

"Comrade Brezhnev! There are now over a thousand people in Red Square, and *they are all eating!*"

"That is *fine!*" beams Brezhnev. "Isn't that proof that in the great Soviet Union there is an abundance of food? That is good news!"

But once more the deputy bursts into the sanctum, shaking with fear.

"Comrade Brezhnev! You must do something quickly!
There are now one hundred thousand people in Red Square, and they are all eating!!"

"Are you a maniac?" shouts the now furious Brezhnev. "What in the name of holy Lenin is wrong with all those people eating?"

"With chopsticks???" wails the shuddering deputy.

....

And a wry comment on how the Soviets bled their satellites:

Fidel Castro implores Leonid Brezhnev for help.

"We desperately need $5 billion dollars in cash!"

"No problem," says Brezhnev with a fatherly smile.

"And this year we must have at least 7 million long tons of wheat!"

"You shall have it," assures Brezhnev.

"...And three thousand tons of construction steel.."

"You will get it all."

"...And black coal, and farming machinery, and automobile parts, and a food processing plant, and...."

"Don't worry," says Brezhnev, "I shall pass on your request, and it shall all be delivered to you by our comrades in Prague."

....

Soviet vs. American technology:

Dog Eat Dog

At the height of the Cold War, the Americans and the Soviets realized that if they continued the arms race they would eventually blow up the entire world. So one day they sat down and decided to settle the whole dispute with a single dogfight. They would each have five years to breed the best fighting dog in the world. Which ever side's dog won, would be entitled to rule the world, and the losing side would have to lay down its arms.

The Soviets found the biggest and meanest Doberman and Rottweiler bitches in the world, and bred them with the biggest and meanest Siberian wolves. They selected only the biggest and strongest puppy from each litter, killed its siblings, and gave it all the milk. They used steroids and merciless trainers, and after five years came up with the biggest, meanest dog the world had ever seen. Its cage needed five-inch thick steel bars, and nobody could even get near it.

When the day came for the dogfight, the Americans showed up with a strange animal. It was a nine-foot long dachshund! What a laugh! Everyone felt sorry for the Americans. There was no way this dog could last five seconds with the huge, slavering, and Soviet beast.

When the cages were opened, the clumsy American dog waddled over toward the Soviet monster, which had leapt out of its cage, drooling and barking in a savage rage. But as it charged, the American dachshund opened it long mouth and consumed the Soviet dog with single bite! There was nothing at all left of the Soviet dog, not even its spiked collar.

The Russian trainers came up to the Americans shaking their heads in disbelief. "How could this have happened???!!!" they moaned. We had our best people working for five years with the meanest Doberman and Rottweiler bitches in the world, bred to the biggest and meanest Siberian Wolves!!!"

"That's nothing," one of the American trainers replied, "We had our best plastic surgeons working for five years to make an crocodile look like a dachshund!"

51 - Not All That Bad

Despite the negative side I've recounted in this history, things were not *all* bad in Communist Czechoslovakia. The Czechs are resourceful people. They knew how to get at least something of what they wanted, and to find ways to have fun and fulfillment. They used to say, "There is *nothing* in Czechoslovakia - but you can get *everything.*"

Let me note some of the ways it could work:

The fact that there had been so many successive waves of emigration from this country meant that nearly everyone had a relative somewhere in the West. With all the negative propaganda Americans heard about life under communism, it was easy for people here to take full advantage of it. They wrote reinforcing letters to their presumably rich relatives abroad. (It was assumed here that all those who left the country became rich.) So, with the easily believed protestations of Czech suffering, many received regular hard currency gifts from abroad.

Of course Czechoslovak citizens were not allowed to actually handle, sniff, or touch the greenbacks. All foreign currency coming into the post offices or banks went straight into the State Treasury. What the recipient got was a notice that the value of X$$ had arrived in his or her name. They would then be able to take this notice to the bank and receive coupons redeemable in an organization named Tuzex. At the Tuzex shops scattered around the cities, one could exchange these coupons for a limited selection of Western goods, or the better Czech goods produced only for export. There were perfumes, whiskey, fancy grocery items, clothing, (jeans!) - all the way up to automobiles. In the first years I was here, a person could not even *enter* a Tuzex shop without showing a guard at the door that he or she actually had Tuzex coupons in hand! People would always save at least one coupon of low value, so they could get into the shops to even have a look.

But patience was a part of life here, and it was possible to get quite a few pleasurable items from Tuzex. A sidelight of this was that I too could get Tuzex coupons by exchanging dollars at a hotel or bank, and thus get better items than in a normal Czech shop. Once I went to the Tuzex head office to order a dishwasher – something that not even the Tuzex shops stocked. The only item you could order, they told me, was an automobile. The stuff in the shops, as glittering as it might appear to Czechs, was often distress merchandise, or older goods no longer profitable to sell in the West, stuff bought on the cheap by the Tuzex organization. While waiting in the office, I read a little booklet in English explaining that "Tuzex is an organization set up so that *foreigners* visiting this country can obtain the products they are used to." Just for fun, I asked the manager about this, and in hushed candor he told me that only about 6% of Tuzex customers were foreigners. 94% were Czechoslovak citizens!

So this "classless" society was actually divided between those who had compliant relatives abroad, and those who didn't. Personally, I was lucky enough to have free travel, and I found I could get what I wanted cheaper, easier, and even *quicker,* by driving to a foreign country, usually West Germany.

Other than that, there was an intricate web of friends and connections that could "get it for you." The best part of any counter was "under" it. In some cases these private perks could even get you a trip abroad, but that was a rarity. Getting things was easier. At any rate, you couldn't get very far without friends and relatives, and it did make for certain togetherness.

In exchange for their denied freedoms, every Czech had at least the following basic "rights"":

❖ Guaranteed employment, (constitutionally guaranteed, though not guaranteed to employ your interests, potential, or talents.)

❖ Free medical and dental care, (long waits, but good doctors.)

❖ Free university tuition, (assuming you had worker parents.)

❖ Strict price control, (with prices actually molded into products.)

❖ Cheap rent, strictly controlled, (if you could get a flat at all.)

❖ Security: Very little street crime; you could walk at night.

❖ A rich cultural life: Concerts, theater, movies, books, newspapers, magazines, museums. (Cheap, and all censored.)

❖ Cheap internal transport. Trams, buses, planes, trains... (very cheap – all very shabby.)

❖ Nobody starved. There were no beggars. (Begging forbidden.)
Wondrous to me was that in this police state it was generally possible to talk

the police out of traffic fines, customs agents out of duty payments, and bureaucrats out of restrictions - if you learned the right tactics. In all my 40 years here, I've never once had to bribe an official! As long as you did not commit a political offense, you could get away with a lot of things. (Just try talking a New York cop out of a traffic ticket!)

Every employer had a social department. For example, one room in the animation studio was full of tents, sleeping bags, backpacks, bicycles - all kinds of recreational equipment, which could be checked out for free. And there was someone on the staff who was a social organizer for parties and trips. Large enterprises even maintained free company hotels in the countryside. A bus could be booked, and employees could sign up for an excursion.

One typical fun trip for the cartoon studio bussed us into the wilderness, where a supposedly charming inn was booked for us.

Traveling in Czechoslovakia in those days required a strong bladder. Finding toilet facilities along any route was next to impossible. Even the few gas stations did not have toilets for customers. If a rare public john could be found along a road, it was a staggeringly smelly booth with a Turkish toilet. If you have never encountered one of those, be happy. They consisted of a square basin on the floor with a hole in the center. You had to straddle and squat to do your stuff. After the effort, if you managed to stand up again with a dry bottom, you were a winner. The usual routine was to avoid anything like that. The bus would pull over when going through a wooded area, and the driver would shout, "Women to the left, men to the right!" The desperate passengers would so divide themselves, each seeking out a tree under which or onto which to relieve themselves.

On this particular excursion we were hit by a monsoon rainstorm, and the bus driver became hopelessly lost. Through the sheets of rain as the day darkened, we came upon what he *thought* was the inn we were seeking. Whatever - we all piled out and dashed inside. The innkeeper was alarmed to see 55 damp animators streaming into his godforsaken keep. His forlorn establishment was in no way prepared for our arrival. But being confronted with the situation, he wiped his hands on his soiled apron, and pronounced the words that made clear the miserable accommodations which awaited us: *"I just hope you that you folks will take it as good sports!"*

The tiny rooms were damp and the mattresses lumpy. I had to grope around behind the building to purloin a few lumps of coal to feed the little stove in the room we were granted. As I was the *American,* Zdenka and I had the "finest" room in the place. We even had the highest quality bedbugs. Most of the others had to cram 10 to a room. But one of our troop had a guitar, and the inn was stocked with plenty of good Moravian wine. I did my best to dance with Zdenka, but that is just another one of my lacking abilities. A half-drunk Gypsy wandered into the place, and decided he wanted to dance with Zdenka. "Forget about your clumsy old man!" he bellowed. We had a wonderful, albeit freezing time, and it was, after all, a socialist freebee.

These problematic glories should not be automatically overlooked. Yes, freedom of choice was encroached upon, but there was a superficial sense of peace and plenty here. Prague is a beautiful city and this is a beautiful country. People had fun - they fell in love, etc. Many of them didn't want to travel abroad. And even when there was little else, you could always buy *"ordinary"* bread. Certainly in America you cannot buy a product labeled "ordinary," but here there was a type of bread actually called "ordinary," and it was great - much better than you could get in any American supermarket until very recently. I always thought that was kind of neat.

Those dedicated and brave few who tried to buck the system had their lives made miserable, but most preferred to play it cool, get what they could, and wait patiently for better times.

This patience, which has, by necessity, defined the Czech character, eventually paid off.

52 – Revolution!

In September 1989, the East German government suddenly decided to let people leave - and people did leave. Multitudes - all swarming into Czechoslovakia, which was perceived as a way station to West Germany. That turned out to be true, but only after the West German embassy in Prague became crammed to the breaking point. I went up there to take some video shots of this historic happening. I filmed people climbing the back fence, handing their babies, prams and all, over the fence, and of the huge embassy garden filled with tents, cots, and masses of refugees.

In a letter to my brother, dated 2 October 1989, and labeled "Trabantiana," I wrote:

On my morning walk today, the "morning after" the Great East German Exodus, I went by the West German embassy, just around the corner and up the street from us. I continued up the hill and into the large Petřín Park, then down again past the rear of the embassy. Police were all over the place, but they were not the main attraction.

Every step of the way, jamming the streets of our Malá Strana district, crammed into every possible spot, even along footpaths leading up to the park, are at least a thousand abandoned East German automobiles. The Malá Strana Square parking lot is at this moment 90% blocked with abandoned East German cars; no room for paying parking customers. In looking over these cars, I noted that many were covered with stickers of Western products, slogans, Playboy rabbits, Garfield, etc., indicating youth and "letch-for-the-West," good or bad.

Most of the cars are typical East German 2-stroke gaspers such as plastic Trabants or tinny Wartburgs, but there are also a number of Western-made cars. Considering that East Germans often wait up to 20 years to get a car, and considering the percentage of their income a car cost - not to mention whatever else they left behind in their homeland - the material sacrifice for freedom is stunningly revealed on our streets.

How or when the local authorities here will be able to free the streets and parks of this mass of abandoned automobiles is anyone's guess. One Czech onlooker volunteered that if it would be announced on the radio that these cars were free for the taking, "they would all be gone by two in the afternoon!" And the minor detail that they are locked and have no keys? "No problem!" the man said.

As the 40th anniversary of the founding of the East German communist state is just a few days away, what stronger statement could be made, than by the preference to leave all and risk all for an uncertain life in the West by these thousands of young people, born, raised, schooled, and indoctrinated in the "German Democratic Republic?" And even as I write this, the West German embassy is filling once again with another batch of refugees; at this moment, 600 more.

The Czech TV news has not shown those rows and rows of forlorn vehicles, even though they are right on the public streets for all to see. They have not shown the cheering, weeping-for-joy refugees arriving in Germany. In contrast to the CNN reports, they show only carefully selected shots, avoiding any smiling faces, and they dwell on the "illegality" of the exodus, the "breaking of diplomatic norms." In the case of Hungary's open border, they say it violates an agreement that fellow communist states will not allow citizens of "brotherly" states to escape. This is an agreement the existence of which had never before been mentioned.

The fact that it was an immoral agreement doesn't seem to
matter. They refuse to address the reason these people are
leaving, nor do they mention the number of people involved.
The last thing the Communists want to do is face reality.
History is bubbling up all around us. Where will all this
lead? Stay tuned.

The Czechoslovak communist government finally realized that its only
hope to end the embarrassment was to allow these unseemly East Germans to
go West. A great bus and train exodus was organized, and off they went. As it
all happened right on our doorstep, I saw a sight that made me realize that
the end of communism was truly near in Czechoslovakia. I saw throngs of
Czechs cheering, smiling, and waving at the East Germans as the buses
roared off through our square.

"Czechs cheering *Germans?*" I thought. "That's a sure sign they're thinking,
'Could we be next?'" My neighbors were skeptical. "Not here," they said. "The
Communists are too strong here."

But the sight of thousands of East Germans using Prague as their escape
route certainly did help raise the local moribund spirits. I knew right then
that nothing could stop the wave of freedom from coming this way too.

Poland, with Lech Walensa, began it. Those living in these (former!) Soviet
Bloc countries had been constantly hammered with "revolutionary" slogans.
But in each case the so-called revolutionary Communists actually had come
to power by a putsch. In Poland, there came a true "workers' revolution" in
1980, not just a Leninist charade. Poland led the way, and, by the grace of
Gorbachev, made possible the chain of events that gave Czechoslovaks their
chance. 1989 was a thrilling year, with an ever-rising rush of stunning events.

It was the harsh, unfeeling suppression of all attempts by the Czechoslovak
people to communicate with the Communist regime that set the spark.
Charter 77 made a glow, but smoke didn't rise until mid-'88 and early '89. The
flame finally burst free in late November. By that time it was far too late for
the Communists to seek dialogue!

When a few brave dissidents, including the playwright Václav Havel, had
written, signed, and published abroad their plea for dialog in 1977, their
Charter was vehemently denounced by the regime. Workers were assembled
in all factories and work places, and lectured that Charter 77 was "counter
-revolutionary," and "anti-State." (The regime's usual label for what was

really just anti-Communist.) Workers were required to sign petitions denouncing the Charter, *but they were not allowed to read it.* Its quite reasonable terms were never printed or spoken in any public media, circulated only in underground "*samizdat.*"

What had thus started as a call for modest reforms, 12 years later became a revolution. The month of November 1989 is now synonymous with revolution. As I noted earlier, the Czech name for November is listopad, which means "falling leaves." So it is symbolic that in listopad, all the "holy leaves" of communism fell to earth and left the tree stark naked.

Following, is my 1989 "*Revolution Report,*" taken from diaries and notes written as these historic events took place. I sent this "report" to many of my American friends and colleagues at the time, and I include it here:

• Spring came to Prague in November this year - 21 years late.

• If you stand the year **68** on its head you will see that "Spring" came in Autumn **89** to Prague.

Can you imagine 300,000 Czechs singing WE SHALL OVERCOME? These are heady days in this country!

The 24th of November was our 25th wedding anniversary, a day that was also the historic climax to the "Great November Czechoslovak Revolution."

Alexander Dubček appeared like a Phoenix from the ashes to address a singing and chanting throng of 300,000 aroused citizens. That was on the eighth consecutive day of mass demonstrations on Wenceslas Square, and the day the Czechoslovak Communist Party politburo cracked.

We will remember that victorious day on every anniversary we have in our lives. But the actions going on in Prague of course overshadowed "our" day. We headed separately for the square at the appointed 4 p.m. Zdenka went with a group of colleagues directly from the animation studio. As production manager, she has to be there every day, whereas I mainly do my film preparation work at home. I walked downtown from home with my video camera. Of course, I had no idea at all where Zdenka was in that throng. She had suggested on the phone that I try to get into the Czechoslovak Filmexport building, right on the square, where I could get some overall shots from above. The day before, on the ground, I couldn't see very much except the people all around me. Of course I wasn't the only person trying to get up into the building, and I was lucky to get to a free window.

Immediately beneath me a projection for large neon sign blocked my view, and I knew that if I leaned out far enough to get a shot down the square, I might not survive for our anniversary dinner. So I just held the video camera out as far as I could reach with one arm. It was the first Sony Video-8 camera, and it was as big and as heavy as a brick!

I panned it back and forth, and hoped the whole scene would make it onto the tape. Then I pointed the camera straight down, and pressed the zoom button.

When I got home and ran the tape, I was astounded to see that on those first "blind" shots, where I had just stuck the camera out the window and hoped, I had zoomed down past 300,000 people directly to Zdenka! Incredible! But that was only one minor miracle in a major day.

Earlier, in the 2nd and 3rd day of this happy, noble, and peaceful revolution, before we could even be sure it was a revolution, the most dramatic (and the word fits) development was in the theaters. Actors were the first group to solidly back the students, who were now striking in protest of their infamous beating by the police on November 17. In theater after theater the arriving audiences would be greeted by cast members on the stage announcing, "There will be no performance of our play tonight, but with your permission we would like to turn this audience into a discussion group." Public meetings were of course forbidden, but theater audiences, people who had bought tickets for plays, became members of a group discussion, difficult for the police to control. Zdenka and I attended one of the first of these impromptu "performances" at the Realistic Theater in the Smichov district of Prague. News had gotten around, of course, so we were lucky to get in past the crush of people, even though we held complimentary tickets. After announcements from the newly formed Civic Forum were read out, person after person rose from their theater seats to add voice to the rising resentment over 40 years of forced silence. It was thrilling how truth and feelings streamed out from people who only a few days before would never have dreamed of speaking such heresies in public.

The most vehement statement from the audience came from a former rector at Charles University, a Dr. Kopecký, who has spent recent years as a night watchman. He rightly pointed out that the success or failure of the revolution would hinge on the control of television. "No matter how many people we get out onto the streets in Prague, the rest of the country, especially those in the smaller villages, won't know why we are doing this. Those people get all their news from TV; they seem to think the students are striking for more money!" A few TV workers were there, and told how powerless they were to tell the truth of what was going on. Two days later there were rumors that the television headquarters were surrounded by the "People's Militia," the Communist Party's private army.

Even as I write this, the Civic Forum organization is only 12 days old (proclaimed November 19 at the Prague Činoherní Klub theater), but already it is the most powerful group in Czechoslovakia. It has the widest following, it has destroyed the seemingly impregnable power of the Communist Party, it has brought down the government, and it has forced the Parliament to rewrite the constitution!

A commentator on British Sky News noted that it took 10 years to bring democracy to Poland, 10 months to accomplish it in Hungary, 10 weeks in East Germany, but only 10 days in Czechoslovakia! To paraphrase one of the Communists' favorite titles, we have just had "Ten Days That Shook the World."

The world of the Communist Party of Czechoslovakia has been shaken to the ground. The Party here has been droning on about "revolution" and "peoples' uprisings" for over 40 years. Now, at last, they have been forced to witness a true revolution!

The students who started the revolution were the most carefully vetted children of Communist and workers families - those considered "safe" by the regime, and thus allowed to study in the universities. That's the real sting for the Communist government!

On the 27th of November, I saw a man losing his mind on live television. A self-described secret policeman, a "fink," amidst the cheering throng on Wenceslas square, he watched his whole world - the only world that gave his life meaning - falling around him in ruins.

The man absolutely flipped out. "I am for socialism!" he shouted hysterically. "I am for the working class!" The man could not be calmed. His eyes shifted wildly. He simply could not comprehend or allow himself to see what was actually happening. This is a document to illustrate what must be searing the minds of the long-time, self-assured rulers of this country... and I have it all on videotape!

The most dramatic TV shot I saw was the secretly taped stormy meeting of the television workers, just two days after the theater event described above. Every effort had been made to seal off the TV facilities. But in the end they could not seal off the inside, and the television staff itself joined the movement. The workers had voted, and were telling their director that they would close down television completely if they could not broadcast the truth. They said their "honor as journalists was at stake." The director shouted down at them from a lighting catwalk that if they didn't follow the official orders they would "no longer be television journalists." He said that the "honor of the Socialist State was at stake," and that if they didn't broadcast as they were told, the militia would take over television completely. There was shouting and whistling at this, with one worker yelling that "liars have no right to talk about honor." The videotape of the meeting was smuggled out, and I saw it broadcast on the British SKY NEWS we receive by satellite. This, I think, was the key moment in the revolution, and during the day of the meeting there were conflicting statements coming from ČSSR TV, with a few bits sneaking through, between the usual official viewpoints. Telephone calls from the TV staff spread the word, and student members of the Civic Forum rushed up to TV headquarters to confront the guards with a large demonstration. All of this got onto world news broadcasts.

The pressure on the Communist government was severe. They had to choose between shooting or backing down. They backed down, and TV was freed to its workers! Then it all burst out. Suddenly, the very same news readers who

264

had for years been pouring out garbage, were now saying the most astounding things. They had started to tell the truth! After that, everything went like the wind.

People we haven't seen on TV for over 20 years, 1968 Prime Minister Oldřich Černík, former Party secretary Čestmír Císař, Alexandr Dubček, Václav Havel, etc., are all now speaking. Ordinary people are interviewed and are saying things on national TV not even dreamed of only days ago! Economists are telling the truth about the catastrophic condition of the economy, hidden by the Communists under a cosmetic surface of "110% fulfilled 5-year plans." Suddenly it is live and lively TV!

The Communists are still having their say too. They had the nerve to cry out that "political questions could not be solved in the streets. What is needed is dialogue!" What hypocrites! They've had their exclusive say for 40 years. They didn't allow a single word of opposition dialogue to intrude on their tightly controlled media. But now they have to defend themselves on camera. It was only because of the overwhelming street demonstrations that they suddenly were interested in "dialogue." Their previous answer to those who petitioned for dialogue was to silence them.

But even now, at the live televised National Congress of Collective Farms (still Communist-dominated at this writing), held at the giant Palace of Culture auditorium, the delegates booed, refusing to listen to a statement from two noted spokespersons from the Civic Forum, actress Jiřina Rázlová and actor Petr Čepek. The farmers were later forced to apologize for this rudeness and refusal to abide by their own newly formed interest in "dialogue." It was a tremendous embarrassment for the Communists, and right on live television. All could see that many Communists have still not gotten the message.

These have been days of hour-to-hour, nearly minute-by-minute astounding and unbelievable developments in this country. I was dashing to join the mass actions, then rushing home to keep my video recorder going. Local TV is now the best show in town! Until the last three days, I had depended on satellite TV and Radio Free Europe to get the news. Now it is local Czechoslovak Television! What is now pouring out of this once stone-dead service boggles the brain. Every forbidden word, song, opinion, personage, is now coming at us in an avalanche. We are astounded. We weep. We stare bug-eyed at the parade of statements and interviews. We are dazzled...

In our brains, we know the hard part lies ahead, but we can't deny ourselves the ecstasy of reveling in these long, long awaited and nearly undreamed of thrilling days of Czechoslovak national renewal! But we also realize these are dangerous days. The Communist Party is no longer in control. The new government is not yet in control, and the Civic Forum is not yet fully organized. Some here nervously worry that if firm control is not quickly established, the army might move in, even though army spokesmen have repeatedly appeared on TV to deny it. But such is the shock that the unbelievable has actually happened, many long suffering and doubting Czechs and Slovaks fear that it will all again be taken away from them. It is still difficult for them to accept that they may actually, really and truly be getting democracy.

My feeling though, seeing how it all reflects movements elsewhere, is that the revolution is now irreversible. There will soon be tremendous business opportunities here. Zdenka and I had just about given up on this country. We went so far as to buy a "retirement" home in San Francisco... But now... All of this may well change our plans for leaving. People with knowledge of the country, who know the language, industrial methods and organizations, could have a great opportunity. We expect that many more animation producers will be coming over, wanting new films. Everything could be suddenly booming here...

The euphoria and excitement is still at a peak after 14 unbelievable days of demonstrations by up to 700,000 people. Every shop window in downtown Prague has become a "Democracy Wall." Every metro station is now a gallery of posters and notices from the Civic Forum. At the end station of one of the Metro lines is a sign, directed at the Communist leadership: "LAST STOP, STEP DOWN!" And the wonder of it all is the discipline, organization, and peacefulness of it. They are calling it the "Velvet Revolution."

There's been no nastiness, no aggressive action to be seen. It was a forceful but good-humored revolution - the Czech way. There has been no violence after that first dreadful night of the 17th, the night when the Communists' goose was cooked. The handmade posters are marvelous, and full of biting humor. Referring to the Communist Party, one poster reads: "THE ONES WHO MADE US SICK CANNOT BE OUR DOCTORS!" One of the most hilarious signs I saw was on a blackboard in front of a fruit and vegetable shop. It usually lists what, if anything, is available. Today the shop was full of fresh fruit, and in a first indication of capitalist advertising technique there was scrawled in chalk:

"VÁCLAV HAVEL LOVES GRAPEFRUIT!"

Václav Havel is the brilliant playwright whose work has been banned for the past 20 years. He has been in and out of jail many times, suffering constant indignities, and was one of the founders of Charter 77. He is now the spokesman for the Civic Forum, which unifies the multitude of opposition factions. The fact that the government has had to negotiate with Havel was the bitterest of pills they were forced to swallow. The communist press recently deigned to mention his name, but only to label him a "political zero." But they were forced by the massive general strike on Monday the 27th to give the Civic Forum legality, to give them facilities in Prague, and to negotiate with Havel. They had to pledge to reform the government to include opposition parties, and to remove the sections in the constitution which gave the Communist Party the leading role in the country.

They also had to delete from the Constitution the paragraph establishing Marxism-Leninism as the guiding philosophy in all aspects of teaching and culture.
Thus ended Communist Party rule!

"UŽ JE TOHO DOST!" ("ENOUGH, ALREADY!") is one of the most often shouted slogans at the rallies. The people are indeed fed up, and want fast and radical change. Here in Prague I followed every minute of the two-hour general strike on Monday with my video camera. I started shooting as I crossed the bridge into the New Town, taking in the gathering crowds as they passed hundreds of handmade posters covering every shop window. Then I just flowed in with the mass of people filling the square. Seeing that I was documenting the event, some people up on a parked truck lifted me onto it so I could get an overall view.

It was spectacular. All the church bells were ringing, sirens wailed, horns blew, and the joyous and united crowd picked up and shouted slogan after slogan, their words the very opposite of what they had been forced to shout in previous staged demonstrations.

This was the real thing; the hundreds of banners were handmade by the people themselves, and the flags they waved were not Soviet, but Czechoslovak flags. I waited 30 years to see the streets of Prague fluttering with only Czechoslovak flags. And today, the red flag has disappeared. There are hundreds of thousands of them lying in the dark somewhere. I doubt that we will ever see them on the streets of this country again; They may well be made into red underwear! The blossoming of thousands of red, white and blue Czechoslovak flags was just one of many sights here in the last ten days which have brought tears to my eyes. It's not only the big things, but the little symbols that have meaning. Calls are made for restoration of the old Czechoslovak state emblem, the Masaryk street names, the removal of Klement Gottwald's name from anything! (Gottwald was the first Communist president, and the old regime's No. 2 saint, after Lenin.)

The Communists well and truly committed suicide in this country; so many unfeeling and unnecessary acts of physical, psychological, and cultural violence against the national pride of the Czechs and Slovaks!

Few were speaking against the Communists in 1968, because it was the Communist Party, under Dubček, that had initiated the reforms and new freedoms at that time. It was communism's last great chance here, and these monkeys shot themselves in the foot (to put it discreetly) by smashing that movement. The present revolution has been made by people outside the Party, and they are indeed anti-Communists. By trying to grab it all, the hardline Communists have now lost it all. The spirit I felt in 1968 has returned to the streets of Prague, and this time there is hope it cannot be stopped.

The people want their history returned to them. The biggest mistake the Communists made was to bury the people's history and natural culture, and to try to overlay a foreign and artificial history. The years between 1918 (when the country was founded by Tomáš Garrigue Masaryk) and 1948, have been officially blank here - a heavy cultural and moral loss.

One of the great "dream scenes" we witnessed was the first post-victory concert by the Czech Philharmonic Orchestra. For 25 years we have had season tickets for Thursday evening concerts. In the florid, Art Nouveau extravagance of Smetana Hall, the concert of November 30 was a very special occasion. With us in the audience were Václav Havel, Alexander Dubček, Čestmír Císař, Jiří Dienstbier, Marta Kubišová (the number one pop singer in 1968, whose entire career was wiped out because of her political stand), and distinguished guests from the past: Ota Šik, Dubček's economic minister in 1968 - who could have reformed the economy way back then, but who was driven into exile -Thomas Bata (Tomáš Baťa) the shoe king whose grandfather virtually created a shoe city out of the Moravian village of Zlín, and even a dimly remembered titled figure from the Habsburg dynasty, Count Karel Schwarzenberg.

The occasion of this concert was special because of the orchestra itself. Under Václav Neuman's direction, the entire orchestra had refused to appear on radio or television because of the regime's persecution of signatories to the "A FEW SENTENCES" petition. That was the regime's habitual knee-jerk reaction to any petition calling for dialogue or reform: never publish or mention the contents of the petition, but only denounce it and persecute the signatories. The Czech Philharmonic orchestra members were the very first group to make a stand, and as such are now national heroes. A huge Czechoslovak flag draped the stage, as well as a banner, "CONCERT FOR CIVIC FORUM." When the orchestra filed in, the audience rose to its feet, applauding and shouting "Bravo! Bravo!" for at least ten minutes non-stop

There were tears in every eye. It was a long time before they could play a short piece by Smetana. The rest of the evening was taken up with speeches from the various new leaders, including Havel, giving thanks for this "Velvet Revolution." Indeed it was the first time I heard them publicly acknowledge that what had started as a protest for a few reforms had indeed become a revolution. That had been clear to me since the 24th, but before then no one had dared say it aloud in public. It was a glorious evening - the evening we all came to face the incredible fact that the people had actually won!

The very next day, Thomas Bata (Tomáš Baťa) went to Moravia for the official restoration of the name Zlín to the town where Bata's worldwide shoe empire was born. From a small village, the original Tomáš Baťa - the country's

"Henry Ford"- had built Czechoslovakia's most modern city. The Communists had renamed the city Gottwaldov, after the first Communist president, Klement Gottwald...[1]

A statue of Gottwald, which stands before the Communist Party headquarters building in Prague, has had its hands painted blood red. The "Gottwald Bridge" leads to the "Gottwald Metro Station." Those names will go, and the Klement Gottwald Museum here will be returned to the building's original function: a capitalist bank.

The young people who finally found the courage and strength to break the long silence are today the heroes of the nation. But it was Gorbachev, and the contagion of glasnost, that made it all possible, resulting in this incredible year that saw Polish Solidarity come to power, the Hungarians and Bulgarians turn, and the tremendous spectacle of the Berlin wall crumbling.

All this made it possible to crack the most impenetrable "wall" of all, the Czechoslovak "elected-by-tanks" Communist leadership. But where will it lead? This is only the beginning. Real democracy, whatever that may be, is not inevitable. This country has been devastated by 41 years of misrule, and the people are so turned off by socialism that reactionary opportunists could possibly take the nation down another dead-end road. It will take continued discipline and care to find a reasonable way forward.

"UNITY IS STRENGTH!" they are now shouting. The Communists had constructed a false unity, but pluralism may result in too little unity, perhaps chaos. They will be learning what we Americans know: that the struggle for democracy is a continuing and never-ending process. Even now, the Communist Party here tries to turn their eyes from the handwriting on the wall. The Party continues to make one blunder after another, and is now totally discredited.

December 9, 1989. Tonight we watched Gustav Husák resign as president of the Czechoslovak Socialist Republic. It was a pitiful sight: this old man, his voice wavering, his eyes swimming behind spectacles thick as submarine port-holes. His words were as vague as his utterly bewildered expression. Like the other Communists, he does not appear to understand what has happened or why. He had nothing substantial to say. He is (supposed to be) a lawyer. He has the title "Doctor of Law," but he had no "closing arguments" to make... There were no words indicating his view as to what happened, and no answers to any of the vital questions, such as why his so-called "scientific socialism" - the infallible Marxism-Leninism - didn't work, why it alienated the people. He said nothing about 1968, why the Soviets were called in; there was certainly no hint of mistakes or failure. He just faded out.

Hitler was comparatively modest: He claimed the Third Reich would last a thousand years. It lasted twelve. The Communists, however, claimed eternity. Their system was "irreversible." They lasted 41 years.

This has been a disciplined, intelligent, happy revolution, won by the sheer power of all the people suddenly waking up and shouting, "Enough is enough!" The Communists here had all the power - guns, militia, tanks, control of every aspect of life, every word printed, publicly spoken, or delivered on television. They controlled employment, unions, housing, education, even hobbies... You name it, they controlled it, and all backed by the immense power of the Soviet Union. They were assumed to be invincible. On the other hand, they were a failure, and in the landslide of events, with all the former Soviet satellites at once shouting "Enough is enough!" they dared not use their tanks again.

And yet only days before, people were telling me, "Nothing can change here." As late as November 11, Czechoslovak television assured its viewers, "It cannot be said that there is a crisis in socialism."

The era of Communist wishful thinking is over at last.

[1] Klement Gottwald was prime minister under President Edvard Beneš when, with Soviet backing, he led the February 1948 putsch that put the Communists in total power. After Beneš resigned, Gottwald was named president, and under his rule the terror of the '50s saw hundreds of officials and ordinary citizens executed and tortured. When he died he was virtually sanctified by the regime. Masaryk's name disappeared into a black hole, and every school child was taught that Klement Gottwald was the "first worker president." Besides the town, streets and bridges were named after him, and as a final blow to Czechoslovak pride, a new 100-crown note was issued featuring his demonic portrait. Every bill that came into people's hands was defaced, Gottwald's face X'd out, the eyes punched, and the word "murderer" scrawled across the forehead, until the bills had to be withdrawn.

53 – Revolution
Reflections

In those heady days following the 1989 revolution, there was much to see and hear, and much to consider - as I tried to reflect in my "Post-Revolution Report" to friends and colleagues in America:

"Immediately after Husák's final words the cameras switched to a live press conference reporting the conclusion of intensive negotiations to form a new government. Exhausted-looking representatives of three parties, including the Communists, and Václav Havel for the Civic Forum, announced agreement on what all called a "government of national understanding." It will have 10 Communist Party members and 11 non-Communist members. A great improvement, but still a standby until the next and most vital step, the holding of free elections.

No one can yet predict all of the consequences and ramifications of the east bloc revolutions. The first rumblings appear to be the imminent breakup of the Soviet Union itself, which could screw up everything if it doesn't happen in an orderly way. On our American side, the financial turmoil could be considerable, at the same time pulling the rug out from under our cozy defense establishment. I know many fine teachers at the DoDDS (Department of Defense Dependent's School) in Germany, whose delightful way of life is already under threat if troop reductions become a reality.

However, we cannot put ourselves in the position of ruing the fact that what we have been hoping and propagandizing for all these years has (incredibly / astoundingly/ unimaginably) happened! Nothing can diminish the present joy in this country at having actually shed the communist yoke. Those who were assumed invincible have collapsed like a cheap deck chair. The doings in Czechoslovakia have suddenly made this place

even more interesting than it has previously been for me.
I feel I am in the midst of a historical process of world-shaking
importance.

Despite its wasteful excesses, our own American market
economy does work, partly because it is subject to constant
regulation and adjustment. Today's "capitalism" is something
else entirely from the one on which Marx based his theories.
The Communists allowed no outside reappraisal of their
system, and at each successive failure they simply announced
that they had corrected "past errors" and were now on the
"correct" path. All "errors" were conveniently in the "past."
But the regime's fatal "error" was that it did not listen
to the people whose wishes it claimed to embody. On the
contrary, the Communists did everything possible to keep
any critical voice or single word from being heard.

The supreme irony in this country was that after 1968 they
expelled from the Party the very people who could have saved it:
Alexander Dub ek, his colleagues, and more than 450,000 Party
members who supported the reforms. In 1968 few voices here
were raised against the Communist Party. Their slogan
then was:
     "JSME S VÁMI, BUDTE S NAMI!" = "We are with you, be with us!"

But this time the revolution was solidly anti-communist.
The Communist Party here shot itself in the foot. I'm not
thrilled with mobs, but the atmosphere here has been
thoroughly contagious. I am not a Czech, but I have been
living and working here during three decades of historic ups and
downs, and this has been the ultimate, undreamed of
reward. Czechoslovakia is not Yugoslavia, thank God.

Now the man who was in jail as an "anti-state criminal" is
president of the republic: Václav Havel, the people's hero!
And his election was presided over by the new president of
the Federal Parliament, none other than Alexander Dub ek!
I imagine all Czechs and Slovaks must be sore from pinching

themselves, not quite able to believe what they're reading in their newly freed newspapers, and what they are seeing on television, is actually true!

In those joyous massed demonstrations, everyone was a friend. There was no pushing, no violence. In the entire revolution, except for the November 17 attack by the police, which triggered it, there were no injuries. For those here that had been critical of the "aimless younger generation," there was a great revelation. It was the youth of the country who dared to start it. These kids, born and raised under totalitarianism, with no experience whatever in democratic organization or action, seemed to know exactly what to do. Of course they were joined and guided by older dissidents, and quickly took on board legal and other experts. They realized their chance, and knew just how far they could go at each stage. Their posters made what seemed to be totally impossible demands:

1.   End one-party rule.
2.   Throw out the entire Communist Party leadership.
3.   Amend the constitution to eliminate the guaranteed leading role of the Communist Party.
4.   End the teaching of Marxism-Leninism in schools.
5.   Open the media to the opposition.
6.   Guarantee free democratic elections with competing parties.
7.   Declare the 1968 invasion of Czechoslovakia an illegal act.
8.   Form a new government with Communists in the minority.
9.   Abolish the People's Militia and the secret police.

And most brazen of all:

10.   Elect the dissident playwright Václav Havel as president!

Incredibly, they accomplished every one of these demands, and more! The new Minister of Foreign Affairs, Ji í Dienstbier,

was actually shoveling coal in a boiler room job the day he was
appointed. A former journalist, he had been forced to work for many years in only the most menial jobs.

A devastating sign of how far the Communist Party has slipped
in this short time was seen in the first 1990 edition of the
Party newspaper, Rudé Právo. It has shrunk from being the
only full-sized paper published here, to a mere scrap of an
8-page tabloid, humbly twisting in the wind...

We cannot even say it is all like a dream come true, because
no one even dared to dream it!

There is a lot of materialism behind the various east bloc
revolutions - certainly here. But this too is the fault of
the Communists, who constantly theorized about the creation
of an unselfish "Socialist Man," but who in fact promoted
selfishness by their very promises and failures.

Could there now, suddenly, be truth? Just a few months ago,
who would have believed it? Few believed it even one month ago,
but it was simmering a long time. It was clear to
me last January, when the police brutally put down
a demonstration in memory of Jan Palach, that the resentment
was going to break through. When this happened again in
August things were beginning to boil, and the heat was
turned up further during the East German exodus.

But no one wanted to believe me. "It can't happen here!"
they said. Even Zdenka, who shares the satellite news with
me, said the students could not win. "The workers are
satisfied. The country people are satisfied. They have
houses, they have cars, they have color TVs. They don't have
to work hard. There is plenty of food - it's not like in
Poland. They are now allowing freer travel, dollar bank
accounts, etc. People won't risk losing their positions..."

I'd heard all of that, but I knew that in spite of relative
comforts, there was deep resentment, even hatred against the
Communists. I knew it would go fast - and yet my remaining hair
whistled in the hurricane force of the winds of change. And still:
every day more sweeping changes and astounding revelations.
Luxurious villas, Communist headquarters in every town, Marxist-
Leninist museums and spas, all are being returned to the people
for use as new schools, libraries, and hospitals. Gottwald statues
are being pulled down, communist street names changed; the original state seal is being restored. New stamps are being issued.

Václav Havel was sworn in as president on December 29. Yesterday,
the 9th of January, presidential postage stamps with his image
were already on sale! In this country there has never been such
speed! Other new stamps, bearing the images of Tomáš Masaryk,
Karel âapek, and other long submerged heroes, have appeared with
the same breathtaking speed. This shows what can be done if the
spirit is there.

When did this revolution actually begin? Well, the seeds were
planted by the tank treads of 1968, but they lay dormant through
nine winters, first pushing up shoots with the declaration of
Charter '77. I think that was the actual beginning. And during the
next twelve years only Havel and those brave few signatories were
the lonely tenders of the greenhouse. Of course it was Gorbi who
opened the door and let the sunshine in. Could he have imagined
how blazing would be the light?

The new umbrella organization, proclaimed by Havel only on
November 19, is now calling all the shots. The Civic Forum is
pledged to be merely a guiding spirit until a new constitution
and free elections can be held. It emphasizes that it is not
a political party, but a "forum," open to all, for the
exchange of ideas and opinions. Let us hope it remains that
way. I did my bit by gifting Forum with a Canon copier, but
the revolution was their thing. As usual, I was just an
observer - this time a happy one!

276

As we all expected, the aftermath of the revolution is not all roses. The Slovaks, suffering from a deep inferiority complex after hundreds, even thousands of years of being second-fiddle to one power or another, fought fiercely in parliament for maximum local power. It was touch and go for a long time whether they would insist on total independence. It took weeks to decide the new name and emblem for the country, both of which now give more prominence to the Slovaks. The country's name, always on the long side for such a small place, is now a real mouthful: "The Czech and Slovak Federative Republic."

As an American, all of this reminds me of the great struggles in the creation and building of our own country; the long tug between "State's Righters" and "Federalists."

Many now fear that the eager rush into a market economy could bury the country's culture. Rising paper prices and new taxes could make books - at least cheap if not free under the Communists - too expensive for less well-off readers. In the meantime, the new press freedom has seen a proliferation of pornographic and junk magazines - perhaps somewhat understandable after so many years of suppression.

On our little street of Mostecká we have a grocery, delicatessen, fruit and vegetable shop, bakery, barber, dry cleaners, record shop, antique store, drug store, ironing service, spice shop, coffee house - just about everything. But the word is that the new private owners will want to throw out much of this and in-stall more pubs and tourist gift shops, etc., which means we re-sidents will have less.[1]

Well, the air is bustling with change - some good, some doubtful, some quite bad. Time will tell, but we still think it was well worth it."

---

[1] This is exactly what happened!

54 – After the Fall

When the revolution actually occurred, Havel insisted on including Dubček on his team, out of respect for his past role. Dubček again became speaker of the parliament, this time the new, *democratic* parliament. But in spite of Havel's generous gesture, Dubček never again had the popularity of 1968. "He's still a communist at heart," many people said. But at the time, as a way to establish the continuity of the long struggle for democracy, the symbolism was important. When the split into two nations took place in January 1993, Dubček was the obvious choice for president of Slovakia. The tragedy of his death in an auto accident, just a month-and-a-half earlier, put an end to that, and sentenced the Slovaks to more political gloom.

For those who lament the breakup of Czechoslovakia, let me remind them that the fusion of these two peoples in the first place was a temporary anomaly in their long history. The Slovaks were a minority group within the Hungarian Empire for over a thousand years. They never even had a Slovak province, let alone a nation state, and following the fall of the Great Moravian Empire in the year 896 - which encompassed Bohemia, Moravia and Slovakia - they had increasingly little in common with the Czechs. The language, culture, and temperament differed. But because of the similarity of language the two Slav regions were artificially joined in 1918.

Masaryk, with the help of Beneš and the Slovak Štefánik, had cobbled together the federation by campaigning for it in one allied nation after another during World War I, culminating in Masaryk's visit to the U.S. and his direct appeal to President Woodrow Wilson. He got his wish, but the long turn of history revealed that the idea was unviable. The Slovak agitation for a separate state began almost before the cheers died down after the November 1989 revolution. The Czechs at first tried to hold them with compromises of local autonomy. A short-lived federal republic was established. But after the Slovaks kept pushing for more, going so far as to adopt their own flag and their own constitution, the Czech government gave up.

Today, the vast majority of Czechs are reconciled to the break. They can at last move forward without the Slovaks vetoing every move. A vital two years was lost in continual haggling. The Czech Republic has shed its past as an outcast Soviet satellite and is today a highly respected democracy with a booming free-market economy and a strong currency. Today's Czech crown is real money! [1]

The good name of this new country is largely the work of Václav Havel, whose initial work following the revolution helped focus attention on this country, and projected his idealism and high moral vision around the world. He may hold the unique distinction of having been the president of three different republics within the space of three years: Before a new constitution could be written, Havel was sworn in as the last president of the Czechoslovak Socialist Republic. Then he became the first and only president of the Czech and Slovak Federative Republic, and now he is the first president of the new Czech Republic!

Time takes its toll on any politician in office. Illness, jealousy, maneuvering for power, and just plain political wear and tear have weakened Havel, and now the great question is about who will have the stature to be his successor. The most covetous appears to be another Václav, Václav Klaus, the first prime minister after the revolution, later president of parliament, and the most powerful and self-assured politician of the post-revolution period. But he frightens many, including me. It was under his watch as premier that the commercial corruption, foreign mafias, and various business scandals first appeared. He is a pure Thatcherite, convinced that the market can cure everything, even the environment. All evidence so far is to the contrary. But we live in hope. I'm not a Czech citizen, but as a long-time resident, I too am affected by the political fiddles. And there have been enough "Enrons" here too!

[1] As I edit this year 2000 update, much of the gloss on the "New Camelot" Czech Republic has faded. Greed, corruption, criminality, and a growing tawdriness have brought home to us the bitter fact that however we fantasized, this is just an ordinary country after all, not intrinsically better than any of the other European states, in spite of its much honored "Poet President." And even Václav Havel, weakened by serious illness, has lost much of his influence on political events. Czechia is now moving on to yet another new faze. Stay tuned! The EU is at last on the horizon, and no one here is quite sure how it and the Euro will work out.
Incidentally, "Czechia" is the linguistically-approved English-language one-word name for The Czech Republic, even though the Czechs, illogically, hate their own language version of a one-word, conversational title for the country (Česko). But it's a mouthful, saying "CzechRepublic-CzechRepublic-CzechRepublic", at every mention of the country. I personally opt for "Czechia." It is as simple and logical in English as "Virginia," "Georgia," "Austria," or "Russia." No?

55 – "Liberators"

In May of 1995, during the celebration of the 50th anniversary of the end of World War II and the liberation of Europe, it was at last possible for the people of this country to officially hear the truth about their liberation from the Nazi German occupation.

Under communism, every year at this time, banners, billboards, newspapers, magazines, radio, and television inevitably used the phrase, "The Liberation of Czechoslovakia By The Soviet Army." It was never written or spoken any other way. It was forbidden to simply phrase this as, "The Liberation of Czechoslovakia." No, it had to be stated almost as if it were a single word, cast-iron and indivisible:

> THELIBERATIONOFCZECHOSLOVAKIABYTHESOVIETARMY

The official line was always the same: The American army of George Patton entered the west of the country, freed the city of Pilsen, and stopped there. They could have easily reached Prague in time to liberate the city by May 5, the same day as the other capitals of Europe were liberated. The Germans were eager to surrender to the Americans. There was virtually no opposition. The people of Prague had risen, and were themselves doing battle with the Germans, who were determined to destroy the glorious city before they retreated. They had in fact already destroyed the historic old town hall. Praguers were being killed. Some had seized the radio station, and were broadcasting appeals to the Americans to come and save them. But our American army did not move. Finally, on the 9th of May, after four days of needless additional losses, the Soviet Army arrived to liberate the city. That is what was told, and sadly, that much was true.

On the basis of the Soviet liberation of Prague, the Czech Communists were able to establish their mythology and justify their alliance with the Soviet Union, "the only ones who answered our pleas. The West betrayed us at Munich, and now they have failed us again!"

Of course, what was never mentioned was that Stalin had insisted that he be allowed to liberate Prague. It was because of his insistence that the needless delay, the deaths, and the destruction took place. The tragedy was that our government agreed to it. Czechoslovakia was not and never had been a top American priority, and in May 1945 we still had the war with Japan. Our atom bomb had not yet been fully tested, and we needed to count on the Soviet Union to help win that war. We were not about to irritate Stalin, to whom we had promised this little country. The conference at Yalta effectively divided Europe. "In payment for the great suffering of the Soviet people during the war" (due in great part to Stalin's military incompetence), many of the countries of central and eastern Europe were handed to him.

General Patton had been eager to liberate Prague, and on the day of remembrance in 1995, his son came to tell that to the Czech people. But Patton had been under strict orders from General Eisenhower to stop at Pilsen, and to wait for the Russians to reach Prague first.

However much we Americans vilified communism in Czechoslovakia, we cannot avoid blame for what happened. Our failure to liberate Prague in 1945 changed the course of history, dooming the Czech and Slovak people to another 40 years of subjugation.

Today, with so much catching up to do, the Czechs are striving to join NATO and the European Union, membership in which might have been long established if we Americans had been the ones to liberate Prague.

Before the war, this country was among the top ten industrial nations of the world, its currency even more valuable than the Swiss franc. By the time the Communists were finally ousted in 1989, Czechoslovakia had slipped in world economic ranking to just below Ecuador. As an American, I feel the shame of responsibility, knowing that much of it was really our fault.

56 – The Other Americans

As much as I had fallen in love with Zdenka and with Prague – and had found ways to get the U.S newspapers and magazines, I sorely missed American conversation. I began to hear about the tiny band of "other Americans" in Prague. Zdenka, always protective and careful, warned me to stay away from them. "They are all communists and spies!" she told me.

I was the exception - the only resident American who was not employed by, or under any control by the regime. Those few other Americans who were here were just as much prisoners of the State as were the Czechs themselves. All who worked at any job here were essentially employees of the State, and earned externally worthless Czechoslovak crowns. Many of those other Americans were refugees from the U.S. courts. Some were actual spies. Some were victims of McCarthyism. Some were left-leaning believers in socialism, entranced with the idea of helping to build a "truly democratic, socialist society." Some saw in the state-supported cultural and scientific setups a chance to do research work they couldn't make a living at in America. By the time I arrived on the scene, many, if not all, were disillusioned with the regime. Some had become actually hostile to it - but trapped nonetheless - for they were living within the Czech economy, earning paper worthless as foreign exchange. Most had lost their passports, and in those days, the U.S. Embassy would not give them the time of day. Even if they had U.S. Passports, they didn't have the exchangeable money with which to live abroad. They would have had to rely on friends or relatives to bail them out. So they were effectively trapped here. By the mid-60s U.S. courts finally decreed that their passports should be issued, but for many, returning to America would have put them into the hands of the hostile FBI, so they stayed on.

They were paying the price for their beliefs. Their plight gave me much to think about in those days. I had my own brush with McCarthyism in 1950. I was accused of being a communist by a government agency, and nearly lost my job at the Detroit Jam Handy Organization animation department, which would have nipped my budding career. Under the influence of my great humanist friend Pete Seeger, I had become active in anti-Jim Crow and pro-labor movements. I had leaned over the left railing, but had never actually fallen overboard. I was eventually cleared. Coming here was of course by mere chance, and had nothing to do with my youthful political ideas, but living here very effectively relieved me of them! I felt sadness for these other Americans, most of them sincere, who had so constrained their lives for the ephemera of a utopian society. I retained my revulsion for the many hypocrisies of American life, but could not find any answers here. I was just plain lucky to not have to choose. I was able to enjoy the best of both worlds, and yet be immune from political control of either!

I was able to enjoy the beauty of Prague, and the consumer advantages of the West. What set me apart financially from these "other Americans" was that I did not work at all within the Czech economy. I always did and still do work for American producers, being paid in U.S. dollars deposited into my U.S. bank account. Thus I was never faced with the problem of trying to get money out of this country. I changed just enough dollars into non-convertible Czechoslovak crowns to cover my daily living expenses. I carried a valid U.S. Passport, and had from the ČSSR government an unlimited entrance/exit visa - two golden documents which gave me a uniquely privileged life. I was in fact the most privileged guest in town, and all because I was producing little childrens's films here that brought a few bucks to the hard-currency-hungry country!

Also importantly, I was to them "apolitical," and they had no ideological hold on me. The irony is that the authorities did not expect me to be a "socialist." They would have been highly suspicious of me if I were. To them, "deviationist socialists" were more the enemy than were capitalists, with whom they could at least do business. To them, there was only one pure Marxism-Leninism, which was whatever the Soviet Union said it was at any given moment. Any alternate opinion, however slight, was seen as a mortal threat. (They were right about that!)

Though I was never politically involved here, I did have my own personal entrapment and limitations. I needed to stay on the right side of the authorities, first of all in order to be with Zdenka, and secondly to protect my clients and my livelihood. I had to live by the policy that I was a guest in the country. I could observe, but I could not change anything. With all my privileges here, I was still of limited financial means in the early years. My tethers were to William L. Snyder, and I could just afford to travel mainly by car within Europe. I only got back to the States when Snyder sent me there and bought my air tickets. So I had a hunger for American friends, and for American--English conversation.

One day in 1961 I suddenly heard an American voice at the Klárov studio. It was Herbert Lass, a broadcaster, I later learned, for Radio Prague International, broadcasting Czechoslovak news - and propaganda - worldwide by shortwave. Lass was also frequently called upon by the Czech State film to do English language translation and narration. When I asked Zdenka who he was, she immediately said, "Be careful! All Americans living here are communists and spies!"

I was about to get into my car, parked in front of the studio, when he emerged, and I was curious enough to risk a casual, "Hi!" I explained who I was, and he said who he was, living here with his wife and two sons since 1948... the exact year of the communist takeover. He said he'd been with the CARE organization, distributing food to areas of devastation and deprivation at the end of World War II. The Lasses were obviously left-leaning Americans, fascinated with the "socialist experiment," going on in Eastern Europe. He made it clear that they had already lived through a great disillusionment during the 50s, but that "things were improving." He didn't sound all that poisonous, and he invited me to visit his family. Zdenka was alarmed that I had "gotten involved," and felt that it would be especially dangerous for her, a citizen of the Czechoslovak Socialist Republic, to visit the home of any American who had asylum here. Fortunately for me, I did not fit into that category, as I was a bona fide customer of Czechoslovak Filmexport, a "foreign" American, and thus she had a right to deal with me... *officially of course!*

But I was fascinated, and curious to know the whys and wherefores of other Americans living here, and I decided to risk a visit. Herb's wife was named Hilda, and she was an editor of an English language "information" magazine, published by the Ministry of Foreign Affairs. So if the Lasses were here officially, and working for the State, they wouldn't be political dissidents, those who I would *definitely* court trouble by visiting.

I convinced Zdenka to come along with me. The Lasses had a generously large apartment in a good building in a good area, far nicer than a Czech family would be likely to get. They had two sons, Joe, 18 and Andy, 12. The boys were both born in America, but went to Czech schools, spoke Czech like natives, and good American English at home, generally without an accent, but curiously devoid of any expressions or slang newer than the mid-forties, when their parents left the States. Speaking with them was like a time warp to my childhood years! Joe, at 20 had never been out of the country since he was a toddler. He got his American passport in 1964, and I wanted to help broaden

284

his outlook and experience. It took a lot of urging to get him to go with me just once for a day or two in Vienna. He had nervous qualms about stepping outside the "Czech garden." He finally agreed, and the experience opened his eyes to the fact that there was another world out there. From then on he was willing to step out of the enclosure more and more. In 1965 he got a scholarship to do his PhD in Physics at Cambridge University in England and after that only returned for short visits. He married a Czech girl, and then he was in a position to help her travel. Joe is a brilliant guy, and had benefited from the Czech technical education, which continued to be on a high standard.

The Lasses were good people and a good family. We became friends, and a ritual of having Thanksgiving dinners with them became established, Thanksgiving being a purely American holiday.

Herb eventually spoke the narration for one of my own films, and the two of us regularly met for lunch at the only place in Prague where one could get grilled chicken, a little eatery attached to the Palace Hotel, now rebuilt as the most expensive and luxurious in Prague.

I gradually met other members of the American community, all political refugees of one kind or another, but the Lasses were the only ones I felt comfortable with, even though they lived by working with the regime. We eventually had a 12-year relationship, and Zdenka and I watched their boys grow up.

It was the upheaval of the 1968 "Prague Spring," and the subsequent Soviet-led invasion that changed everything. That had been the last straw for them, and Herb quit his job at Radio Prague, refusing to broadcast the garbage now being sent out. Hilda too quit her magazine-editing job. She had begun doing free-lance reporting for a US medical newsletter since the mid-sixties, and that kept her going. Quitting was a clear indication to the authorities that a person was now not to be trusted. Herb became an accredited correspondent for the London Financial Times, and covered the long sad aftermath of the Russian invasion for them as well as for CBS. That is what caught up with him. He was de-accredited, and then in 1973 expelled for "activity inimical to the Republic." After that, even the two boys, completely innocent of anything, and feeling almost Czech, were persistently denied visas, and were unable to visit the land they were raised in until 16 years later, after the Velvet Revolution of 1989. Today, Joe is an industrial research scientist in Munich. He and his Czech wife Olga have reclaimed their family *chalupa* in Bohemia, and visit here regularly. So does Andy, now a lofty professor. He has been administering a Mellon Foundation project to computerize the library systems in the Czech Republic and Slovakia. Herb and Hilda live in Boston, and we keep in touch by e-mail.

In a recent exchange we realized why we had differing perceptions of the 60s in this country. The Lasses had lived through the terror and total deprivations, disillusionment, show trials, executions... the *horrors* of the 50s. For them, the 60s were an *improvement*, the gradual lifting of cultural restraints, the blossoming of Czech films, the appearance of tiny theaters, able to put on veiled satire... (including the first plays by the then little known Václav Havel) ... and gradually leading up to the Prague Spring of 1968.

I came in at the end of the 50s and experienced the pits of the early 60s, to me plenty grim enough. So our experiences overlapped. The Lasses had lived here through the deconstructing 50s; we both experienced the early 60s, and the rising hopes, but they missed the grim "normalization" of the 70s and 80s, when the communist dogma retroed to its primordial permafrost. I learned from all this that even degrees of rottenness are relative. The Lasses lived here for 24 years, and I marveled at them as Prague veterans. I never imagined it possible for me then, but I am now here 40 years and counting. In a recent letter to me Hilda Lass put this positive spin on their own lives in Prague:

"Did the American guy who was teaching chemistry at the university level, and changing the whole approach to chemical engineering in Czechoslovakia, feel trapped? Or the agricultural economist who kept trying to tell the Czechs what they were doing wrong? Not to our knowledge. Sure, there were things we all thought were terribly wrong. There were frustrations and some hardships. Of course there were no real channels for protest, but like a lot of Czechs we tried wherever we could to edge things in a more sane direction on our particular turf. And also we had fun. We had friends in, we had visitors from abroad, we went out to dinner, to the theatre, to lots of wonderful cheap concerts. We went on picnics with our friends and their children. We took the kids to puppet shows. We took the kids on trips. We visited our friends' cottages. We had a week's skiing holiday every year. We travelled the length and breadth of Czechoslovakia, visiting all the natural and historical beauty spots and learning more history than we ever did in school... and all of us loved Prague and got to know it intimately. We got our passports back in 1964, and other

Americans who had lost theirs did too, about the same time, following a Supreme Court Decision. That same year we started to travel to the West, Italy, and France, you name it, summer holidays in Yugoslavia, and continued to do so as long as we remained in Prague.

"Would we ever have seen all these places had we remained in America? In 1966 we went back to the U.S. for the first time, visited in New York, went to Grand Canyon and other parks, drove to SF and stayed with friends. But we came back! [to Prague] We were having a fascinating experience which we have never regretted." So wrote Hilda Lass.

One couple who couldn't go anywhere were the Sterns, Alfred and Martha. They were in the political-refugee category I mentioned at the beginning of this chapter. They had fled America and taken refuge in Prague after being indicted on espionage charges during the McCarthy period, accused of being part of a Soviet spy network. Out of the blue, in the mid-80s, we received a phone call from them, inviting us to dinner. Actually, the call came from their *secretary!* We didn't get exactly why they called us. It simply seemed that they hungered for American company, and had heard about me.

We were astonished when we arrived at their place. They lived like no one else here in those days, except for high Party people; a luxurious villa, elegantly furnished, many paintings on the walls, a private chauffeur with a Mercedes limo, (He picked us up and brought us there and back), and a personal secretary. The Sterns had lived in Prague for nearly 30 years by that time and still did not speak a word of Czech. All of their dealings, from grocery shopping on up, were handled by their secretary. Alfred had inherited a fortune, so money was no problem for them, but there were things in Prague at that time that money could not buy. It was the State that provided them with the villa, and made sure that they had access to the best of everything. In return, Alfred kept his hard currency reserves in Czechoslovak banks, out of reach of the US government. By the autumn of 1990 both had died. But for the last 30+ years of their lives they were among those few who definitely had it better under communism! With such special privileged conditions, life here offered many pleasures. The truth of their past has died with them, but in fact, they had been cleared of the espionage charges in 1978 by US courts. But it was already too late for them to re-establish their lives in America, so they stayed on here. Ironically, these people, thought to be dangerous spies, and rumored to have been involved with the executed Julius & Ethel Rosenberg did not at all work for nor collaborate with the Czechoslovak communist government, whereas the Lasses did. The difference of course was money. The Sterns had plenty of it, and had simply transferred their elite life style to Prague. What was little known, but gleaned from reliable sources, was that in her last years, Martha Stern gave money to the Charter 77 dissident group! She kept in touch with us, always calling us "dears," until her death in 1990.

But is there an American who has lived in Prague longer than I have? Yes, there is. She is Joy Kohoutová, born Joy Moss, who has lived in Prague for over 50 years so far! As a young student, she came here from New New York in 1947, just a year before the Communist putsch, to study Russian. The Soviet Union wouldn't take her, and she heard it was possible to study the Russian language, along with Czech, in Prague. She met and married a Czech student, Jiří Kohout, and in order to be able to stay here with him, (by then the Communists were in power, and Jiří could not get out), Joy took Czech citizenship, thereby losing her American passport.) Being young and in love, she hadn't fully considered the consequences. But in fact, she tells me she had a good life here. In her youthful enthusiasm for the new regime, she even tried to join the Communist Party, but she was rejected as "an enemy of the State!" Joy retained the American habit of speaking her mind, and that of course was out of the question here. Jiří became a lexicographer and had to be a Party member, but he was expelled after the 1968 Soviet invasion, and was relegated to washing windows. (Shades of Kundera!) Later, when the publishers realized they needed him, he was able to return to his work of compiling dictionaries, but his name was not allowed to be printed in any of the books he produced. Their daughter and son were each refused entrance to any university here. But Joy was gutsy and determined enough to pull off a ploy similar to what Zdenka had done to save David's army career. She told the education ministry authorities that her son and daughter had been offered scholarships at a prominent American university, and if the offer was publicized in the western press, (making the point that the Czechoslovak government was denying education to two brilliant young people), it would bring great shame to the State. It was a complete bluff, but it worked, and both son and daughter are now successful professionals, and of course citizens of the Czech Republic. But the struggle, and the entire degrading and demoralizing experience, according to Joy, led to her husband's deteriorating health and premature death.

But Joy is properly named. In her late 70's she remains an optimistic and lively personality. Now retired from her translation work, and for several years again in possession of an American passport, she is an intense movie fan, and I am happy to be able to provide her each year, after I've voted, with the dozens of movie tapes I receive for Oscar consideration. She looks at them over and over again. It's possible that the anticipation of the latest free movies each year is what keeps her going. Looking back over her life in Prague, she says she has no regrets. The political uglies aside, she has enjoyed the people, the culture, and the place.

We all, the other Americans and I, took advantage of what was here in those days, and within our circumstances, enjoyed what we could. It was, after all, "For The Love of Prague!"

57 - Happy Endings

I. A Dog Named Roosevelt

The most fascinating young animator, when I arrived here was uniquely an independent, named Pavel Fierlinger. He had assumed the name "Fala," after former U.S. president Franklin Roosevelt's pet dog. Rounding out the joke, he named his own dog "Roosevelt."

Why did he want to be known as Pavel Fala? It was an act of open defiance against his father, Jan, a high Communist official, and his uncle, Zdeněk Fierlinger, the first Prime Minister of Communist Czechoslovakia. Pavel had actually been born in Japan, where his father was ambassador of the still democratic post-war Czechoslovakia. During that volatile post-war period, in which the Communists were maneuvering for power, his father managed to move his family to America, where he could wait out the situation at a distance. So young Pavel spent his early boyhood in New York, growing up as "Paul." But as his father's brother Zdeněk began to climb the upper levels of power after his homeland was taken over by the Communists, his father too saw his own golden opportunity.

He suddenly became a Marxist-Leninist, and brought young Pavel and his mother back home. Finding himself the scion of one of the leading Communist families, Pavel was sent to a special school that had originally been set up as a private school for children of the rich. His roommates at school were future Oscar-winning film director Miloš Forman, and future president of the restored democratic Czechoslovakia, Václav Havel! Of course at that time they were just privileged kids, like he. Both he and Havel were already rebels at the school, and both endured the standard punishment of being cane-whipped on their bare bottoms. As Pavel told us, in retrospect it would be a comic sight to see the both of them sitting deep in adjacent toilets in the school's washroom, constantly having to flush so that the rushing water could cool their throbbing fannies! This is an image that has never left Pavel - or Havel either, I'm sure!

As Pavel became more estranged from his opportunist father, his only driving passion was to escape from this country and somehow get back to America, the country of his young boyhood. He made several wild attempts, once even paying a shadowy figure who promised to guide him to a thinly guarded section of the black forest, bordering Bavaria in the then West

Germany. But he was caught by border guards, and would have faced certain imprisonment had his father not quickly covered up the affair, letting Pavel off with only a severe reprimand. He nonetheless persisted in trying to embarrass his apparatchik relatives, getting into one pickle after another, and eventually sinking into alcoholism. But no matter what he did, the police would not touch him. He was a Fierlinger. His one hope was that he would become such an embarrassment that they would send him out of the country. His chance finally came when one of his animated films was selected for a festival in Holland, and he was allowed to attend. When he sought asylum there he was threatened with forcible return to Czechoslovakia on the assumption that a Fierlinger was likely to be communist spy! But a sympathetic Dutch colleague managed to sneak him across the border into Belgium. From there he was finally able to get an American immigration visa. He settled in Philadelphia, where he set up his own small studio and built a reputation as a talented and original animator.

Just as I have felt it necessary to tell my story in this book, Pavel - once again Paul, and now proudly bringing proper fame to the name Fierlinger - devoted himself to animating his own story. His film is called *"Drawn From Memory."* It may well be the first animated film autobiography. It's a beautifully made and devastatingly candid telling of the story I have just skimmed over, encompassing years of hard work, and utilizing Paul's animation skills as a form of personal catharsis.

Paul showed us a video copy of his film when he was here as a guest at the 1996 Prague Film Festival. We were glad to see him again, especially rejoicing that his turbulent youth has finally resolved in success as an adult on his own terms.

II. Real Estate Gold

Věra Hainzová (sounds like Heinzová) is an animator in Zdenka's studio, and worked on many of my films. Though she no longer has to work, she remains there purely for the love of it. During all the years I've known her, Věra was just barely able to scrape by on her salary. Most of what she made always went to her children, even when it seemed to Zdenka and me that they were old enough to take care of themselves.

Věra had married into a family of clockmakers who ran a little shop in a small building they owned on Old Town Square. Of course it was confiscated by the Communist regime, and the family was left without resources. The clock shop continued under state ownership, but it was stocked with only the lowest quality clocks, and became increasingly shabby.

As with most people in this position - former shopkeepers and small businessmen who were not members of the "working class" - they had to forget about their former "bourgeois" life and accept the typically meager lifestyle of the socialist society. But Věra had drawing talent, and found work she enjoyed in animation.

After 1989, the unexpected miracle of restitution gave them back their building on Old Town Square, and it is now one of the most valuable pieces of property in Prague. As a point of comparison, just imagine you had inherited a house in midtown-Manhattan!

With perfect 20-20 hindsight, Zdenka and I still kick ourselves for not buying a house here. We had so many chances to buy a villa in Prague for prices ranging around $8,000. The same houses today cost $600,000. No, that is not a typo! Assuming that communism would never end in our lifetimes, we decided to enter our retirement years by buying a house in San Francisco. That was in 1985. Granted, it's a very nice house, but in the meantime everything in Prague has changed, and now we want to stay. But real estate property today typically costs more in Prague than San Francisco, so we have to be glad we can still hang on to our two-room Malá Strana apartment.

But Věra Hainzová was lucky. Now her sons are millionaires, and at last, after 40 years of just getting by, she has been able to restore her old family home and give her children and grandchildren something of the good life she was deprived of for so many years.

III. The Fateful Album

Back in 1979 BCD, (before CD's) David's eye was caught by a strangely familiar LP album cover in a Prague record shop window. The album was the recording debut of a then little known jazz pianist, Martin Kratochvil, and his quartet.

The cover painting was by a young illustrator just out of graphic school named Aleš Vyjidák. What immediately shocked David, and impelled him to buy the album and rush it home to me, was that Vyjidák's cover illustration had exact copies of the monster figures from Maurice Sendak's famous book, „Where The Wild Things Are."

As I had done the animation film version of that book, as well as two other films with Maurice, I knew well that a giant lawsuit would surely fall on the head of this young Czech artist. On the back cover of the album was a notice that the record was intended for export by the Prague Artia distributor. Big trouble! No one messes with Maurice Sendak, the king of children's book illustrators!

On the other side, there was poor innocent Martin Kratochvíl. I didn't know him personally, but I knew many other Czech jazz musicians, and I knew how long they had to wait to get an album released, usually taking at least a year after the recording session! I often heard the dismay of musicians, when one of their records finally appeared, that in the meantime they had changed or developed their style, or had new sidemen, or whatever, and felt that the late release of their work gave the public the wrong impression of their current music.

So I knew that if I should blow the whistle on this Kratochvíl "Jazz-Q" album it would be a terrible blow to him, especially if the record were to be withdrawn from circulation.

One of the main reasons records took so long to get out was because of the difficulties in printing the album covers. A change in album design could delay the release for another year. Bad, but not nearly so bad as what would happen if this record were actually exported to any Western country! As I am a friend of Maurice Sendak, I felt I had to be the one to try to resolve the matter. I managed to contact the young artist, who naively admitted that he had seen a reproduction of Sendak's drawings in a graphic magazine in his school library and thought they were real neat, so he just blithely copied them, not understanding at all that such things were copyrighted, nor that he was stealing art from the most famous children's picture book of all! "*Where The Wild Things Are*" had already been published in almost every country in the world except Czechoslovakia!

I wrote Maurice, and sent him a copy of the album, explaining the innocence of Martin Kratochvíl, and how much it would hurt him if this album had to be withdrawn because of the cover. To my surprise and relief, Maurice agreed to let the record stay on sale in this country, but only if a sticker would be attached with his copyright notice. And of course it could not be exported with the present cover.

The director of Supraphon Records, the then State-owned recording monopoly, had been sweating bullets over the affair, and was relieved and grateful for the solution I had managed to get for him. The cost of a new cover would have meant the record would have been scrapped.

The end of this story is that, right after the revolution, Martin Kratochvíl started his own record company, BonTon, which quickly became a tremendous success. He then set up a BonTon radio station and branched out into film production, and then to film distribution. Today BonTon is the largest film distribution agency in the country. Martin Kratochvíl's company now owns Supraphon! It runs the largest record and video megastore in this country. Today he is a multi-millionaire, listed among the 50 richest men in the Czech Republic. He established a "Millionaire Entrepeneur's Club" called "Golem", a spiffy cellar in the Old Town, and he put Zdenka and me on the invitational list. A nice perk for what we did in saving his first album! He still plays his complex jazz piano there in little private concerts.

IV. The Underground Wedding

Madness has by no means vanished with the Communists. This is still "Absurdistan," which is part of the fun of being here. On Tuesday, 25 April 1995, Zdenka and I attended a very special wedding.

In the late '70s and early '80s a statuesque and eccentric young girl named Pavla Bratská worked for Zdenka as an animation in-betweener. She worked on many of my films. She was always a special, rather far-out girl. Tall, dark, quite beautiful, slim and charming, she nevertheless had always given Zdenka a lot of trouble at work. She was, as they say, on the wild side.

She married a talented Czech guitar player named Slávek Hanzlík. He performed in of one of the early groups in Prague that were learning to play American country and western music. The couple managed an escape from the country, gaining political asylum in West Germany. But Slávek's dream was to get to Nashville. As they were in West Germany, a free country by the U.S. measure, they no longer qualified as refugees, so the closest to America they were eventually able to wangle was Canada. They settled in Winnipeg. They had difficulty surviving. Pavla tried to sell paintings, and also worked as a waitress. For Slávek, work as a musician was minimal, especially for a poor Slav wanting to do American country-style music.

One way or another, they managed to spend a lot of time in the States, especially in Nashville, where Slávek became more and more adept at American-style guitar work. Pavla is a strong, charming personality, and they managed somehow to get by, even without U.S. residency. We met from time to time when we were abroad, always hearing of their adventures, but not realizing just how much musical growth Slávek was achieving.

He developed into a really sensational guitarist, moving to the top of the heap in virtuoso fingering technique - real flashy country style guitar picking. He produced a couple of remarkable CDs. However, he and Pavla grew apart, and eventually they divorced. Pavla went to Florida, where she met Fred Reed, a skindiving instructor. They fell in love, and decided to get married in Prague, in the presence of her family and old friends. After the revolution here, this was possible.

As automatically happened in the communist era, Pavla's family, especially her brother Petr, suffered because of her escape. Petr was barred from any travel, and relegated to a dusty corner of the Prague housing bureau, where he worked as a lowly clerk. We often had to carry letters to and from Pavla that he was afraid to mail directly.

But in a stunning reversal after the 1989 revolution, Petr Bratský actually rose from obscurity to become the mayor of West Prague!

A subway station in his section of Prague is decorated with palm trees enclosed in glass towers. Quite striking. This gave Pavla the inspiration for her wedding. As her brother is the mayor, he is empowered to perform wedding ceremonies, and as the metro station in his district is decorated with palm trees - and Fred Reed is a Floridian - she decided they would be married right on the subway platform, as the subway trains continued to pull in and roll out on either side! As a cool touch, she also decided that the wedding music would be that of her former husband, Slávek!

Zdenka and I arrived on one of the trains, and I was immediately commandeered to be Best Man. They pinned an iris corsage on my lapel, the photographers snapped and flashed, and this extraordinary ceremony began. Here was the scene on that wedding day:

Right on the platform of the Lužiny metro station, under an elaborate skylight opened to the heavens, a little oak-wood counter was set up, the State Seal of the Czech Republic was hung, and Petr Bratský, the mayor of West Prague, with his medal of office hung around his neck on a wide red-white -and-blue sash, by the power vested in him by his office - and while the subway trains continued to roar in and out, hissing as their doors opened and closed, disgorging and receiving astonished passengers - performed the marriage ceremony for his sister, while in the background a sound system played the guitar music of her former husband!

Surely it was the first wedding ever on a Prague subway platform, and surely the only one with such an intertwining cast of characters.

V. So Surreal

Among the most fascinating people on the current Prague scene are Jan & Eva Švankmajer. Jan Švankmajer is today recognized as one of the world's great contemporary surrealist filmmakers, and Eva is not only his collaborator, but a leading surrealist painter. For Jan Švankmajer, filmmaking was all but forbidden to him during the communist period. This usually soft-spoken man is an uncompromising tiger in relation to his work, and rather than buckle under to the State Film's attempt to bend him, he and Eva took to making surrealist pottery at their country place, which they sold privately out of their home in the ancient "New World" quarter behind the Prague Castle. We bought many of their pieces, for ourselves and as gifts. Today, both Švankmajers have achieved world aclaim, and only our sugar bowl, water pitcher, and other bizarre pieces remind us of their old struggles.

Those are just a few of the happy endings of people close to us. There are thousands more who have suddenly found themselves free to express themselves, or affluent through property restitution. But just as Zdenka married a non-sportsman whom she had to support for years, I married a woman with nothing to inherit. So it goes!

VI. John Lee Hooker rescurrected!

But I do have a new little personal success story - a happy ending directly resulting from the previous edition of this book. I still receive lovely letters each week, and occasionally a reader appears at our door. One early morning in late 1999, (was that really in the last century?), I came rushing out our front door, still munching on a piece of toast, when I surprised a strange bearded man peering at our doorbell. He quickly walked away, embarrassed, but then decided to take off after me. "Are you Gene Deitch? I figured out where you must live from your book! I really dug your book," he crooned, "but I was also a fan of your "CAT" cartoons in the old Record Changer jazz magazine!" It was Paul Vernon, born a Brit, but now an American citizen, and working right around the corner at the American Embassy. Paul turned out to be an encyclopedia of blues, and the only possible way I could impress him as we palavered over lunch, was to mention that I had recorded John Lee Hooker at my Detroit home in 1949. With this revelation, the breath went out of the man. *"Do - you – still – have – that – tape???"* were his next half-whispered words. For a moment of panic I thought, "Am I conning this guy?" Wallowing in self-doubt, I ran down to my dusty basement locker, and among hundreds of old tapes, there it was! But it was marked, "JOHN LEE HOOKER, REEL 2." Where was reel 1?

Desperate emails to my sons in New York revealed the answer. "Dad, I remember that you loaned a reel of your Hooker tapes to Tony Schwartz!" My God, that was in the mid-50s when I worked in Manhattan. I had completely forgotten about loaning that tape to Schwartz, the well-known music and sounds collector. He was now 80 years old and ill, but on a phone call he remembered the tape. Within a few days I had it. A true miracle!

In 1949, when I worked in Detroit as a budding animation director, I was told of a sensational young blues singer named John Lee Hooker, then virtually unknown, playing in a dive in Detroit's black district. I ventured down there, gingerly approached him and told him about our group of blues lovers up the white suburb of Pleasant Ridge, and said we could scrape up a few bucks and a great dinner if he would agree to come up and play for us. In 1949, portable tape recorders were still a new thing, nowhere near today's hifi stereo, but I had a business class machine with a fairly good crystal microphone. Hooker was already aiming to be a successful city blues man, and about this time – either just before or just after our session – he'd made one commercial recording for a local Detroit label, already trying for city appeal. But we coaxed him to record for us some of the old songs he remembered from the south – the true country blues. "I don't think anyone wants to hear that old stuff today," he said.

"We do!" I exclaimed. What John laid down for us that night was unforgettable, *songs he never recorded again,* played and sung magnificently! My recording was only as a personal souvenir, and the home recording tape then was actually made of *paper* – I couldn't possibly get it released, but I enjoyed listening to it over the years. That reel was among the few precious possessions I took with me when I began working in Prague in 1960. In the meantime John Lee Hooker had become a major blues star. I knew that the music on my tape belonged to him, not me. So it laid in my dusty Prague storeroom for 35 years, until that amazing morning in late 1999. By that time, 50 years after it was recorded, it was at last possible to release this tape! *"The*

Unknown John Lee Hooker!" And all because of Paul Vernon, who came up with a British record company, Interstate Music Ltd. that eagerly and magically restored it on CD! I later signed a contract with John Lee, shortly before he died, and "The Unknown" is being prepared to be known on Virgin Records!

Happy Ending!

One of the things that infuriated the Czech people the most about the communist regime was the desecration of the most cherished graphic symbol of their nation from the very beginnings of the Czech kingdom: the twin-tailed, crowned lion. The communists replaced the crown with the red star of socialism, within the shape of a Hussite shield, presumed as a symbol of a peasant revolution. On the awkward-looking lion's breast they placed what was supposed to be a symbol of the Slovak uprising against the nazi occupiers. One of the first acts of newly elected president Václav Havel, was to restore the traditional crowned lion, in its historic form. The shield on the left is now called the "Small State Seal" and appears as a rubber stamp, etc. on documents. On the right is the "Grand State Seal of The Czech Republic," with the lions representing Bohemia, (the Czech lands), and the two eagles being the historic shields of the provinces of Moravia and Silesia respectively. Thus, the nation's graphic connection to its history has been restored.

58 – Unhappy Ending

Bill Snyder.

Extravagantly optimistic: *"Snyder & Deitch will rule the world!"*
Supremely self-assured: *"I never catch a cold. I refuse to believe in colds!"*
Openly narcissistic: *"I am a beautiful man!"*

This unfazeable, unstoppable, unreasonable, endlessly resourceful man came finally to an end none could have imagined for him. He fell victim to Alzheimer's syndrome and died in his sleep on June 4th, 1998 at the mere age of 80, though he seemed to me to have enough steam to reach 100. He once told me matter-of-factly that neither of us could expect to live more than another 20 years, so we had to "make it now." That was 40 years ago.

Snyder evoked so many mixed reactions from people that he is impossible to summarize. My two oldest sons thought he was a con man. The women in the Prague film organizations loved him. They giggled at his outrageous remarks. He reveled in the outrageous, and loved to show his bravery by uttering politically taboo remarks while in communist Prague. The women loved him especially because he always brought them rare presents from the West.

I have the greatest problem in measuring him. He discovered the possibility of producing animation films in Prague. He had excellent taste. He chose great books to adapt. But he came on too strong for me. He was a show off. He was exasperating. He didn't hesitate to embarrass. We would be sitting in a luncheonette, I trying to have a serious discussion with him, when the waitress arrived. Snyder would grasp her hand and plow right in: *"Darling, you are a nice looking girl, but you are really wearing too much makeup!"* At such moments – and there were many such moments – I wished I could fall through the floor.

He was insufferable in many ways. Whenever we were outside he was constantly hacking a spitting, and there was that omnipresent cigar; cigar smoke makes me nauseous.

When we walked along together, he insisted on stopping when he had a point to make, to ensure he had my full attention. He was extremely critical of my character, as contrasted to his, and he missed few opportunities to lecture me. I left my wife and kids for Zdenka, but he was "loyal to his wife." Yet he reveled in his tales of philandery. *"So I leave a little semen in Europe. So what?"*

We were different, that's all. Bill Snyder evokes such a mix of emotions in me that I can hardly make a sum of the man. He changed my life. He brought me to Zdenka, (albeit unwittingly). He also brought me to collywobbled anxiety and economic distress.

I could never prevail in a confrontation with him. He was a master of attack as defense. Once I went to his office in New York, determined to get a settlement of money he owed me. Before I could open my mouth, and without a word of greeting, he leaned forward angrily: *"Gene, there are three things I can never forgive you for!"* and launched into a litany of nonsense, forced me into long rebuttals, smothering any chance of my getting to my own points. He had a sixth sense.

Only Fate was able to defeat him, and I get no joy in making my points now. For Zdenka and me, there is much to think about, and much to remember. Zdenka still loves him. Bill Snyder did change our lives for the better, and we cannot forget that. And I also cannot forget the great fun we had together, and the marvelous creative burn we both raced through in the early days of our productions. He exuded confidence and optimism; he projected the image of a winner, and yet he lost; he never made his million. He was a person no one could forget, and no one could cope with. We neither can cope with his inexplicable end.

59
PRAGUE/PRAHA
Your Free Secret Guidebook!

The name of Prague in Czech is Praha, which is based on the Czech word for threshold. The goddess Libuše, the mythic founder of Prague, proclaimed it the threshold to a new home for her tribe. And for me, Prague was the threshold I crossed over into my own new life. So the name seemed very appropriate to me, and still does.

Part of the mystery of the old towns which make up today's Prague, is that nothing you look at is any one thing. Prague is a city of layers, one style of architecture layered onto another. Another simile might be to the video trick called "morphing." You may have seen it first in the movie, "Terminator 2," and later in nearly every television commercial wherein one object smoothly transforms into another. Prague is a town, which has been "morphing" throughout its history, every structure seemingly in the process of mutating into something else.

For example, the old Judith Bridge tower, the smaller of the famous double towers on the Malá Strana end of the Charles Bridge, started as Romanesque style. A Gothic peak was added, and later a Baroque escutcheon was pasted on the front.

The huge Gothic Vladislav Hall up in the castle has Renaissance windows. From outside, you can almost see the "morphing" as the Gothic spires seem about to be absorbed into the evolving building. Everywhere you look in Prague, one building superimposes itself onto another, all in a kind of hodgepodge of houses. And yet, there's also a strangely harmonic wholeness that's...well, Praha. The very name suggests movement, the threshold, the midpoint between the outside and the inside.

Here are some things to see that are not usually in the guidebooks:

- Look closely at the saint on the right of the lower window of the Renaissance house, "At the Golden Well," on Karlová Street in the Old Town. He is Saint Rocus or Rocko, and he is holding up his tunic to reveal blood running down his leg. Look at the little dog at his feet with its cheeks all puffed out. In order to insure his celibacy, St. Rocko has had the dog bite off his testicles!

- At the Old Town end of the Charles Bridge, just before you pass through the tower onto the bridge, lean (just a bit!) over the balustrade on your left, and see a medieval carving of a man pushing his hand up a woman's skirt. Look on the right-hand corner of the tower and see a man with his hand on a woman's breast.

- On the bridge is the famous cross with the Corpus Christi, probably unique in the entire world, as it is emblazoned with gilded Hebrew lettering. Why? What does it say? American Jewish tourists wonder, and when they find out they are offended, as are Israelis who read Hebrew. The story is complex, and dates back three centuries to 1694, when a Czech court, dominated by Catholics, accepted highly dubious evidence that a Jew named Backoffen committed a disrespect to the cross. (It is said he didn't remove his hat when passing.) They levied a heavy fine and ordered the lettering attached to the cross as a punishment to him, and as a warning to other Jews. But there is far more to the story, involving big money, revenge, intrigue and corruption... what else? The lettering says, "Holy, holy, holy, is the Spirit of God!" a sacred Jewish chant, which does not belong on a Christian Cross! Again we have the layers of meaning, typical of Prague. It's clearly and intentionally anti-Semitic, but it's also 300 years old and part of Prague history. Finally, in March, 2000 explanatory plaques in Czech, English, and Hebrew have been mounted below the cross. Holy, Holy, Holy!

- From the bridge, as it extends over the island of Kampa, you can see the eternal light at the Shrine of the Washerwomen. On the sides of the painting of Mary you'll see the two rollers of a washing-wringer. Washerwomen traditionally lived on Kampa, and washed their noble clients' clothes on the banks of the Vltava River.

- In the Old Jewish cemetery is one monument that breaks the Jewish law, forbidding one's own likeness to be used on a gravestone. If you look very carefully, close to the ground, around the corner of the old mortuary building, you can find a stone with the graven image of a rich merchant and his wife!

- Fasces - not feces - fasces are bundles of rods tied together around an ax, with the blade projecting. It was the ancient Romans' symbol of power and strength - (one can easily break a single rod, but when bundled together they are almost impossible to break). Mussolini adapted the symbol, and proudly proclaimed himself and his government to be "fascist." OK, you know all that, but for really weird irony take a close look at the classic triangular peak of the German embassy on Prague's, Vlašská Street. Way up there, among the gilded artifacts of ancient battle, are actually a couple of fasces. I wonder how many people notice this, or even how many of the Germans working in their embassy realize that their building is ironically emblazoned with the original symbol of fascism!

- The naked bronze boy in the courtyard of the Children's palace, inside the Prague castle *(Hradčany)*, is a delightful example of Czech attitudes. When this area was rebuilt and dedicated to children in the mid-1960s, a bronze statue of a pubescent nude boy, appearing to be maybe 13-14 years old, was installed in the center of the courtyard. However, where his penis was supposed to be, there was only a discreet *bronze smear.* There was an immediate public uproar. Here was something about which people felt able to vent their rage. *"Do we want our children raised to be ashamed of their body parts?"* This was something the authorities had to give in on. They ordered the sculptor to repair and recast this life-sized bronze statue, at great expense. Today you can see it proudly standing in the middle of that courtyard, fully endowed! Our colleague, Paul Fierlinger sent me this additional note: " There is more to the penis story. I remember when this happened and as you will know, everything in those days had to pass through the [communist era] *Svazova komise.* [League Commission] When the sculptor was commissioned to create the addition, the little thing had to pass the *komise,* like everything else. My friend, Honza Brychta was there. He described it as a hilarious, absurd scene, when the sculptor took the little bronze penis out of a box and placed it in the middle of the table. The entire *komise* stood up from their seats to bend over and get a closer look.

- The pink building just to the left of the orloj clock, in Old Town Square, is where Zdenka and I were married - behind the Renaissance window under the letters, "Praga Caput Regni." This part of The Old Town Hall is still the most popular wedding site.

- On the Smetanovo Nabřeží, (Smetana Embankment), the broad street with tram tracks, running right alongside the river Vltava, (and with the best view of the Charles Bridge and Prague castle beyond), is the small "Park of National Awakening." Right in the center of its well-kept lawn stands an imposing and elegantly statue-embellished neo-gothic, tall spire. There is an opening in the spire, wherein is a large podium. Standing on the podium is... nothing!

  Once, there stood a heroic likeness the Austro-Hungarian Emperor Franz-Joseph. But after the establishment of the first Czechoslovak independent republic, old Franz-Joseph's statue was banished. However, his elaborate but empty enclosure is still there... It is doubtful if the "memorial" even remembers whom it was once memorializing! Interestingly, even the Communists were reluctant to install in it one of their own idols!

- The paper model of Prague is mentioned in some guidebooks, but is one of the city's wonders that's largely overlooked. It was created by Antonín Langweil in the 1830s. He spent years measuring every street, every building, and every window, to create an exact model of the entire city at that time. This spectacular work is on permanent display at the City (Mětské) Museum (not the National Museum!).

- The main tower of Hradčany is that of St. Vitus cathedral, probably the only cathedral in the world that drastically changes architectural style on its way to the heavens! The huge square tower is Gothic up to a straight horizontal line, and then suddenly switches to Baroque from there up. It is the crowning statement of Prague morphing, and the preeminent symbol of the Catholicization of the Protestant Kingdom of Bohemia, after its defeat by the Hapsburgs in 1620. The Catholics despised gothic architecture.

• One of the hidden wonders of Prague is the Vrtbovská zahrada. On the noisy, traffic-smelly street of Karmelitská, near the Malostranské náměstí, is an unpreposessing brown doorway, (No.25/373). Open that door, and enter a lovely courtyard. (Be sure to close the door so the roar of the street will be shut out!) Go all the way to the rear of the courtyard where a tiny stairway will transport you to Paradise! (You will have to buy a ticket!) At the very top of this hidden wonder, with its unique viewpoints, you will come right up against the fence of the backyard of the American Embassy. No wonder this gorgeous corner was off-limits during the communist years!

• A really cool addition to the Prague scene is the Museum of Communism, right on the main luxury-shopping street of Prague, Na Příkopě, exactly at the Palace Savarin. Don't be put off by the big "Casino" sign; the Museum shares the space, but doesn't have enough signs or posters to guide you in. When you go up the plush staircase, the Casino will be on the right, and the Museum on the left. (Fitting!) If you turn right at the top of the staircase, you're wrong, because you'll lose your money! At the left, The Museum of Communism is cleverly laid out to take you on a condensed tour of the 40 years of horror this country suffered under communism. You'll see full-size mockups of a grocery shop, a workshop, offices, statues, posters, and many artifacts rescued from the thankfully bygone era. With the present-day luxury and freedoms in this country, many young people, and even some older, have forgotten or don't know what it was like in those gray days. This museum, though necessarily but a glimpse of what was here for a period of forty long years, is an important place to visit, for Czechs and tourists alike - lest we forget! Another new addition, along the same lines, is the Memorial To The Victims of Communism, which can be seen at the foot of the Petřín Park, right where Vítězná (Victory) Street ends at Újezd.

And so it is with Prague, from the beginning into the present: changing, evolving, surviving, always elusive, always contentious. Everything in Prague is some kind of an argument; an argument between architectural styles, between religious beliefs, cultures, languages, street names, nationalities, classes, between moralists and hedonists, between believers and skeptics, dreamers and cynics, politicians and historians... The arguments only seem capable of being settled when one takes a distant view of the dynamic whole.

Nothing you see is any one thing. It's the same with the Czech people and the Czech life: ambiguity is the norm. Don't look for definite answers. It's better to believe in the legends than to pry after any one truth. The legends are more interesting.

The famous Pink Tank, mentioned in Chapter 49, was not a legend, but it is gone - with mixed emotions. During the entire communist era, a Soviet tank, said to be the first one to enter Prague during the liberation from Nazi occupation in May 1945, was displayed on a pedestal in the Smichov district. During the heady days following the 1989 Velvet Revolution, a spunky art student and a few friends climbed up onto the tank in the middle of one night and painted it a brilliant pink. It was a terrible affront to the Soviet Embassy in Prague, but a hilarious sensation to nearly everyone else. Crowds of tourists gathered every day to photograph it. I did the same. It was made into postcards and t-shirts, but it was ultimately decided to remove the tank and pedestal completely. It was just too embarrassing. All you will see there today is a patch of lawn.

If you want to get a handle on what Prague is really about, I recommend reading Prague, the Mystical City, by Joseph Wechsberg (Macmillan).

But we have to remember that the when we speak of the Prague we love, we are nearly always focussing on the 5 historic core towns, The Malá Strana, (The Little Side), The Staré Město (The Old Town), Hradčany (Site of the Prague Castle), Josefov (Area of the Old Jewish Ghetto) and the Nové Město, ("New" Town). Today's Prague sprawls over 308 square miles (4962 km^2), and much of it suffered architectural devastation at the hands of the communists, from which it may not recover for decades. Like herds of concrete elephants, hundreds, perhaps thousands of gray, grungy, and characterless concrete panel apartment buildings blight former meadows. These monstrosities were quickly assembled, like houses of concrete cards, and often years later some grass-like weeds were planted around them. In the meantime, the tenants who were "lucky" enough to get an assignment for an apartment in them would have to wade through mud to get home. If you have heart to see the Prague most citizens actually live in, you should at least once venture outside the historic core, and see what ticky-tacky really is; see what the communists' promise of "flats for everyone," was worth. It will be a depressing sight; it was for me when I first encountered them. Fortunately, the outer areas are now being slowly rebuilt.

An exhibit in the Museum of Communism, right on the main luxury-shopping street of Prague, Na Příkopě 10, at the Palace Savarin. Go upstairs and to the left. (Naturally!)

I was thrust into a country that at the time presented a diametrically opposite ideology to my own, and presented its share of dangers and negatives. But look at what it got me: a fantastic wife, a unique opportunity to develop my art and craft, and a chance to see, think about, and experience many things I'd previously had no occasion to consider. Not only that, but I discovered Prague in a way that is no longer possible to see. Watching the hordes of tourists stream down our ancient Mostecká street today - with their sweaty faces and summer shorts, carrying their bottled water and congregating in front of McDonald's - I wonder if any of them really catch the atmosphere of this town. Over 100 million tourists are officially recorded in the Czech Republic each year, almost all of whom crowd into this city of just over a million and-a-quarter inhabitants. Prague was not designed for masses of people streaming through its narrow old streets, littering as they go. (I never saw a Czech drop a piece of paper on the street. They would carry it, crumpled, for blocks until they came to a trashcan.) It's wonderful that people from the outside world have at last discovered this town, but the lonely, quiet charm of gas lit Praha is gone.

However deviant people thought I was in those early days, I did see and experience Prague when it was still possible to be lost in its ancient atmosphere. I'm glad I experienced it in its dark, lonely times, when Zdenka and I could walk the narrow gas lit lanes all by ourselves!

Many beautiful picture books of Prague and the Czech and Slovak republics exist. To best enjoy, and feel the atmosphere of what I have written about in this memoir, you should really look through a good book of Prague photographs! Best of all, buy a book of the paintings of Jakub Schikaneder. He captured the mood and glow of prewar Prague as no one has ever done!

G.D.

Color illustrations from this chapter are in the second color folio.

O.K. – This was worse than communism.
Our Mostecká Street, decked in Nazi flags - 1942

Epilogue 2002

Today, millions of tourists pass through Prague, in the new, democratic, and intensely market-oriented Czech Republic. They see the glittering shopping malls and hypermarkets here, crammed with a vast assortment of high-quality products, and view it all as "*so what?*" The young Czechs who throw on their backpacks and nip across the border, as if it's their every right, (which it is), and even the older Czechs, who jump into their shiny new cars and do the same thing, may not remember - and some may not even know - how it was. As an American, I was raised with all these freedoms and plenitude, but having lived here for 30 years during the gray depression of communism, I don't take any of it for granted. I am like a little boy in a toy store. Every day when I go for a walk I see something new and exciting. I get a thrill from it every time.

Of course, there is the bitter with the better. We all know that the capitalist system is not all roses, and that the Czech Republic did not become Camelot after the 1989 Velvet Revolution. It would seem that no one here in his or her right mind would willfully return to the brain dead days of slogans such as, "THE SOVIET UNION IS OUR EXAMPLE!" And yet, as I update this Epilogue in the spring of 2002, over twelve years after the revolution, there are mixed feelings in the public mind about the cosmic changes here. Some polls indicate that only a slim majority of the population feel the present regime is better than the communist one! It is shocking to me that memories are so short. Some have said "What does the freedom to travel mean to me if I can't afford to do so?" That is an overstatement. Czechs are travelling maniacs, and the shops and malls are full of eager buyers. When we see the new immense hypermarkets, some with 45 checkout counters, jammed with buyers pushing huge heaped shopping carts, it's evident that the average citizen is far better off. The Czech crown is once again of the strong currencies in Europe. But the dog-eat-dog political power plays, the invading mafias, the financial scandals have induced in some a twisted nostalgia for the certainties of totalitarianism - for a government that did the thinking for all.

The old Alcron hotel was reborn in the late 90s as the sleek Radisson-SAS Alcron . The old-world atmosphere, however dingy, that made the Alcron a legend was slicked up in art deco style, very nice, but not quite like the old creepy focal point for foxy traders, news hawks, and intriguers. But the "New" Alcron is a fine hotel, with possibly the best restaurant in town, and they have a policy of using jazz music for their entertainment! They even proudly proclaim that Louis Armstrong stayed there in 1964 - the year Z&I were married. Perhaps the old ghosts are still there, lurking in the background. If you ever stay there, perhaps you will see them shimmying to the old jazz tunes! So in Prague, if you want to be where it all happened, the Radisson SAS Alcron hotel is the place to stay!

In retrospect, I could say that I miss the fun of doing what was difficult /"impossible"/forbidden, the satisfaction of sidestepping the satraps, overcoming the constant challenges. I could do what others could not: get a good car, travel when I wanted to, get the unavailable, get Time, Newsweek, and the Herald-Tribune, spirit my stepson out of the country, outwit the communist customs authorities, get nearly everything I needed into the country - bypass the roadblocks - get an ungettable apartment, a telephone - do private recording in the great halls, cathedrals, and jazz dens. Obviously, the hazards were well mixed with fun and accomplishment.

Every little victory was an adventure and a satisfaction. Now it's all too easy. The thrill is gone. Whatever I want is at a corner shop, mega market, or mall. My Mercedes-Benz is just one of thousands, (and it's not even the latest model!) A Czech passport is now as good as my American one. I am no longer unique. I'm just another resident American among the hordes. So should I fret? Should I long for the "good old commie days?" No thanks. I've had it, and I am happy to see that everyone here can now have it.

What fascinated me in communist Czechoslovakia was how the people found ways to wring every drop of positive out of the pervasive negative - how oppression brought out foxiness - how a humorless regime inspired a continuous stream of hilarious jokes - how ordinary people made the most of every rusty spot on the iron curtain. I found the truth of the central slogan of the population: "*In Czechoslovakia everything is forbidden, and everything is possible!*" The Czechs and Slovaks actually relished the sport of overcoming!

At the same time, I am happy to say that some old slogans still do hold true. In our earliest days together, Zdenka would look at me with her clear blue eyes and lovingly say, *"Nothing change!"*

Well of course we have changed, but our love for each other has not. We will this year celebrate our 38th wedding anniversary. It was not just a fling, but an intense, bi-cultural relationship based on love, understanding, tolerance, complete trust, and true friendship.

I realize how lucky we've been. For every "dream that comes true" there is usually a flip side. Disappointment can come to even the biggest lottery winner. Unfortunately or fortunately, I don't have first hand experience with that, and I can look back without regret on the big dream I had when I first fell in love with Zdenka.

I had imagined - even with my financial weakness at the time, and all my uncertainties, that I somehow still had the power to change someone's life for the better. So on New Year's Eve, 1959, I made the secret resolution that I would open up this woman's life - that I would take her to places she could never have seen, and bring her things she would never have had - in short, give her a new life that none of her people could realistically hope for. If I were to directly ask her now if I had fulfilled my 1959 New Year's resolution, I know exactly what she would say: "I would have managed it anyway." And she just might have!

Something I have brought her is more housework and much exasperation. Zdenka loves order, a clean and orderly apartment, and a minimum of gadgetry. I live in disorder; I have filled our place with gadgetry, which I cannot resist. And even though I am very good at household chores and all manner of handymanery, it is never enough: Zdenka notices only the things I have not done. Of course, this is somewhat disappointing, but I do know I have improved her life. I do know I have broadened her outlook and her possibilities, improved her English, and have raised her standard of living. I can take some satisfaction from that, even though money, as such, is not Zdenka's craving. Beyond all that, after 42 years (and counting), I know she loves me and I love her. I also know that she is devoted to my well-being, in spite of many criticisms, and in spite of any lingering disappointment that my sporty red sweater of 1959 did not, in fact, clothe a genuine sportsman, but just a 164-pound weakling.

Zdenka never allows the notion of personal illness, nor any form of lassitude, enter her consciousness, and she expects the same from me. Picture a broiling summer day at our mountain cottage. Picture vast acreage of ankle-deep scrub grass I somehow managed to avoid mowing the previous weekend. And see that anvil-heavy lawnmower, which, though electric, needs to be pushed by sweaty hand? "Look, I just don't think I'm up to it today," I whine. "What? A big man like you? Do it, or else I will do it myself!" That is the unassailable challenge. I do it. Driving home from our chalupa, and listening to the BBC on our car radio, we once happened to catch a discussion of Buddhism, which mentioned the Buddhist aim of seeking perfection of self. "What do I need that for?" huffed Zdenka. "I'm already perfect!"

When Zdenka finally decided to apply for her pension, nominally retiring from her job as animation studio producer, it was a full ten years after she had a right to do so. She did it only because she was told she had already earned the maximum possible pension, and *that she could still continue to work at full salary.* She "retired," but she still doesn't miss a day's work. 57 years in the studio and still happily at it!

When the studio clerk was toting up her pension a few years ago, she came to Zdenka's desk with a sheaf of papers and a puzzled look. "There must be an error here, Mrs. Deitchová. The records indicate that in over 50 years in the studio, aside from your short maternity leave, you were only out sick for a total of two weeks!"

It was true. A seriously misguided virus had the temerity to actually move in on her that one time. She fought it so furiously that it never made that mistake again, turning it's attention instead to weaker mortals, such as I. Zdenka has never read, "The Power of Positive Thinking." She lives it naturally.

Zdenka started at the very beginning of the "Bratři v triku!" animation studio, in 1945 when she was 17 years old. 57 years later, as she passed her 74th birthday, she is still there, now the Studio Manager and hands-on Senior Producer. She has produced hundreds of classic children's films there, and her studio is the jewel in the crown of Krátký Film, the parent company. No longer supported by the state, it must now master modern marketing and cost accounting. Though we will continue to produce what comes our way, younger talents will be more and more taking over. But for the time being, (and it may yet be a longish "time-being), Zdenka will continue to be their boss!" I always used to joke that the only way Zdenka would ever retire would be if the studio collapsed under her. It almost did at one point, but the owners realized that the studio is a national icon, and for the animators who work there, it is not just a place to work for (low) pay, but a place for a lifetime of mutual creativity and camaraderie which people like Zdenka could not easily abandon. Financing was found, and, (so far), it goes on!

Prague is still Prague. Regimes come and go. The Castle is still there. We still don't know who will succeed Václav Havel as president, nor nothing of the future in this highly unpredictable world. I look at a book of photographs of Prague of 100 years ago; the historic streets and palaces, the sky pierced by a hundred towers - our own square - and it's all still here to see and feel!

Prague, "Praha" has long since adapted to the passage of time.

G.D. Prague, May, 2002

Backwords:

First, my thanks and pleas of forbearance to all those whose names appear in this book. They are, or were, all real people, referred to wherever possible by their real names. To any that might be offended enough to want to sue me, be advised that I have my air ticket to Bogotá, Colombia always in my pocket. I hope I don't have to use it, as I really do love Prague.

Many friends, relatives, and colleagues were patient enough to read various drafts of this history, and to supply me with valuable suggestions and literary precautions. Some I actually heeded.

I extend my grateful thanks to Lynn and Steve Peterson for scouring an early draft of this book and identifying tons of terrifying typos and sloppy syntax, and for coming up with positive and purifying suggestions. I absolve them from responsibility for mistakes in the large amount of material I've added since they read the draft.

My thanks to Allen Swift for upgrading my memory on some mutual adventures, for contributing an entire chapter, and for his professional advice. Also to Allen's wife, Lenore Loveman, for her instructive notes. Thanks to Larry Ravitz for his approving comments and sharp eye. My great thanks to Adam Snyder for his forbearance regarding my portrayal of his father. "He was my father," he told me, "and I also know how he was."

Thanks to my youngest son Seth, who read for the first time the details of what his father had been up to all those years when he was growing up. On my knees to Zdenka for not insisting on her original order to trash the entire project. "It's our private thing," she insisted. I suppose she's right, but I just had a great need to write it all down. Once started, I couldn't stop. So many things came back to me in a flood that I had to have my notebook with me at all times, even at my bedside, to be sure I didn't miss including a particularly strange, ridiculous, exasperating, amazing, or dramatic event that impinged on our lives together.

Luckily, I am something of a diarist and I wrote an account of most of the episodes just after they occurred, so I can assure you it is all unembroidered. I am also a dedicated letter writer who saves copies of everything. Reading through all of my correspondence over the years reinforced my memory of things I might have forgotten. The good news for those whose boredom thres-

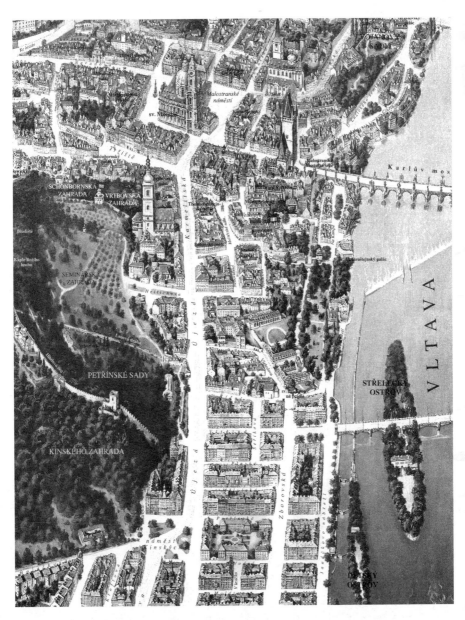

This is the Malá Strana quarter of Prague, where we live

hold was approached and/or crossed, I can assure you that there was a lot more stuff I could have thrown in. (Every good filmmaker leaves room for a sequel!)

I wish to express appreciation to my Prague editor David Speranza, who waded through my disjointed tales and run-on sentences in the first version of this book, and put them in the best possible order - he did a great job of cleaning up after me – and to Alan Levy, editor-in-chief of The Prague Post, who graciously gave his time and editorial eagle-eye in an effort to save me from grammatical and factual shame. I take full responsibility for the veracity of the included incidents as I have set them down.

"JUST WHEN I THINK I'VE HEARD EVERYTHING, HERE'S A STOMACH THAT GURGLES LOUIS' INTRO TO WEST END BLUES!"

Thanks to Robert Němec of Pragma publishers for taking a chance on the first edition of this book, even though it did not fit into his Czech language list, and to Miloš Uhlíř of Baset Books, Prague, for taking on the continuing editions.

My greatest thanks of all I extend to you, the reader, for being interested enough to share with me my true tale.

Gene Deitch, Prague, 2002

"*I was there the night John Lee Hooker ate his guitar!*"

An archive photo by Josef Illík, taken from inside Eduard Čapek's old iron shop.